super
foods
super
easy

super
foods
super
easy

Published by The Reader's Digest Association, Inc.
London • New York • Sydney • Montreal

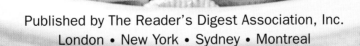

Contents

INTRODUCTION 6

SUPERFOOD BENEFITS CHART 10

Soups, starters & snacks 12

Vegetables & salads 64

Fish & seafood 98

Poultry & game 134

Meat 164

Pasta, pulses & grains 196

Desserts 244

INDEX 282

ACKNOWLEDGMENTS 288

NOTE TO READERS

While the creators of this work have made every effort to be as accurate and up to date as possible, medical and pharmacological knowledge is constantly changing. Readers are recommended to consult a qualified medical specialist for individual advice. The writers, researchers, editors and publishers of this work cannot be held liable for any errors and omissions, or actions that may be taken as a consequence of information contained within this work.

Welcome to the next stage of
the healthy food revolution

Put down your health books, take up your knife and fork and discover how to eat your way to a healthier lifestyle, easily, quickly and deliciously. So, savour our recipes and move into the superfood nutritional fast lane.

Superfoods Supereasy is a cookery book with a difference – a fantastic selection of tasty, modern and easy recipes for everyday living, each of them packed with foods that have been demonstrated to promote long-term health, aid healing, and even help to fight some diseases. And all this can be done without fuss, complicated preparation and lengthy cooking time – and with supermarket staples.

What is a superfood?

Superfoods, such as broccoli, blueberries and salmon, contain natural ingredients with exceptional nutritional values or protective qualities. They contain natural chemicals, compounds and nutrients that, for example, may help to protect against the impact of diseases such as cancer and Type 2 diabetes, as well as fight the effects of ageing, help to lower cholesterol levels and improve mental alertness.

Here are five top reasons for including more superfoods in your daily diet:

★ Superfoods will help you to meet the 5-a-day fruit and vegetable target that health professionals recommend as a minimum daily amount to protect your body and maintain well-being.

★ Many superfoods such as lentils and oats have a low Glycaemic Index (GI) value, which means that their carbohydrates are absorbed slowly into the bloodstream. Such foods stave off hunger and keep you feeling full for longer, so helping with weight control.

★ Many superfoods such as wholewheat pasta and carrots are a good source of fibre. This helps your digestive system to work effectively, and some forms of fibre can help to lower cholesterol.

★ All superfoods are low in, or free from, the 'bad' fats, such as saturates and trans fats, which can increase the risk of heart disease.

★ Superfoods naturally provide high levels of the essential vitamins and minerals that your body needs for a healthy nervous system, a fully functioning brain and other key bodily processes, such as the regulation of blood clotting and the efficient working of your cells and organs.

Turn to the Superfood Benefits Chart (see pages 10-11) for a list of the main superfoods featured in our recipes and the conditions they can help to reduce and possibly even prevent, as well as their positive health benefits in the body.

Making yours a balanced diet

Superfoods should form a large part of a healthy, well-balanced diet. Follow this checklist of what food types to include regularly to keep your mind and body performing at its best.

Protein
Essential for building and maintaining muscles and internal organs, protein is also needed to build new cells and repair damaged tissue in your body. High-protein foods include lean meat, poultry, fish, seafood, milk, hard cheese, eggs, beans and pulses.

Carbohydrate
The staple of most diets, starchy carbohydrates provide energy for your body throughout the day and as you sleep. About 50 per cent of your daily energy should come mainly from starchy wholegrain foods, such as potatoes, brown rice, wholewheat pasta and wholegrain bread. Within this total, no more than 10 per cent should come from sugary foods. The best type of sugar is found naturally in fruit and vegetables.

Fat
Providing your body with energy and fat-soluble vitamins, and protecting your vital organs, are among the many roles fat has to play. Eating too much fat, though, especially saturated fat, can lead to weight problems and obesity. The good fats are unsaturated fats, such as olive oil or sunflower oil. Other healthy fats include omega-3, found in oily fish, nuts and seeds.

Vitamins and minerals
The main vitamins we need are vitamins A, the B group, C, D, E and K. These are essential for keeping your body in good working order. Major minerals (those found in relatively large amounts in the body) are iron, calcium, zinc, selenium, magnesium and potassium. Vitamins and minerals appear in small quantities in lots of different foods, so a varied diet is the best way to obtain them all.

Dietary fibre
You need around 24g of fibre per day to keep your digestive system in good working order. Some types of fibre also help to lower cholesterol levels, which is vital if you want to maintain a healthy heart. Unrefined (unprocessed) plant-based foods contain the most amounts of fibre. Good examples include wholegrains, pulses such as lentils, beans, dried fruit and fresh fruit and vegetables.

Fluids
Water is vital for physical well-being. An average adult needs to drink 1.2 litres of fluid every day. Water is the best thirst quencher, but other choices could be fruit teas, unsweetened fruit juice or milk. Food can also supply some of your fluid requirements – many fruit and salad ingredients have a high water content.

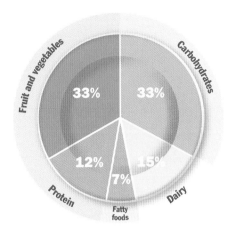

EATING WELL
Build your food intake around the main food groups for healthy living. The optimum amount of nutrients needed to maintain health varies from person to person – depending on sex, age, height, weight and activity levels – but as a rule of thumb, about one-third of the food you eat should come from high fibre, starchy foods such as wholegrains, pulses and potatoes, another third from fruit and vegetables, with the rest made up from fish, poultry, lean meat and low-fat dairy foods, with only limited amounts of processed fatty or sugary foods.

A note on seasoning
Salt Use a light hand when adding salt to your cooking and when serving – too much can lead to high blood pressure. Choose low-salt stock granules or cubes, or make your own stock. Salt is not added to the cooking water of vegetables, rice and pasta in our recipes. We have not seasoned the recipes needlessly, but suggested where salt might be added to suit your taste.

Herbs Use herbs and spices to boost flavour – many have their own health properties. Fresh is best but use dried, if preferred.

Sugar Replace processed sugar with natural sweetness whenever you can from fresh and dried fruit.

Freezing superfoods

Using a freezer to store food ready to use at any time is a great idea – vegetables, fruit, meat, poultry, fish and even some fresh herbs and spices retain their nutritional value when frozen.

When buying meat, poultry and fish to freeze, look out for 'suitable for freezing' labels. Freeze on the day of purchase and do not store it for longer than 3 months. Never re-freeze meat, fish or poultry, even when cooked.

Frozen vegetables are so handy – either when shop-bought or fresh from the garden. If freezing your own produce, always freeze as soon as possible after picking to avoid losing essential vitamins and minerals. Wash and chop the vegetables ready for freezing, then blanch in a pan of boiling water for 2-3 minutes. Lift out with a slotted spoon, refresh under cold water and pack into labelled containers. Once opened, reseal bags of frozen vegetables with a tie. Salad vegetables cannot be frozen.

Always defrost food thoroughly at room temperature before cooking. Do not cook raw poultry or meat from frozen as it may not cook right through. Some seafood and fish can be cooked from frozen – follow the recipe instructions.

Supereasy planning and shopping

Healthy cooking does not mean costly lists of little-known ingredients. Much of it is about making a few easy changes to your usual routine and planning ahead, such as making best use of your freezer (see left).

A WELL-STOCKED STORECUPBOARD

Build up your superfood storecupboard staples and you will always be able to make delicious, healthy food even if you forget to plan ahead. These are the staples that should always be on your shelves:

★ grain products such as brown rice, rolled oats, bulgur wheat, couscous, a few different wholewheat pasta shapes, noodles and flour
★ dried and canned pulses, including lentils, cannellini beans, kidney beans and chickpeas
★ a variety of unsalted nuts and seeds
★ oils for cooking and salads – sunflower oil and olive oil are best
★ natural sweeteners such as dark and light brown sugar, honey and maple syrup
★ whole and ground spices, plus a selection of seasonings, such as low-salt soy sauce, stock cubes, herbs and pepper.

THE SAVVY SHOPPER

All the ingredients in our recipes are easy to find in supermarkets. If your local store has a fish or meat counter, ask the fishmonger or butcher to prepare the food fresh for you. You are likely to end up with less waste – and even save money.

Also try speciality shops either on the high street or online, and make use of local farmers' markets for top-quality produce that is locally and ethically farmed. Choose organic ingredients whenever possible as they should be free from pesticides and artificial additives.

Fish When buying white fish, look for sustainable sources – try to avoid endangered cod and haddock, and use more abundant varieties such as coley, hake and pollock.

Poultry Choose free-range chicken and turkey meat wherever possible. It is slightly more expensive than 'basic' ranges but will have a better flavour. Breasts and steaks are the most versatile cuts.

Meat Beef, pork and lamb are sold ready cubed, sliced or minced, which will save on preparation time. Steaks, chops and tenderloin are best for quick cooking. Always choose lean mince.

Fruit and vegetables Fresh is best, but ready-prepared packs will save you time.

Let's get cooking

Superfoods Supereasy contains 184 health-boosting recipes, and all include at least one superfood. Each recipe page offers clear step-by-step cooking instructions, ingredient information and invaluable tips.

- **Ingredients** Each ingredient is listed on the page in the order that it is needed in the recipe, with exact quantities given, either in weight or numbers. Unless otherwise stated, all ingredients such as eggs, fruit and vegetables are medium in size.

- **Alternative ingredients** The majority of recipes in this book include different ingredient suggestions so you can include the foods you prefer – or adapt the recipe to what you have available.

- **Nutritional values** If you need to keep an eye on the calories or your intake of fat, protein and fibre, these values supply guidance at a glance.

- **Cook's tips** Expert practical advice to get the most from our recipes, from how to remove seeds from a cardamom pod to which cut of lamb to choose for a stir-fry, and the best way to cook raw beetroot.

- **Superfood information** Every recipe page tells you about the health benefits of one superfood ingredient. Refer to the Glossary (right) if there are any terms that are unfamiliar to you. Also, special features on 14 major superfoods appear throughout the book. Each provides information on the food's health-promoting benefits and includes five simple mouth-watering recipes.

Conversion chart

Food in the United Kingdom is sold according to its metric weight. If you feel more confident with imperial measures, use this conversion chart. Remember to use either metric or imperial – do not mix the two together or the recipes will not work.

Weight

Metric	Imperial (approx)	Metric	Imperial (approx)
10g	¼oz	55g	2oz
15g	½oz	60g	2¼oz
20g	¾oz	70g	2½oz
25g	1oz	75g	2¾oz
35g	1¼oz	85g	3oz
40g	1½oz	90g	3¼oz
50g	1¾oz	100g	3½oz
		1kg	2lb 4oz

Volume

Metric	Imperial (approx)	Metric	Imperial (approx)
30ml	1fl oz	90ml	3¼fl oz
50ml	2fl oz	100ml	3½fl oz
75ml	2½fl oz	1 litre	1¾ pints
85ml	3fl oz		

Glossary

anthocyanin: a type of plant pigment that may help to protect the body against heart disease (see also flavonoid).

antioxidant: a substance that helps to protect against and destroys harmful free radicals that can damage the body's cells.

beta-carotene: part of a family of natural antioxidants found in many fruit and vegetables. It can be converted to vitamin A in the body.

cholesterol: fatty substance made predominantly by the body from saturated fat in the diet. Too much cholesterol in the blood can increase the risk of heart disease.

ellagic acid: a plant chemical that may have anti-cancer properties.

flavonoid: a plant pigment with beneficial antioxidant properties.

folate: form of B vitamin folic acid that occurs naturally in food. Folate helps to produce and maintain new red blood cells in the body.

glycaemic index (GI): a ranking of carbohydrate foods based on the rate at which they raise blood sugar levels after eating. A low GI rating means only a gradual rise in blood sugar levels, which may help with weight control and reduce the risk of heart disease and diabetes.

immune system: the body's defence system, composed of cells, tissues and organs, which protects the body against infection.

monounsaturated fat: can help to lower harmful cholesterol in the blood and keep the heart healthy.

phytochemical: describes a wide variety of compounds produced by plants that may help to reduce the risk of cancer.

polyunsaturated fat: heart-healthy fats that lower harmful cholesterol in the bloodstream. Provides essential fatty acids.

saturated fat: can raise harmful cholesterol in the blood, increasing the risk of heart disease.

vitamin: a substance found in food that is essential to maintain a healthy body.

Superfood Benefits Chart

The chart below lists top superfoods and shows you where they may be particularly beneficial when eaten as part of a balanced diet for the health issues, diseases and conditions indicated in the headings. Use this chart as a guide only – always talk to your doctor if you have any concerns about your health.

	Ageing (skin)	Cancer	Cholesterol lowering	Depression	Diabetes (Type 2)	Digestive health	Eye health	Fatigue	Heart health	Immune function	Menopause	Mental alertness	Osteoporosis	Rheumatoid arthritis	Stroke prevention	Weight control
Apples	•	•	•	•	•	•	•		•	•	•	•		•	•	•
Apricots	•	•	•	•	•	•	•		•	•	•	•	•		•	•
Aubergines	•	•	•	•	•	•			•	•	•	•			•	
Avocados	•	•	•	•	•	•	•		•	•	•	•	•		•	•
Bananas	•	•	•	•	•	•		•	•	•	•	•	•	•	•	•
Beans		•	•	•	•	•		•	•	•			•		•	•
Beef (lean)	•			•				•	•		•	•	•			•
Beetroot	•	•	•	•	•	•	•		•	•	•	•			•	•
Berries	•	•	•	•	•	•	•		•	•	•	•	•	•	•	•
Broccoli	•	•	•	•	•	•	•		•	•	•	•	•	•	•	•
Cabbage	•	•	•	•	•	•	•		•	•	•	•	•	•	•	•
Carrots	•	•	•	•	•	•	•		•	•	•	•	•	•	•	•
Cauliflower	•	•	•	•	•	•			•	•	•	•		•	•	•
Cherries	•	•	•	•	•	•			•	•		•	•	•	•	•
Chicken		•		•	•		•	•	•	•		•	•	•	•	•
Chicken livers		•		•	•		•	•	•	•		•	•	•	•	•
Citrus	•	•	•	•	•	•	•		•	•	•	•	•	•	•	•
Courgettes	•	•	•	•	•	•			•	•	•	•		•	•	•
Dried fruit	•	•	•	•	•	•		•	•	•	•	•	•	•	•	•
Eggs		•		•			•	•	•	•	•		•	•	•	•
Garlic		•	•		•	•			•					•		•
Grains		•	•	•	•	•		•	•	•	•	•		•	•	•
Grapes	•			•	•				•	•	•	•		•	•	•
Lentils		•	•	•	•			•	•	•	•	•	•		•	•

	Ageing (skin)	Cancer	Cholesterol lowering	Depression	Diabetes (Type 2)	Digestive health	Eye health	Fatigue	Heart health	Immune function	Menopause	Mental alertness	Osteoporosis	Rheumatoid arthritis	Stroke prevention	Weight control
Low-fat dairy	●	●		●	●	●		●	●	●	●	●	●	●	●	●
Mangos	●	●	●	●	●	●	●		●	●	●	●	●	●	●	●
Mushrooms	●	●	●	●	●	●	●	●		●	●		●	●	●	●
Nuts	●	●	●	●	●		●		●	●	●	●	●	●	●	●
Oats		●	●	●	●			●	●	●	●	●			●	●
Oily fish	●	●	●	●	●				●	●	●	●	●	●	●	
Olive oil	●	●	●		●				●	●		●	●	●	●	
Onion		●	●			●			●	●	●				●	●
Pears	●	●	●	●		●			●	●	●				●	●
Peas	●	●	●	●	●	●	●	●	●	●	●	●	●	●		●
Peppers	●	●	●	●	●	●			●	●	●	●	●	●	●	●
Pineapples	●	●	●	●	●	●			●	●	●	●			●	●
Pomegranates	●	●	●	●	●	●	●		●	●	●	●	●	●		●
Seafood	●	●	●	●	●			●	●	●	●	●	●	●	●	●
Seeds	●	●	●	●	●	●	●	●	●	●	●	●	●	●	●	●
Soya beans	●	●	●	●	●	●		●	●	●	●	●	●	●	●	●
Spinach	●	●	●	●	●	●	●	●	●	●	●	●	●	●	●	●
Squash, butternut	●	●	●	●	●	●	●	●	●	●	●	●		●	●	●
Sweet potatoes		●	●	●	●	●	●	●	●	●	●	●		●	●	●
Tomatoes	●	●	●	●	●	●	●		●	●	●		●	●		●
Turkey		●	●	●	●		●	●	●	●		●	●	●	●	●
White fish		●	●	●	●			●	●	●		●	●	●	●	●
Wholegrain bread		●	●	●	●	●		●	●	●	●	●	●	●	●	●
Wholegrain rice		●	●	●	●	●		●	●	●	●	●	●	●	●	●

Soups, starters & snacks

Boost your energy with delicious and moreish light bites crammed with nutritional goodness. These quick-to-fix healthy choices will also help you to avoid the high-calorie snack trap.

Chunky **vegetable** soup with **pasta**

A real Italian-inspired meal in a bowl – nutritious wholewheat spaghetti bathed in a rich minestrone-style soup chock-full of tender vegetables. Serve with warmed olive focaccia for a heartening treat.

Serves 4
Preparation 10 minutes
Cooking 30 minutes

Each serving provides • 270kcal
• 11g protein • 29g carbohydrates
of which 13g sugars • 13g fat of which
4g saturates • 7g fibre

1 onion
1 carrot
1 celery stick
1 yellow pepper
1 parsnip
100g mushrooms
2 tbsp olive oil
1 bay leaf
1 garlic clove, crushed
400g can chopped tomatoes
500ml hot chicken or vegetable
   stock
75g wholewheat spaghetti
50g grated Parmesan cheese,
   to serve

ALTERNATIVE INGREDIENTS
• For a meaty version of this soup,
dry-fry 50g diced smoked bacon,
chorizo or pancetta for 1 minute
before starting step 1.
• Leave out the parsnip and add
150g fresh or frozen green beans
or broad beans with the pasta.

1 Finely chop the onion. Dice the carrot, celery, pepper and parsnip, and chop the mushrooms. Heat the oil in a large saucepan over a high heat. Add the bay leaf, onion, carrot, celery and garlic, reduce the heat to low, then cover and cook for 2 minutes.

2 Stir in the pepper and mushrooms, re-cover and cook for a further 2 minutes. Add the parsnip and tomatoes, then pour in the hot stock and bring back to the boil. Reduce the heat and simmer, covered, for 20 minutes or until the vegetables are tender.

3 Snap the spaghetti into 4cm pieces and stir them into the soup. Bring back to the boil, reduce the heat and simmer for 5 minutes until the pasta is tender. Ladle the soup into four bowls and sprinkle with Parmesan cheese.

COOK'S TIPS
★ Frozen vegetables are great for everyday meals, saving on shopping and preparation. There is a wide variety of mixtures, some with peppers, celery and mushrooms as well as the usual carrots, peas and beans. Use fresh onion and garlic, then add frozen mixed vegetables in step 2 in place of the fresh ingredients. Reduce the cooking time by 5 minutes.

SUPERFOOD

WHOLEWHEAT PASTA
Most of the goodness of wholegrains
is concentrated in the outer bran layer.
Wholewheat pasta retains that bran
and so contains up to 75 per cent
more nutrients than pasta made
from refined grains. Regularly eating
wholewheat pasta protects against
heart disease and may lower the
risk from some forms of cancer of
the digestive tract.

Chilled **carrot** and **orange** soup

For a refreshing and healthy cold soup, try a fusion of yogurt, herbs and two juices whose vibrant orange colour is the product of the cancer-fighting pigment beta-carotene.

Serves 4
Preparation 10 minutes
Cooking 2 minutes

700ml carrot juice, chilled
150ml plain yogurt
grated zest of ½ orange and juice
   of 1 orange, about 75ml
4 tbsp snipped fresh chives
2 tbsp chopped fresh tarragon
1 tbsp olive oil
4 slices wholemeal bread

Each serving provides • 181kcal
• 7g protein • 26g carbohydrates of
which 11g sugars • 6g fat of which
1g saturates • 3g fibre

ALTERNATIVE INGREDIENTS
• For a slightly thicker soup with
a 'nutty' flavour, cut the crusts off
3 extra slices of wholemeal bread,
about 100g, and whizz the bread in
a blender with the carrot juice, yogurt
and chives.
• Fresh coriander works well instead
of tarragon.
• Try tomato juice in place of carrot
juice and add a dash of chilli sauce
for a piquant tomato soup.

1 Preheat the grill to the hottest setting. Pour the carrot juice into a large bowl and whisk in the yogurt until smooth. Add the orange zest, juice and chives, then whisk again. Ladle into four soup bowls.

2 Mix the tarragon with the olive oil. Toast the bread for 1 minute on one side under the grill, then turn and lightly brush the untoasted side with the tarragon oil. Toast for another 1 minute until golden and crisp. Season the soup with ground black pepper to taste, and serve.

COOK'S TIPS
★ You can make this soup in advance and chill for several hours in the fridge before serving. Add chopped tarragon to the oil well in advance to infuse it with the herb flavour and then store it in an airtight jar in the fridge until needed.
★ If you cannot get carrot juice from your supermarket, make it with an electric juicer or in a blender. For this recipe you will need 1kg of peeled or scrubbed carrots. Either juice the carrots according to the juicer instructions or whizz them in a blender until finely mashed. Add a little water if the mixture becomes too dry and the blades stick. Pour the carrot juice into a jug and add 500ml of water. Leave it to stand for 30 minutes, then strain through a fine-meshed sieve.

SUPERFOOD

CARROTS
Beta-carotene, found in abundance in carrots and other brightly coloured fruits and vegetables, has strong antioxidant properties and may help to protect against cancer. It is converted to vitamin A in the body, which helps to promote healthy skin and improve vision in dim light.

Carrots

SUPERFOOD

It is no myth that carrots help you to see in the dark, thanks to their high level of beta-carotene, which the body converts to vision-enhancing vitamin A. Yet carrots offer much more – cell-protecting properties for great-looking skin, plenty of fibre to aid digestion, and a low fat and calorie count to make them a healthy anytime snack.

Herby carrot and coriander soup

Serves 4
Preparation 10 minutes Cooking 45 minutes

Each serving provides • 112kcal • 2g protein • 16g carbohydrates of which 13g sugars •5g fat of which 1g saturates • 4g fibre

Heat **1 tablespoon vegetable oil** in a saucepan over a medium-low heat and then add **5 chopped carrots** and **1 large chopped onion**. Stir-fry for 5 minutes or until softened. Add **2 crushed garlic cloves** and **1 teaspoon ground coriander**, and stir occasionally for 1 minute. Pour in **1 litre hot vegetable stock** and bring to a simmer. Cover and cook for 30 minutes. Take off the heat, leave to cool a little then purée in a blender or in the pan with a stick blender until smooth. Stir in the **juice of ½ lemon**, and add seasoning to taste. Gently reheat the soup but do not boil. Just before serving, stir in **4 tablespoons chopped fresh coriander**. Ladle into four bowls and drizzle **1 teaspoon plain yogurt** over each one before serving.

COOK'S TIPS

★ Give the soup a slightly different flavour by using ground cumin instead of gound coriander.

Layered veggie casserole

Serves 4
Preparation 15 minutes Cooking 60 minutes

Each serving provides • 381kcal • 13g protein • 62g carbohydrates of which 20g sugars • 8g fat of which 2g saturates • 3g fibre

Heat **1 tablespoon olive oil** in a flameproof casserole dish and cook **1 large thinly sliced onion** over a medium-low heat for 5 minutes to soften, stirring occasionally. Add **1 tablespoon chopped fresh parsley**, **1 tablespoon snipped fresh chives** and **2 crushed garlic cloves**, and stir through the onions. Remove the onion mixture from the casserole dish with a slotted spoon. Cover the bottom of the dish with **500g thickly sliced potatoes** then sprinkle **40g dried split peas** and a third of the onion mixture over the potatoes. Add the next layer of **5 sliced carrots** and cover with **40g dried split peas** and one-third of the onion mixture. Top with a layer of **2 sliced parsnips** then **40g dried split peas** and the remaining third of the onion mixture. Pour in **1 litre hot vegetable stock** and bring to the boil.

Reduce the heat, cover and simmer for 30 minutes. Remove the lid and cook for a further 20 minutes or until the vegetables are tender and the sauce has thickened. Serve each portion with **1 tablespoon soured cream** on top.

COOK'S TIPS
★ The dried split peas cook in the casserole stock, and so there is no need to pre-soak or pre-cook them.
★ Serve the casserole with a steamed green vegetable such as broccoli, spinach or savoy cabbage.

Honey-braised carrots with petit pois

Serves 4
Preparation 5 minutes Cooking 12 minutes

Each serving provides • 137kcal • 3g protein • 15g carbohydrates of which 14g sugars • 8g fat of which 3g saturates • 5g fibre

Place **500g whole baby carrots** in a saucepan and add **15g butter, 1 tablespoon olive oil, 3 tablespoons hot vegetable stock, ½ teaspoon grated nutmeg** and **1½ tablespoons runny honey**. Bring to a simmer, cover and cook for 8 minutes or until the carrots are just tender. Add **125g frozen petit pois** to the pan and heat through for 1-2 minutes. Serve the carrots garnished with **1 tablespoon snipped fresh chives**.

COOK'S TIPS
★ If baby carrots are not available, use large ones and cut them in half widthways and lengthways.
★ Serve as a side dish to roast beef or venison to complement their rich meat flavours.

Brown rice, lentil and carrot salad

Serves 4
Preparation 10 minutes Cooking 35 minutes

Each serving provides • 137kcal • 3g protein • 15g carbohydrates of which 14g sugars • 8g fat of which 2g saturates • 5g fibre

Cook **150g brown rice** in a saucepan in **300ml hot vegetable stock** and boil, covered, for 30 minutes or until tender and the stock is absorbed. Cut **3 carrots** into 1-2cm chunks and boil with **200g broccoli florets** for 10 minutes or until tender. Remove the rice from the heat and add a **150g can green lentils** to the rice. Stir in gently and allow to cool. Stir the cooked vegetables

into the rice with **1 tablespoon finely chopped sun-dried tomatoes**. Make a dressing with **2 tablespoons olive oil, 2 tablespoons sesame oil, 1 tablespoon balsamic vinegar, 2 teaspoons finely grated fresh root ginger** and a dash of **readymade hot pepper sauce**. Stir the dressing and **2 tablespoons chopped parsley** into the rice mixture. Sprinkle **1 tablespoon sesame seeds** over the salad and serve.

COOK'S TIPS
★ To cook dried lentils, place 150g green lentils in boiling water and simmer for 25 minutes until tender. Drain before adding to the rice.
★ If the rice is not cooked through by the time the stock is absorbed, add a little more hot stock or boiling water and continue cooking until tender. Rice varies in cooking time according to the age and variety of the grains.
★ Handy for a buffet, this salad can be stored overnight in the fridge. It will taste even better when brought back to room temperature and the flavours have infused.

Sweet and sour noodles

Serves 4
Preparation 10 minutes Cooking 10 minutes

Each serving provides • 334kcal • 7g protein • 52g carbohydrates of which 16g sugars • 12g fat of which 2g saturates • 5g fibre

Cook **200g medium egg noodles** for 4 minutes or according to the packet instructions. In another pan, heat **2 tablespoons vegetable oil** over a high heat and add **3 thinly sliced carrots** and **1 sliced leek**. Stir-fry for 3 minutes. Diagonally slice **6 spring onions** and add to the pan with **2 chopped garlic cloves** and **1 chopped mild green chilli**. Stir-fry for 1 minute. Add **1 teaspoon ground cumin, 1 tablespoon light soy sauce** and **2 teaspoons runny honey** and stir for another 1 minute. Add the noodles and stir gently to heat through. Add **1 teaspoon whole cumin seeds** before serving.

COOK'S TIPS
★ Adjust the level of chilli heat to your preference with mild, medium or hot chillies.
★ For a heartier meal add leftover cooked meat, or thin slices of pork or chicken fillet stir-fried in 1 tablespoon vegetable oil, when adding the noodles.

Chicken and rice broth with shredded omelette

Sesame oil, juicy chicken and vitamin-rich pak choi are just three of the good-for-you ingredients in this delectable soup. Laced with strips of protein-packed omelette, it is a perfect light meal.

Serves 4
Preparation 15 minutes
Cooking 35 minutes

Each serving provides • 315kcal • 22g protein • 22g carbohydrates of which 5g sugars • 16g fat of which 3g saturates • 2g fibre

ALTERNATIVE INGREDIENTS
• Ready-prepared stir-fry chicken strips are available in the chiller cabinets at supermarkets. If you cannot find any, use the same quantity of chicken breast and cut it into small slices.
• Choi sum, or mustard greens, is delicious instead of pak choi. Alternatively, replace with purple sprouting broccoli and allow an extra 1 minute cooking time in step 4.

SUPERFOOD

EGGS
Two medium eggs will provide 100 per cent of your recommended daily amount of vitamin B12. Researchers believe this vitamin may help to retain mental alertness and protect against Alzheimer's disease. Eggs are also rich in protein and other key nutrients.

1 small onion
2 celery sticks
2 carrots
2 tbsp vegetable oil
1 tbsp sesame oil
250g stir-fry chicken strips

75g brown rice
2 garlic cloves, crushed
1.2 litres hot chicken stock
2 eggs
250g pak choi
2 spring onions

1 Thinly slice the onion and chop the celery into 1cm chunks. Cut the carrots into 5mm sticks. Heat 1 tablespoon vegetable oil and the sesame oil in a large saucepan. Add the chicken and cook over a high heat for 1 minute. Stir in the rice, garlic, onion, celery and carrots. Cook for 1 minute more.

2 Add the hot chicken stock and bring back to the boil, then reduce the heat. Cover and simmer for 30 minutes or until the chicken and vegetables are cooked and the rice is tender.

3 Meanwhile, heat the remaining 1 tablespoon vegetable oil in a frying pan over a high heat. Beat the eggs together and pour them into the pan. Cook over a high heat for 1 minute, tilting the pan and lifting the edges of the omelette as the egg sets. Remove from the pan, roll up the omelette and slice into 1cm wide strips.

4 Slice the pak choi and shred the spring onions. When the soup is cooked, add the pak choi and spring onions, bring back to a simmer and cook for 1 minute more. Season to taste, add the omelette rolls and ladle into four bowls to serve.

COOK'S TIPS
★ To wash and prepare pak choi, swish the head in a bowl of water. Rinse between the leaves with running water then shake well. This keeps the head intact and makes slicing easy. Trim off the base and slice as required.

Beetroot and cranberry borscht

Cranberry juice brings sweetness and fruity goodness to red cabbage and purple beetroot in a soup that is full of vitamins and antioxidants. Wholemeal bread makes a tasty accompaniment.

Serves 4
Preparation 5 minutes
Cooking 10 minutes

1 onion
2 celery sticks
1 tbsp olive oil
2 garlic cloves, crushed
pinch of ground mace
300g red cabbage
500g cooked beetroot
600ml hot chicken stock
600ml cranberry juice drink
1 tsp red wine vinegar or
   cider vinegar
4 tbsp plain yogurt
2 tbsp snipped chives

Each serving provides • 237kcal • 6g protein • 40g carbohydrates of which 17g sugars • 6g fat of which 1g saturates • 5g fibre

ALTERNATIVE INGREDIENTS
• Use fresh beetroot instead of cooked. Wash, trim, peel and dice 500g fresh beetroot and add it to the onion mixture instead of the cabbage in step 2. Add the stock and water, bring to the boil then reduce the heat, cover and simmer for 10 minutes. Add the cabbage and cranberry juice drink and continue from step 2.
• Try pomegranate juice drink instead of cranberry for a stronger sweet-sour soup. Increase the quantity of vinegar to 2-3 teaspoons, tasting as you add, to balance the sweeter fruit juice.

1 Chop the onion and dice the celery. Heat the olive oil in a large saucepan over a high heat and add the onion, celery, garlic and mace. Stir the vegetables and reduce the heat to medium, then cover and cook for 4 minutes or until the vegetables begin to soften.

2 Finely shred the red cabbage and dice the beetroot. Add the cabbage to the pan and cook, stirring, for 1 minute. Add 600ml hot chicken stock and the cranberry juice drink. Stir in the beetroot and bring to the boil. Reduce the heat to low, so that the soup simmers steadily. Cover and cook for 10 minutes.

3 Stir in the vinegar, season to taste and ladle the soup into four bowls. Top each serving with 1 tablespoon of yogurt and sprinkle with chives.

COOK'S TIPS
★ Cut red cabbage into short fine shreds by slicing it into slim wedges and then finely slicing the wedges – the cabbage should then fall apart.
★ Vacuum-packed cooked beetroot is a brilliant storecupboard ingredient with a long shelf life. It works well in this recipe – just make sure it is not the kind preserved with vinegar or acetic acid. If using fresh beetroot, chop any large beets in half, then boil for 20 minutes or until tender.

SUPERFOOD

RED CABBAGE
Cabbage belongs to the brassica family, along with Brussels sprouts, broccoli and watercress. It is bursting with antioxidant nutrients, and also provides vitamin C and B vitamins, such as folate. There is some evidence to link brassicas with a reduced risk of getting cancer, especially cancer of the digestive tract.

Springtime **vegetable** soup

The gentle aniseed flavour of fennel, the firm texture of new potatoes and a kick of fresh parsley merge temptingly in a hearty soup inspired by a Polish recipe. Serve with bread and cheese.

Serves 4
Preparation 15 minutes
Cooking 25 minutes

1 fennel bulb
2 large onions
2 carrots
1 tbsp olive oil
1 small rosemary sprig
3 garlic cloves, crushed
500g small new potatoes
900ml hot vegetable stock
4 tbsp chopped fresh parsley

Each serving provides • 202kcal
• 5g protein • 36g carbohydrates of
which 13g sugars • 5g fat of which
1g saturates • 6g fibre

ALTERNATIVE INGREDIENTS
• Add 4-6 diced celery sticks instead of the fennel for a milder flavour with less aniseed.
• If new potatoes are out of season, use maincrop potatoes that are recommended for boiling. Peel and cut them into bite-size chunks.
• For some extra colour, add the tips of 200g tenderstem broccoli spears to the soup for the final 5 minutes of cooking. Bring the soup back to a simmer before covering the pan to ensure that the broccoli cooks.
• Boost the flavour of the soup by adding 100g diced bacon or pancetta in step 2.

1 Trim and chop the stalk and feathery leaves of the fennel and set aside. Cut the bulb into slim wedges, remove the core from the base and thinly slice the wedges into bite-size pieces.

2 Chop the onions and coarsely dice the carrots. Place the oil, fennel stalk and leaves, rosemary, onions, carrots and garlic in a large saucepan and cook, stirring occasionally, over a high heat for about 3 minutes. Stir in the diced fennel bulb, cover and reduce the heat to low. Cook for a further 5 minutes, stirring once or until the vegetables have softened.

3 Scrub the potatoes, cut in half and add them to the pan, then add the hot stock. Bring back to the boil and adjust the heat so that the soup simmers steadily. Cover and cook for 10-15 minutes or until the potatoes are tender. Season to taste and stir in the parsley just before serving.

COOK'S TIPS
★ Use good-quality cubed, powdered and chilled stocks for the best flavour when making soup.
★ If making your own stock, simmer the leftovers of a roast chicken with an onion, carrot and celery stick.

SUPERFOOD

PARSLEY
Though usually served and eaten only in small amounts, parsley is highly nutritious. It contains fibre for a healthy digestive system, the antioxidant vitamin C for cancer prevention and folate (a B vitamin) for heart health.

Creamy **lentil** soup with **croutons**

Perk up the rich flavours of hearty, hunger-busting lentil soup with an unexpected zingy topping of avocado, spring onion and lemon zest. Crispy wholemeal croutons add crunch appeal.

Serves 4
Preparation 15 minutes
Cooking 22 minutes

Each serving provides • 164kcal • 8g protein • 24g carbohydrates of which 9g sugars • 5g fat of which 1g saturates • 4g fibre

1 onion
2 celery sticks
1 large carrot
200g swede
1 tbsp olive oil
1 garlic clove, crushed
100g red lentils
1 bay leaf
2 fresh thyme sprigs
1 tbsp tomato purée
900ml hot chicken or vegetable
   stock

Croutons
2 slices wholemeal bread
1 tbsp olive oil
1 avocado
1 spring onion
finely pared zest of 1 lemon

ALTERNATIVE INGREDIENTS
• As a change to red lentils, use 150g green or brown lentils and increase the quantity of stock to 1.2 litres. Simmer the soup for 30-35 minutes until the lentils are tender. Do not blend but serve as a chunky soup.
• Add 1 large diced parsnip instead of the swede for a sweeter flavour.

1 Preheat the grill to high. Chop the onion then dice the celery, carrot and swede into 3cm pieces. Heat the oil in a large saucepan over a high heat. Add the onion, celery, carrot, swede and garlic. Reduce the heat to low, cover and cook for 2 minutes.

2 Rinse the lentils in a sieve under cold running water. Add the lentils, bay leaf, thyme and tomato purée to the pan. Pour in the hot stock, stir and bring back to the boil. Reduce the heat, cover and simmer for 20 minutes until the lentils have disintegrated.

3 Meanwhile, make the croutons. Brush one side of the bread slices with ½ tablespoon of the olive oil and grill for 1 minute or until golden. Turn them over, brush with the remaining ½ tablespoon of oil and grill for 1 minute more. Cut the toast into 2cm croutons.

4 Dice the avocado and place in a bowl. Finely chop the spring onion and add it to the avocado. Stir in the lemon zest. Remove the thyme and bay leaf from the soup. Purée the soup in a blender or in the pan with a stick blender until smooth. Season to taste and ladle the soup into four bowls. Top with the croutons and avocado mixture.

COOK'S TIPS
★ If using a blender, return the soup to the pan after blending and reheat for 1-2 minutes to make sure that it is piping hot when served.
★ Use a potato peeler or zester to remove, or pare, the lemon zest. Make sure that you remove only the yellow skin and not the white pith as well, as this tastes bitter.

SUPERFOOD

LENTILS
Rich in starchy carbohydrates, lentils have a low glycaemic index (GI) rating, so are great for keeping hunger at bay. Their high fibre content is good news for the digestive system, and with iron, B vitamins and immunity-boosting zinc, lentils are an all-round healthy choice.

Spinach and pea soup
with minty yogurt

This beautiful, garden-fresh soup is just bursting with the flavours of energy-boosting spinach and peas. It is quick to make, too – simply add a refreshing yogurt swirl and then serve.

Serves 4
Preparation 10 minutes
Cooking 18 minutes

Each serving provides • 129kcal • 10g protein • 16g carbohydrates of which 9g sugars • 3g fat of which 1g saturates • 7g fibre

1 onion
1 large potato
1 spring onion
200g plain yogurt
2 tbsp chopped fresh mint
1 tbsp olive oil
1 garlic clove, crushed
600ml hot chicken stock
350g frozen peas or petit pois
200g fresh spinach

ALTERNATIVE INGREDIENTS
• Swiss chard, Chinese leaves or lettuce work well in this recipe as an alternative to the spinach.
• Use a peeled and diced whole cucumber instead of the spinach.
• As a change to the yogurt topping, dice the flesh from 2 ripe avocados and toss them with 2 tablespoons chopped fresh coriander and the grated zest and juice of ½ lime. Spoon over the soup just before serving.

1 Chop the onion and dice the potato into 2cm cubes, then finely chop the spring onion. Spoon the yogurt into a bowl and add the spring onion and mint. Heat the oil, garlic, onion and potato in a large saucepan over a medium heat. Cook for 2 minutes, stirring occasionally, until the onion softens slightly. Add the hot chicken stock, stir, bring the contents of the pan back to the boil, then cover and simmer for 10 minutes.

2 Add the frozen peas or petit pois, bring back to the boil, cover and simmer for 2 minutes. Stir in the spinach, cover and cook for a further 3 minutes.

3 Remove the pan from the heat and leave the soup for 1 minute to cool slightly. Purée using a blender. Reheat for 1-2 minutes, if necessary. Pour the soup into four bowls and serve with generous helpings of the mint yogurt.

COOK'S TIPS
★ This soup freezes well, without the yogurt topping, for up to 3 months. Make twice the quantity and store half immediately in a lidded container. Thaw completely, then reheat to boiling point, stirring frequently, before serving with the yogurt swirl.

SUPERFOOD

SPINACH
Rich in nutrients, spinach is an excellent source of folate – a vitamin needed for good blood circulation and a healthy pregnancy. The vegetable also contains fibre to promote digestive health and iron to help to prevent anaemia.

Warming **cock-a-leekie** soup with **kale**

A thoroughly comforting meal for the family, with chunks of tender chicken, sweet kale, soft leeks and vitamin-filled prunes to keep you energised throughout the day. Serve with a crusty baguette.

Serves 4
Preparation 15 minutes
Cooking 20 minutes

400g skinless chicken breast fillets
350g leeks
1 tbsp vegetable oil
2 carrots, about 150g
1.2 litres hot chicken stock
350g kale
100g ready-to-eat prunes

Each serving provides • 240kcal • 24g protein • 15g carbohydrates of which 14g sugars • 7g fat of which 1g saturates • 7g fibre

ALTERNATIVE INGREDIENTS
• Fresh savoy cabbage or spring greens make good alternatives to kale.

1 Cut the chicken breast fillets into 3cm cubes. Trim, slice and rinse the leeks. Heat the oil in a large saucepan over a high heat. Add the chicken and leeks and cook for 5 minutes, reducing the heat to medium after the first 1-2 minutes. Stir occasionally.

2 Slice the carrots. Pour the hot stock into the pan. Add the carrots and bring to the boil over a high heat, stirring, then reduce the heat to low. Cover and simmer for 10 minutes or until the carrots are tender.

3 Finely shred the kale and stir into the pan. Bring back to the boil then reduce the heat, re-cover and simmer for 4 minutes. Chop the prunes into quarters and stir them into the soup. Simmer for 1 minute, season to taste and then pour into four bowls to serve.

COOK'S TIPS

★ To shred leafy green vegetables such as kale, tightly roll up a few leaves together and slice them thinly with a sharp knife. For short shreds, cut the slices in half. Alternatively, ready-prepared vegetables, especially frozen, are a labour-saving option for everyday cooking.
★ Organic chicken stock is a good choice as it has a light flavour and is not too high in salt.
★ If fresh vegetables are not to hand, use mixed frozen broccoli and cauliflower instead of kale. Add the florets with the prunes in step 3 so that they remain crunchy.

SUPERFOOD

LEEKS

Among a leek's many phytochemicals is a rich amount of carotenoids, especially beta-carotene, a natural antioxidant. With potassium to help to regulate blood pressure, and B vitamins, including folate, leeks are a good all-rounder for heart and digestive health.

Pepper and tomato soup with a spicy egg

For a bowl of sunshine, try a rustic soup packed with the vivid goodness of tomato and red pepper, topped with a chilli-flecked fried egg. It makes a filling snack or light supper with oodles of taste.

Serves 4
Preparation 10 minutes
Cooking 25 minutes

1 onion
1 celery stick
2 red peppers
3 tbsp olive oil
400g can chopped tomatoes
600ml hot chicken stock
1 spring onion
4 eggs
pinch of chilli flakes

Each serving provides • 251kcal • 10g protein • 11g carbohydrates of which 10g sugars • 19g fat of which 4g saturates • 3g fibre

ALTERNATIVE INGREDIENTS
• To boost the fibre content of this dish, drain a 400g can of cannellini beans or red kidney beans and add them in step 2.
• For a meaty soup, slice 100g chorizo sausage and add it to the soup at the end of step 3 to warm through while the eggs are frying.
• For a complete meal in a bowl, add 50g miniature pasta shapes in step 2 during the final 5 minutes of cooking.

1 Chop the onion, trim and dice the celery and dice the peppers. Place 1 tablespoon of the oil in a large saucepan over a high heat. Add the onion, celery and peppers and cook for about 30 seconds until sizzling. Reduce the heat to medium-high, cover with a lid and cook for 5 minutes, shaking the pan occasionally, until the vegetables are softened.

2 Add the tomatoes and stir in the hot stock. Bring back to the boil. Reduce the heat, re-cover and simmer the soup for 15 minutes. Trim and finely chop the spring onion.

3 Heat the remaining 2 tablespoons of oil in a large frying pan over a medium-high heat. Break in the eggs and fry for 1-2 minutes or until the whites are set but the yolks are soft. Season the soup to taste and ladle into bowls. Float an egg on each portion and sprinkle with the chopped spring onion and chilli flakes.

COOK'S TIPS
★ If you feel adventurous, break the eggs directly into the soup and allow them to poach for 1-1½ minutes. The trick is to have the soup bubbling steadily when the eggs are added, then regulate the heat to keep the liquid simmering gently. Use a slotted spoon to transfer the eggs to each bowl before ladling in the soup.

SUPERFOOD

TOMATOES
It is the antioxidant lycopene in tomatoes that gives them their wonderful rich colour. Lycopene is more easily absorbed by the body from processed or cooked tomatoes, so it pays to enjoy them canned or in a paste, as well as fresh. As a rich source of potassium, tomatoes can help to regulate blood pressure, reducing the risk of stroke.

Chunky **fish** and **vegetable** soup

Aromatic lemon and herbs blend brilliantly with leeks and broad beans to make a perfect match for pieces of succulent white fish. This chunky soup is low in fat and really satisfying.

Serves 4
Preparation 10 minutes
Cooking 20 minutes

Each serving provides • 312kcal • 28g protein • 29g carbohydrates of which 9g sugars • 10g fat of which 1g saturates • 7g fibre

1 large leek
2 tbsp olive oil
2 garlic cloves, crushed
4 fresh thyme sprigs
2 bay leaves
2 x 400g cans chopped tomatoes
600ml hot fish stock
450g skinless white fish, such as haddock, coley, pollack or hoki
¼ cucumber
200g frozen baby broad beans
grated zest of 1 lemon
100g readymade croutons

ALTERNATIVE INGREDIENTS
• Try a mixture of salmon and white fish or mixed seafood. If using frozen mixed seafood, add an extra 1 minute of cooking time in step 3.
• For a subtle aniseed flavour, add 1 large fennel bulb and cut it into slim wedges, then slice these across into shreds. Cook the fennel with the leek in step 1.
• Frozen peas or sweetcorn can be used instead of the broad beans.
• For a more substantial soup, add a drained 400g can of cannellini or black-eyed beans with the broad beans.

1 Finely chop the leek. Heat the oil in a large saucepan over a high heat, then add the leek, garlic, thyme and bay leaves. Cover and cook for 2 minutes, reducing the heat if the vegetables begin to brown too quickly.

2 Stir in the tomatoes and the hot fish stock. Bring back to the boil, cover, reduce the heat to low and simmer for 15 minutes. Meanwhile, cut the fish into 3cm square chunks and dice the cucumber.

3 Add the broad beans to the pan, cover and bring back to the boil. Reduce the heat so that the soup is bubbling gently then add the fish, lemon zest and cucumber. Cover and simmer for 3 minutes until the fish is cooked through. Ladle into four bowls, add a sprinkling of readymade croutons to each one and serve.

COOK'S TIPS
★ When buying fresh fish, choose fillets or steaks that are firm and translucent. Fish that smells fishy is probably past its best. If you are concerned about sustainability, buy fish that is responsibly caught or farmed. When buying fish in a supermarket, look for the blue Marine Stewardship Council (MSC) logo that guarantees the fish has come from a sustainable source.
★ Readymade croutons are available in different sizes and flavours, so you can add your own twist to the presentation and taste.

SUPERFOOD

WHITE FISH
Government guidelines recommend that we eat more fish – at least one serving of white fish per week – to maintain good health. White fish is low in fat, high in protein and rich in iodine, vital for a healthy metabolism.

Fresh **tuna** and zesty **bean** salad

What better way could there be to get those all-important omega-3 oils? Arrange strips of lightly seared tuna next to a lemony bean salad infused with garlic and basil for a tangy lunch or starter.

Serves 4
Preparation 20 minutes
Cooking 1 minute

Each serving provides • 220kcal
• 17g protein • 15g carbohydrates
of which 2g sugars • 10g fat of which
2g saturates • 5g fibre

1 small red onion
400g can cannellini beans
1 small garlic clove, chopped
pared zest of 1 lemon
4 tbsp chopped fresh parsley
8 finely shredded fresh basil leaves,
   plus extra whole leaves, to garnish
2 tbsp olive oil
150g tuna steak
4 lemon wedges, to garnish

ALTERNATIVE INGREDIENTS
• Use 200g smoked mackerel, boned
and flaked, instead of the tuna.
• Grilled halloumi cheese is a
delicious vegetarian alternative with
the bean salad. Brown the slices under
a hot grill for 30 seconds on each side.
• This salad also makes a good base
for grilled salmon fillet. Cook the fillets
flesh side up under a very hot grill for
about 1 minute until just firm.

1 Thinly slice the onion. Drain and rinse the cannellini beans. In a bowl, mix the cannellini beans with the garlic, onion, lemon zest, parsley, basil leaves and olive oil. Cover and leave to stand for 15 minutes.

2 Meanwhile, cut the tuna steak into slices about 5mm thick. Heat a heavy nonstick frying pan over a high heat, add the tuna slices and fry for 30 seconds to brown. Turn over the fish and fry for a further 30 seconds. Remove from the heat immediately.

3 Divide the bean salad between four plates. Arrange 3-4 tuna slices on one side and garnish each portion with a lemon wedge and whole basil leaves.

COOK'S TIPS

★ The frying pan must be very hot so that the tuna browns and cooks almost immediately. If you do not have a nonstick pan, add 1 tablespoon vegetable oil before adding the tuna. Use tongs for turning the tuna, or try a spatula and fork.
★ For rare tuna still pink in the middle, cook the steak whole, browning it for 30-60 seconds on each side, then remove from the heat and slice. This method is best suited to really fresh tuna. Pre-packed or frozen tuna is better cooked until opaque.

SUPERFOOD

TUNA
Unlike canned tuna, fresh tuna is rich in health-promoting omega-3 fatty acids. In addition to their proven heart benefits, these oils can alleviate inflammatory conditions such as rheumatoid arthritis and joint stiffness. One weekly serving of oily fish, such as herring, salmon, mackerel or fresh tuna, provides your daily requirement.

SUPERFOOD

Beans

In all its forms, from tender garden-fresh green beans to robust dried kidney beans, this humble vegetable soaks up flavours while contributing a generous helping of fibre for gut health and enriching the blood with iron. Beans fill you up but are low in fat, and as most beans contain at least 20 per cent protein they are an excellent alternative to meat for vegetarians.

Warm citrus bean salad

Serves 4
Preparation 10 minutes Cooking 15 minutes

Each serving provides • 104kcal • 6g protein • 9g carbohydrates of which 2g sugars • 5g fat of which 1g saturates • 7g fibre

Boil **400g frozen baby broad beans** in a saucepan of boiling water for 3 minutes or until just tender, then drain and set aside. Heat **1 tablespoon olive oil** in a frying pan and add **2 finely chopped shallots** and **1 crushed garlic clove**. Stir-fry over a medium heat for 8 minutes or until softened. Add the beans to the onions in the frying pan with **2 tablespoons finely chopped fresh mint, 2 tablespoons finely chopped fresh parsley** and the **juice of ½ lemon**. Cook for 2 minutes, stirring occasionally, before serving.

COOK'S TIPS
★ If the broad beans are large, remove the outer pale green cases. Pour boiling water over them, leave for 2-3 minutes, then strain and refresh with cold water. Pop the beans out of the cases.
★ This dish works really well with grilled chicken or smoky bacon.
★ Use the juice of 1 lemon to sharpen the flavour and serve with steamed white fish fillets.

Summer bean risotto

Serves 4
Preparation 5 minutes Cooking 30 minutes

Each serving provides • 596kcal • 19g protein • 110g carbohydrates of which 5g sugars • 12g fat of which 4g saturates • 7g fibre

Heat **1 tablespoon olive oil** in a large frying pan and add **1 thinly sliced large onion**. Cook over a medium-low heat for 5 minutes or until softened. Add **2 finely chopped garlic cloves** and stir in. Add **400g risotto rice**, turn up the heat to medium-high, and stir to coat all the rice with oil. Add **1 tablespoon fresh thyme** and the **juice of 1 lemon**. Begin to add **1 litre hot vegetable stock** to the pan in 200ml batches, allowing the rice to absorb each amount of stock before adding more. Drain and rinse **600g cannellini beans** and add to the pan when half the stock is used up. Season to taste with plenty of **ground black pepper**. After about 25 minutes or when all the liquid is absorbed, the grains will be soft and creamy. If the rice is not tender, continue to add more hot vegetable stock or water until cooked. Divide the risotto between four bowls and top each portion with **1 tablespoon Parmesan cheese shavings**.

COOK'S TIPS
★ Replace 100ml of the stock with dry white wine for a more sophisticated flavour.
★ Add 150g chopped cooked green beans towards the end of the cooking time to boost colour and nutrition.
★ Serve the risotto with a crisp green salad.

Mediterranean green beans

Serves 4
Preparation 5 minutes   Cooking 15 minutes

Each serving provides • 102kcal • 3g protein • 8g carbohydrates of which 6g sugars • 7g fat of which 1g saturates • 4g fibre

Top and tail **450g green beans** and boil in a saucepan for 3 minutes or until just cooked but still firm. Refresh the beans under cold running water, drain and pat dry. Heat **1 tablespoon olive oil** in a frying pan and stir-fry **1 thinly sliced onion** over a medium heat for about 8 minutes or until softened. Stir **16 whole red cherry tomatoes** and **2 teaspoons olive oil** into the onions. Cook for 2 minutes, turning the tomatoes gently once or twice. Add the cooked green beans to the pan and stir for 1 minute over the heat to warm through.

COOK'S TIPS
★ This tasty and healthy side dish goes very well with beef or chicken. Add 200g diced cooked potatoes to the pan with the onions for a main dish.
★ For extra crunch add 30g flaked toasted almonds to the dish before serving.

Spicy Caribbean rice

Serves 4
Preparation 15 minutes   Cooking 35 minutes

Each serving provides • 540kcal • 16g protein • 81g carbohydrates of which 15g sugars • 19g fat of which 9g saturates • 10g fibre

Heat **2 tablespoons vegetable oil** in a large frying pan over a medium heat and add **2 finely chopped red onions** and **2 sliced red peppers** to the pan. Cook for 5 minutes to soften the vegetables, then add **2 finely chopped garlic cloves** and **1 or 2 finely chopped chillies, 1 teaspoon medium pepper sauce** and **2-3 teaspoons paprika**. Stir for 1 minute or until the

aromas are released then add **200g long grain brown rice**. Stir to coat all the grains of rice with oil. Pour in **250ml hot vegetable stock** and **400ml light coconut milk**. Bring to a simmer then reduce the heat, cover and cook for 15 minutes. Drain and rinse a **200g can red kidney beans** and a **200g can black-eyed beans**. Add to the rice with **2 teaspoons dried thyme** and **2 teaspoons dried oregano**. Cover again, simmer for 10 minutes then stir in **4 chopped tomatoes**. Cook uncovered for a further 15 minutes or until the rice is tender. To serve the dish moist, you may need to add more hot stock or water to leave a small amount of liquid in the pan by the time the rice is cooked.

COOK'S TIPS
★ For a heartier dish add small pieces of cooked chicken or bacon to the pan with the tomatoes.

Rich chicken and bean hotpot

Serves 4
Preparation 10 minutes   Cooking 1 hour

Each serving provides • 311kcal • 37g protein • 24g carbohydrates of which 11g sugars • 8g fat of which 1g saturates • 7g fibre

Heat **2 teaspoons olive oil** in a flameproof casserole dish and add **4 skinned chicken breast fillets**. Cook for 5 minutes, turning occasionally, until browned on both sides. Remove from the dish and keep warm. Add **1 tablespoon olive oil** to the dish with **2 sliced onions** and **1 chopped celery stick**. Cook over a medium-low heat for 5 minutes or until softened. Stir in **4 chopped garlic cloves, 200ml hot chicken stock, 1 bay leaf, 1 teaspoon dried rosemary, 5 skinned chopped tomatoes** (see page 56, No-cook tomato pasta sauce, for how to skin tomatoes) and **100ml passata**. Cover and cook over a low heat for 20 minutes. Drain and rinse a **250g can borlotti beans** and add them to the casserole dish with the browned chicken fillets. Simmer for a further 30 minutes with the lid off the pan, stirring occasionally, until the chicken is cooked through and a thick, rich sauce has formed. Serve sprinkled with **2 tablespoons fresh chopped parsley**.

COOK'S TIPS
★ Sides of crusty bread and a green salad add extra dimensions of flavour and texture.

Carrot pancakes with prosciutto and silky mango

Freshen up these golden pancakes and high-protein prosciutto slivers with delicious slices of firm, ripe mangos. Bursting with antioxidants and vitamin C, it tastes fabulous, too.

Serves 4
Preparation 10 minutes
Cooking 10 minutes

Each serving provides • 494kcal
• 11g protein • 27g carbohydrates of which 8g sugars • 39g fat of which 6g saturates • 3g fibre

For the pancakes
1 small carrot
100g self-raising flour
1 egg
100ml semi-skimmed milk
2 tbsp chopped fresh parsley
1 tbsp vegetable oil

For the mango salad
1 ripe mango
8 slices prosciutto
4 fresh basil sprigs, to garnish
8 tsp olive oil

ALTERNATIVE INGREDIENTS
• Try other types of air-dried ham such as Westphalian or Serrano instead of prosciutto.
• Use papaya either as an alternative to mango or combined with it. Halve the fruit, scoop out and discard the seeds, then peel and slice the papaya.
• For a lighter fruit flavour with a contrasting crunchy texture, slice 1 star fruit instead of mango, sprinkle the ham with 1 teaspoon lightly toasted pine nuts per portion and drizzle over walnut oil instead of olive oil.

1 First make the pancakes. Finely grate the carrot. Sift the flour into a bowl, add the egg and 25ml of the milk, then stir the mixture to form a thick paste and beat until smooth. Gradually beat in the remaining 75ml milk to make a thick batter. Stir in the carrot and parsley.

2 Heat a griddle pan or heavy-based frying pan and brush with a little of the vegetable oil. Drop 4 separate dessertspoons of batter into the pan, spacing them well apart. Cook for 2 minutes until browned underneath and bubbling on top. Turn and cook the second side for about 1 minute. Transfer the pancakes to a plate lined with a tea towel and wrap them to keep warm. Repeat twice more to make 12 small pancakes.

3 Peel the mango and cut the flesh off the stone in small neat slices (see Cook's Tips). Divide the mango between four plates. Trim any fat from around the edges of the prosciutto and arrange the slices on the plates then scatter the basil leaves. Drizzle 2 teaspoons olive oil over each portion of prosciutto and serve with the pancakes.

COOK'S TIPS
★ To slice mango flesh, use a large knife to make one cut straight down into the stone, then cut the fruit at an angle to remove the first slice. Work outwards, cutting off slices at an angle until the fruit is removed from one flat side. Turn the stone over and repeat for the second half. Peel each slice before serving.

SUPERFOOD

MANGOS
Thanks to its high vitamin C and carotenoid content, the exotic mango is a great source of antioxidants, good for boosting immunity and offering protection from heart disease and some cancers. Mangos can also help you to maintain a healthy weight.

Beetroot and mozzarella with raspberry dressing

A piquant fruit dressing spices up this salad of creamy mozzarella cheese and mellow beetroot. The raspberries contain natural antioxidants that may help to protect against heart disease.

Serves 4
Preparation 10 minutes

100g raspberries
2 tsp honey
2 tsp cider vinegar
500g peeled cooked beetroot
150g mozzarella
50g fresh flat-leaf parsley
a few whole raspberries, to garnish

Each serving provides • 167kcal • 10g protein • 15g carbohydrates of which 14g sugars • 8g fat of which 5g saturates • 4g fibre

ALTERNATIVE INGREDIENTS
• Blackberries taste as good with beetroot as raspberries.
• For a contrasting flavour, use a cheese with a more pronounced taste, such as Roquefort or goat's cheese.
• For a tangy flavour, use feta cheese instead of mozzarella and tender basil leaves instead of parsley.
• Add orange slices to the beetroot for a citrus kick. Drizzle with a little olive oil, then add the mozzarella. A few fresh oregano leaves make a tasty garnish.

1 Put the raspberries in a bowl and crush them with a fork. Drizzle in the honey before mixing in the vinegar to make a thick dressing.

2 Thinly slice the beetroot and arrange the slices on four plates. Dice the mozzarella into 1cm cubes. Spoon the raspberry dressing over the beetroot and add the mozzarella. Strip the leaves from the flat-leaf parsley, roughly chop and sprinkle over the dish, then garnish with whole raspberries and serve.

COOK'S TIPS
★ Make this salad as close to mealtime as possible because the raspberries (and raspberry vinegar) will lose their flavour if left for more than an hour.
★ Frozen raspberries are ideal for the dressing here. Either microwave them on high for 30 seconds, or let them defrost naturally at room temperature for a couple of hours.
★ For a more substantial salad serve with boiled new potatoes – they are great for soaking up the delicious salad juices.
★ You can cook beetroot from fresh or, to save time, buy it ready-cooked (see Cook's Tips on page 22).

SUPERFOOD

BEETROOT
Known for its distinctive, deep purple colour, beetroot contains a range of essential vitamins and minerals, including vitamin C, magnesium, potassium and folate. Betaine, a compound important for heart health, is also abundant in beetroot.

Tangy **sardine** pâté

Lemon, garlic and dill deliver flavour punches to a robust fish pâté that is great as a tasty starter or snack. Serve with vine-ripened tomatoes, thin cucumber sticks and a round of crunchy toast.

Serves 4
Preparation 5 minutes

120g can sardines in sunflower oil,
  drained
1 garlic clove, crushed
grated zest of 1 lemon and juice
  of ½ lemon
125g low-fat soft cheese
1 small spring onion
2 tbsp chopped fresh dill

Each serving provides • 117kcal
• 10g protein • 2g carbohydrates of
which 1g sugars • 8g fat of which
3g saturates • no fibre

ALTERNATIVE INGREDIENTS
• For a fabulous, firm-textured mustard
and dill pâté, reduce the quantity of
low-fat soft cheese to 50g and omit
the spring onion. Use 2 tablespoons
wholegrain mustard instead of the
garlic and reduce the zest to ½ lemon
and the juice to 1 tablespoon.
• Use canned mackerel in oil instead
of sardines. Canned smoked mackerel
or sild (small smoked fish) also make
tasty alternatives to sardines.
• A number of herbs complement
sardines. Try chopped fresh parsley
as an alternative to dill, adding 4 finely
shredded fresh basil leaves to the
parsley for a distinct aroma.

1 Use a fork to mash the sardines with the garlic and lemon zest in a bowl. Stir in the lemon juice when the sardines have a smooth consistency. Add the low-fat soft cheese and beat the mixture until all the ingredients are combined.

2 Season to taste and divide the pâté between four ramekins, or spoon it onto plates. Finely chop the spring onion and sprinkle a little over each portion together with the dill.

COOK'S TIPS
★ Use leftover pâté to fill rolls or sandwiches. The pâté will keep for up to two days in the fridge; store in a sealed container to prevent the strong smell of garlic and fish contaminating other food.
★ Make double the quantity of pâté and freeze half of it to use on another occasion. Store in an airtight container for up to two months.

SUPERFOOD

SARDINES
One of the few foods rich in vitamin D, sardines help to boost dietary intake of this essential vitamin. It is needed for the formation and maintenance of bones and the absorption of calcium into the body. It may also play a role in protecting against breast, prostate and colon cancers, and heart disease.

Asparagus and ham grill

With a no-fuss cheesy sauce, this delicious combination is a favourite for a hot, tasty lunch. Asparagus provides a host of health benefits, so make the most of it when it is in season.

Serves 4
Preparation 5 minutes
Cooking 12 minutes

Each serving provides • 185kcal • 18g protein • 4g carbohydrates of which 4g sugars • 11g fat of which 6g saturates • 1g fibre

12 asparagus spears
4 large slices cooked ham, about 150g
150g low-fat soft cheese
1 tsp cornflour
50g Parmesan cheese
3 tbsp milk
2 tbsp snipped fresh chives

ALTERNATIVE INGREDIENTS
• Substitute canned or bottled white asparagus if you cannot buy fresh green asparagus.
• Try baby leeks instead of asparagus. Allow 2-3 leeks per portion and poach them in a pan of boiling water for 3-5 minutes or until tender.
• Use crumbled blue cheese instead of Parmesan.

1 Trim any tough ends off the asparagus (see Cook's Tips) and lay the spears in a large frying pan. Add just enough boiling water to cover, then bring back to the boil over a high heat. Reduce the heat, cover the pan and simmer for about 5 minutes, or until the spears are just tender.

2 Meanwhile, lay the ham on a board. Preheat the grill to medium-high and have a large ovenproof dish or four gratin dishes ready for step 3. In a bowl, mix the soft cheese and cornflour. Finely grate the Parmesan cheese. Reserve 1 tablespoon of the Parmesan cheese and stir the rest into the mixture. Whisk in the milk.

3 Drain the asparagus and lay three spears over each slice of ham. Roll up and place in the prepared dish. Spoon the soft cheese mixture over the ham and sprinkle with the remaining 1 tablespoon of Parmesan cheese. Cover any protuding asparagus tips with tin foil.

4 Grill the asparagus and ham rolls for 5-6 minutes, or until the cheese topping is bubbling and browned. Sprinkle over the snipped chives before serving.

COOK'S TIPS

★ If the spears have slightly tough ends, trim them off with a knife or snap them off – the stems will break at their weakest point, where the tender spear meets the woody end. Use the woody parts to flavour a stock, straining and discarding them before use.

SUPERFOOD

ASPARAGUS
This colourful vegetable is a good source of energy-releasing B vitamins, including folate, which lowers the risk of heart disease and stroke. With calcium and magnesium to maintain strong bones, asparagus is an all-round superfood.

Juicy garlic **mushrooms** with **sun-dried tomatoes**

Great for soaking up the garlic flavour and as a contrast to intense sweet tomatoes, mushrooms are also low in calories and a good source of fibre. It all adds up to a mouth-watering, satisfying dish, delicious hot or cold.

Serves 4
Preparation 5 minutes
Cooking 5 minutes

Each serving provides • 205kcal • 5g protein • 10g carbohydrates of which 7g sugars • 16g fat of which 2g saturates • 6g fibre

500g button mushrooms
4 tbsp olive oil
4 garlic cloves, crushed
12 sun-dried tomato halves
20g chopped fresh flat-leaved parsley
lemon wedges, to garnish

ALTERNATIVE INGREDIENTS
• Use chestnut mushrooms instead of button mushrooms for a slightly stronger flavour.
• Try nut oils instead of olive oil. Cook the garlic in the olive oil then add walnut or hazelnut oil in step 2.
• Add sunflower seeds to the ingredients. Roast 2-3 tablespoons sunflower seeds in a dry pan and remove them before adding the oil and garlic. Sprinkle the seeds over the mushrooms before serving.

1 Halve the mushrooms and trim any long stalks. Place 1 tablespoon of the oil in a large saucepan. Add the garlic and cook for 1 minute over a high heat until it begins to sizzle.

2 Add the mushrooms and continue to cook, stirring occasionally, for 4 minutes. When the mushrooms begin to brown, remove the pan from the heat and toss them in the remaining olive oil.

3 Slice the sun-dried tomatoes and stir them into the mushrooms together with the parsley. Season to taste and garnish with lemon wedges before serving.

COOK'S TIPS

★ To serve cold, add the sun-dried tomatoes in step 3, then transfer the mushroom mixture to a bowl, cover and marinate for 15 minutes. Add the parsley just before serving.
★ Larger mushrooms also work well in this recipe if they are quartered, but do not use open cap mushrooms, with the soft gills exposed, as they are not firm enough.

SUPERFOOD

MUSHROOMS
A useful source of fibre, mushrooms contain energy-releasing B vitamins and minerals, too. They are rich in selenium, an important antioxidant that may help to prevent heart disease and cancer, as well as being high in folate for healthy blood and circulation.

Ginger and apricot rarebit

Here is a lively and unusual version of an old favourite that combines the zing of ginger and the succulence of apricots with a high-calcium cheese for a really nutritious snack.

Serves 4
Preparation 10 minutes
Cooking 5 minutes

50g fresh root ginger
75g ready-to-eat dried apricots
4 thick slices multigrain bread
125g grated Cheddar cheese
50g rocket
50g watercress
lemon wedges, to garnish

Each serving provides • 272kcal • 13g protein • 29g carbohydrates of which 9g sugars • 12g fat of which 7g saturates • 3g fibre

ALTERNATIVE INGREDIENTS
• To help to achieve your 5-a-day, dice 1 eating apple and add it to the toast in addition to the ginger and apricots.
• Leave out the ginger and use 50g chopped dates instead of the apricots.
• Top with crumbled feta instead of Cheddar cheese.

1 Preheat the grill to the hottest setting. Cut the ginger into fine strips and slice the apricots. Toast the bread slices on one side under the grill. Turn the slices and lay them close together in the grill pan.

2 Scatter the ginger and apricots evenly over the bread, then sprinkle with the cheese, right up to the edges. Toast for 5 minutes until the cheese is bubbling and golden.

3 Divide the rarebits between four plates and serve with the rocket and watercress leaves garnished with lemon wedges.

COOK'S TIPS
★ Adding the topping to the untoasted side of the bread means that the crusts do not burn before the cheese has melted. The result is a crisp base with a moist top.
★ Instead of grating the cheese, pare off thin slices using a potato peeler to get a more even covering.

SUPERFOOD

CHEESE
Just 30g hard cheese provides up to one-fifth of your daily recommended intake for protein and calcium, which is essential for maintaining strong bones. With the added benefits of vitamin A for healthy skin and zinc to boost immunity, small amounts of hard cheese make a highly nutritious contribution to a balanced diet.

Minted **celery** houmous

Celery gives a lovely light crunch to this high-fibre chickpea dip, while mint imparts a clean, fresh flavour. Serve with vegetable sticks and warm pitta bread for a quick, healthy low-fat snack.

Serves 4
Preparation 10 minutes

Each serving provides • 251kcal • 7g protein • 13g carbohydrates of which 1g sugars • 19g fat of which 3g saturates • 1g fibre

400g can chickpeas, drained
4 large fresh mint leaves
1 garlic clove
1 tbsp tahini paste
4 tbsp olive oil
1 celery stick
grated zest and juice of 1 lemon
mint sprigs, to garnish

1 Put the chickpeas, mint, garlic and tahini paste in a food processor and reduce to a crumbly mixture.

2 With the processor motor running, gradually pour in the olive oil until the mixture forms a thick paste. Continue to process, adding 2 tablespoons of water to soften the houmous if it is very thick.

3 Dice the celery and add it to the processor with the lemon zest and half of the lemon juice. Process for 3 seconds to avoid crushing the celery. Stir in the remaining lemon juice, season to taste and transfer the houmous to a bowl. Serve garnished with mint sprigs.

COOK'S TIPS

★ Tahini is a sesame seed paste. It is thick and pale, usually with a layer of oil on the surface when the ground seeds have sunk. Stir well before use.

★ If you do not have a food processor, make the houmous in a blender. Use a spatula to scrape the mixture down the sides occasionally so that it processes evenly. Stir in the celery with the remaining lemon juice.

★ This houmous will keep in a sealed container in the fridge for 3 days.

ALTERNATIVE INGREDIENTS
• Fennel is delicious and delicate in houmous instead of celery. Use a quarter of a fennel bulb, finely diced, and do not use mint. For a more pronounced flavour, slice off the top of a fennel bulb – the remains of the stalk and any feathery leaves – chop and add them to the houmous with the garlic and chickpeas.
• For a houmous with a rich tomato flavour, finely chop 4 sun-dried tomatoes (drained if stored in olive oil) and add them with the celery in step 3. Leave out the mint leaves and stir in a finely shredded basil sprig. Leave the houmous to stand for 30 minutes and stir before serving.

SUPERFOOD

CHICKPEAS
A low-fat, starchy, high-fibre food, chickpeas are good for digestive health. They also contain calcium, which helps to maintain healthy bones and teeth, and are a useful source of iron, making them a great alternative to red meat.

Cheesy **vegetable** frittata

Tender baby turnips add peppery punch, and plenty of fibre, to courgettes and tomatoes in a layered set omelette. For sheer deliciousness, savour the toasted Brie topping.

Serves 4
Preparation 10 minutes
Cooking 25 minutes

Each serving provides • 388kcal • 21g protein • 8g carbohydrates of which 7g sugars • 31g fat of which 13g saturates • 3g fibre

1 onion
250g baby turnips
2 courgettes
2 tbsp olive oil
1 garlic clove, crushed
5 eggs
3 tbsp chopped fresh parsley
2 large plum tomatoes
200g Brie

ALTERNATIVE INGREDIENTS
• Use 250g small cauliflower florets instead of the baby turnips. Check that they are tender, but not soft, by piercing with the tip of a sharp knife before adding the courgettes.
• Celeriac makes a change to turnips. Use 250g diced celeriac and top the frittata with Roquefort, Gorgonzola or smoked cheese.
• Butternut squash goes well with turnip instead of courgettes. Peel and dice 300g squash and add it with the turnips in step 1.

1 Finely chop the onion. Peel, halve and thinly slice the turnips. Finely slice the courgettes. Heat 1 tablespoon of the oil in a large lidded frying pan over a high heat. Add the onion, garlic and turnips then turn down the heat to medium-low. Cover and cook for 5 minutes, stirring occasionally, until the turnip slices are tender. Stir in the courgettes, cover and cook for another 4 minutes or until the courgettes are tender and beginning to brown in places.

2 Preheat the grill to the hottest setting. Beat the eggs with seasoning and the parsley. Add the remaining oil to the pan with the vegetables and heat for a few seconds until sizzling. Pour in the eggs, cover and cook for 10 minutes. After 2 minutes of cooking, using a slice or spatula, lift the set egg off the pan.

3 Slice the tomatoes and cut the Brie into four wedges. Place the frying pan under the grill, with the handle sticking out, and grill the frittata for 1 minute to set any uncooked egg. Arrange the tomatoes and the Brie slices on top. Grill for another 4 minutes until the Brie is lightly golden. Cool for 2-3 minutes before cutting into wedges.

COOK'S TIPS
★ The trick with set omelettes – Italian frittata or Spanish tortilla – is to cover the pan to keep in the heat, which helps to set the egg mixture and prevent the underneath from overbrowning on the pan. Regulate the heat – and be patient – for good results.
★ The frittata is also delicious cold for picnics or in lunchboxes. Cool the cooked frittata for 20-30 minutes, cover and chill in the fridge until needed or for up to 24 hours.

SUPERFOOD

TURNIPS
A winter root crop, turnips contain more starchy energy-giving carbohydrates than many other vegetables. They are a good source of fibre, which makes them beneficial for digestive health, and their potassium content can help to regulate blood pressure.

SUPERFOOD

Tomatoes

Fruit or vegetable? Who cares when tomatoes are jam-packed with health-giving nutrients. Eat just one large tomato and you get over half of your daily vitamin C needs, potassium to aid the control of high blood pressure, a rich supply of carotenes and lycopene, which may help to reduce the risk of cancer.

Cheesy-crust baked tomatoes

Serves 4
Preparation 10 minutes Cooking 45 minutes

Each serving provides • 180kcal • 6g protein • 26g carbohydrates of which 8g sugars • 7g fat of which 2g saturates • 3g fibre

Preheat the oven to 190°C (170°C fan oven), gas 6. Cook **75g brown rice** in a saucepan of boiling water with **½ teaspoon saffron threads** for 20 minutes or until tender. Slice the tops off **4 beefsteak tomatoes** and scoop out the insides, leaving the walls intact. Reserve any juice. Heat **1 tablespoon olive oil** in a frying pan and fry **1 small finely chopped onion** for 5 minutes over a medium heat or until softened. Add **150g chopped chestnut mushrooms** and stir-fry for 1 minute. When the rice is cooked, drain and combine with the onion and mushroom mix, **2 tablespoons chopped parsley**, and the **reserved tomato juice**. Fill the tomatoes with the mixture. Combine **2 tablespoons fresh breadcrumbs** with **2 tablespoons grated Parmesan cheese**, then sprinkle over the tomato tops. Place on a lightly oiled baking sheet and brush the tomato skins with a little vegetable oil. Bake in the oven for 20 minutes or until the tomatoes are tender.

COOK'S TIPS
★ The stuffed tomatoes are ideal as a starter, or a light lunch served with salad leaves.

No-cook tomato sauce with pasta

Serves 4
Preparation 10 minutes, plus 15 minutes standing
Cooking 12 minutes

Each serving provides • 125kcal • 1g protein • 4g carbohydrates of which 4g sugars • 12g fat of which 2g saturates • 2g fibre

Skin **6 ripe tomatoes**. The best way to do this is to remove any stalks, make a cross with a sharp knife on the stalk end and blanch (submerge the tomatoes in boiling water) for 1-2 minutes or until the skins start to split. Drain and peel off the skins. Chop the tomatoes and transfer to a bowl. Crush **2 garlic cloves** with **1 teaspoon sea salt** in a pestle and mortar or small bowl and mix until you have a paste, then add this to the tomatoes. Stir in **2 tablespoons chopped parsley, 2 tablespoons finely shredded basil leaves,**

3 tablespoons olive oil, 1 tablespoon red wine vinegar and add **ground black pepper** to taste. Leave to stand for 15 minutes, covered but not in the fridge, then stir again. Cook **300g pasta** for 12 minutes or according to the manufacturer's instructions. Drain the pasta, return to the pan and stir in the tomato sauce. The heat of the pasta will warm the sauce through.

COOK'S TIPS
★ If you prefer, you can heat the sauce for a short while in a bowl in the microwave or in a saucepan.

Summer seafood salad

Serves 4
Preparation 10 minutes Marinating 30 minutes

Each serving provides • 349kcal • 15g protein • 9g carbohydrates of which 7g sugars • 28g fat of which 5g saturates • 4g fibre

Thaw **300g frozen mixed cooked seafood** overnight in the fridge or, if available, use the equivalent weight of fresh, cooked mussels, prawns and sliced squid. Halve **350g ripe cherry tomatoes** and place in a large bowl. Rinse and drain the seafood and add to the bowl with **1 thinly sliced small red pepper** and **2 peeled sliced ripe avocados**. In a small bowl combine **3 tablespoons olive oil** with **2 teaspoons chilli sauce** (optional), **2 teaspoons white wine vinegar, a pinch of paprika** and **ground black pepper** to season. Cover and set aside in a cool place for 30 minutes to allow flavours to develop at room temperature. Place a handful of salad leaves on four plates then spoon a quarter of the seafood mix onto each plate. Garnish with **1 tablespoon chopped fresh coriander** per portion.

COOK'S TIPS
★ Using a mixture of golden, orange and red tomato varieties will make this salad look even more appetising.
★ Replace the seafood with the same quantity of prawns or dressed crab for a more conventional salad.

Classic tomato soup

Serves 4
Preparation 35 minutes Cooking 35 minutes

Each serving provides • 145kcal • 4g protein • 16g carbohydrates of which 15g sugars • 7g fat of which 2g saturates • 3g fibre

Skin and chop **1kg firm ripe tomatoes** (see opposite, No-cook tomato sauce with pasta, for how to skin tomatoes). Heat **1 tablespoon olive oil** over a medium heat and add **1 finely chopped onion**. Stir-fry the onions for 3 minutes or until just softened. Add **1 large chopped garlic clove** and **1 teaspoon paprika** and continue to stir-fry for 1 minute. Stir in **2 tablespoons tomato purée**, cooking for a further 2 minutes. Add the chopped tomatoes, without the juice if watery, **2 teaspoons caster sugar, 1 bay leaf, 600ml hot vegetable stock** and **125ml semi-skimmed milk**. Bring the soup to a simmer and cook, uncovered, for 20 minutes. Remove the bay leaf, allow the soup to cool a little, then purée in blender or with a stick blender until smooth. Reheat, season to taste and ladle into four bowls. Sprinkle each bowl with **1 teaspoon fresh snipped chives**.

COOK'S TIPS
★ Classic tomato soup is often made with cream instead of milk, but the semi-skimmed milk still gives a creamy texture to the finished soup and is lower in fat.
★ Drizzle 1-2 teaspoons of single cream into each bowl for a touch of indulgence.

Tricolore tomato towers

Serves 4
Preparation 15 minutes

Each serving provides • 447kcal • 25g protein • 8g carbohydrates of which 8g sugars • 35g fat of which 17g saturates • 3g fibre

Lightly crush **2 tablespoons pine nuts** in a bowl and combine with **3 tablespoons readymade basil pesto** and **4 finely chopped spring onions**. Rinse and pat dry **2 soft Italian mozzarella balls (about 200g)** then carefully cut each one into 8 thin slices. Slice the bottom off each of **4 beefsteak tomatoes** to make a flat base, then cut each tomato into five horizontal layers. Reassemble each tomato on a serving plate, spreading a little pesto mix and adding a slice of mozzarella between each tomato layer. Slowly drizzle **½ teaspoon olive oil** over each tomato and garnish with **2-3 small fresh basil leaves**.

COOK'S TIPS
★ Make sure that the tomatoes are ripe yet firm, or they will be hard to slice evenly and will not retain their shape when stacked.
★ If you are concerned about the layers slipping, insert a cocktail stick down through the centre of the tomato, but tell your diners before serving.

Walnut and basil pesto pasta

Packed with Italian flavour and the intense aroma of basil, pesto sauce makes a brilliant partner for wholewheat pasta. For a tasty twist, walnuts are in the pesto instead of the more usual pine nuts.

Serves 4
Preparation 5 minutes
Cooking 15 minutes

25g Parmesan cheese
1 small garlic clove
50g walnuts
10g fresh basil leaves
4 tbsp olive oil
300g wholewheat pasta, either
    fusilli, penne or spaghetti

Each serving provides • 510kcal
• 13g protein • 58g carbohydrates
of which 2g sugars • 27g fat of which
4g saturates • 3g fibre

ALTERNATIVE INGREDIENTS
• For a traditional pesto, replace
the walnuts with 50g pine nuts.
• Rather than serving the pesto with
pasta, use it in rolls, sandwiches
or wraps. Spread the pesto thinly
instead of butter or mayonnaise as
a base for salad-leaf fillings, tomatoes,
sliced hard-boiled eggs or cooked,
diced chicken.
• For a more substantial meal with
added protein, grill four plain fish
steaks, such as cod, salmon or tuna,
and place one on top of each portion
of pesto pasta just before serving.

1 Cut the Parmesan cheese into 1cm pieces. Mix together the garlic, Parmesan, walnuts and basil (reserving a few leaves to garnish) in a food processor until reduced to a crumbly paste. Alternatively, use a blender or a vegetable chopper.

2 With the motor running, gradually pour in the olive oil to create a coarse, thick paste.

3 Fill a large saucepan with boiling water. Add the pasta, bring back to the boil and cook for 12-15 minutes, or refer to the packet instructions for specific cooking times.

4 Drain the pasta in a colander and return it to the pan. Add the pesto and toss to coat evenly. Transfer the pesto pasta to four warmed plates, garnish with the reserved basil leaves and serve.

COOK'S TIPS
★ To test if the pasta is cooked, carefully remove a piece with a slotted spoon, cool under cold running water and taste. It should be firm but not crunchy – and certainly not mushy.
★ Pesto freezes well and is a great way of preserving home-grown basil leaves. Freeze the pesto in pots that contain sufficient sauce for one meal. Thaw it in the fridge overnight or at room temperature for 2-3 hours before use.

SUPERFOOD

OLIVE OIL
Eighty per cent of the fats in olive oil
are heart-healthy monounsaturated
and polyunsaturated fats. Virgin olive
oil, and particularly extra virgin,
contains vitamin E, which helps to
protect against heart disease. Like
all oils, it is high in calories, so should
be used sparingly for weight control.

Fruity **banana** and **date** breakfast bagel

Bananas and wholemeal bagels release energy slowly, so here is a satisfying snack guaranteed to keep you alert and to stave off hunger until lunchtime. The mixed seeds are full of protein.

Serves 4
Preparation 10 minutes
Cooking 5 minutes

4 wholemeal bagels
120g low-fat soft cheese
2 large bananas
12 stoned dates, about 85g
8 tbsp mixed seeds
  (see Cook's Tips)
4 tsp runny honey

Each serving provides • 509kcal
• 18g protein • 74g carbohydrates of
which 37g sugars • 15g fat of which
4g saturates • 10g fibre

ALTERNATIVE INGREDIENTS
• Allow 2 stoned and sliced fresh
apricots per bagel instead of banana.
• Ring the changes by using different
bread bases. English muffins have a
similar soft bready texture to bagels,
while French brioche rolls are richer
and slightly sweet. Thin slices of dark
rye bread or linseed bread also work
well. Increase the quantity of honey to
6 teaspoons when using firmer breads.
• For added fibre, include 1 tablespoon
each of rye grain and whole flaked
oats in the seed mix before sprinkling
over the bagels.

1 Preheat the grill to the hottest setting. Cut the bagels in half
horizontally and toast them, cut sides down, for 2 minutes until
warm but not overly browned.

2 Spread the untoasted sides of the bagels with soft cheese, then
place them, cheese-side up, in a large ovenproof dish. Alternatively,
cover the grill pan with foil before adding the bagels, but be careful as
the pan will be hot.

3 Slice the bananas at a slight angle and arrange the slices over the
bagels. Chop the dates into thirds and place the pieces on and
around the banana. Sprinkle each bagel half with seeds then drizzle with
honey. Grill the bagels for 3 minutes or until the topping is hot. Watch
carefully to ensure that the seeds do not burn.

COOK'S TIPS

★ There are many brands of mixed seeds in shops and supermarkets
and most contain sunflower, sesame and pumpkin seeds as the main
ingredients. Store any leftover seeds in an airtight container.
★ Buy raw seeds and toast them lightly in a dry, heavy-based frying
pan over a medium heat, stirring frequently until lightly browned. Cool
completely before storing in an airtight container.

SUPERFOOD

BANANAS
Ripe bananas are great energy
boosters, and with their low to
moderate glycaemic index (GI) rating
provide a sustained energy supply.
Full of essential potassium, bananas
can help to regulate blood pressure,
reducing the risk of a stroke.

Scrumptious **raspberry, banana** and **oat** smoothie

Beautiful to look at and delightful to taste, this feel-good high-fibre drink provides both quick-release and slow-burning energy that lasts for hours. Raspberries are high in antioxidants, too.

Serves 4
Preparation 5 minutes

2 large bananas
60g rolled oats
200g raspberries
1 tbsp honey
8 raspberries, to garnish

Each serving provides • 150kcal
• 3g protein • 32g carbohydrates
of which 20g sugars • 2g fat
(no saturates) • 3g fibre

ALTERNATIVE INGREDIENTS
• Use 200g blackberries, redcurrants or blackcurrants instead of the raspberries for an equally refreshing and good-for-you smoothie.
• For a chilled smoothie, substitute frozen mixed autumn or summer fruit for fresh raspberries.

1 Peel the bananas and cut them into 3cm chunks. Place the bananas, oats and raspberries in a blender. Pour in the honey and 250ml of cold water. Purée until smooth, then add another 250ml of water and blend for a further 4-5 seconds.

2 Pour the smoothie into four tall glasses. Garnish with 2 raspberries per glass and serve immediately.

COOK'S TIPS
★ For a refreshing raspberry drink that is zingy rather than sweet, use just-ripe bananas, which contain less sugar than very ripe fruit.
★ Rolled oats are large flakes often sold as porridge oats. Do not buy fine, medium or coarse oatmeal as it will not amalgamate into the drink.

SUPERFOOD

RASPBERRIES
Raspberries are full of nutrient goodness – they are a valuable source of fibre, contain potassium, which helps to regulate blood pressure, and pack an antioxidant punch thanks to their high levels of vitamin C and flavonoids.

Vegetables & salads

High in fibre and disease-fighting antioxidants, vegetables are among the top superfood heroes. Transform them into tasty and easy-to-prepare side dishes, and supercharge with fruit, nuts and other wholesome choices for sensational salads.

Golden **squash** with **peppers** and **almonds**

Succulent is the word for a sunny medley of vitamin-rich butternut squash and yellow peppers in a nut and honey glaze. It is ideal as a side dish or a vegetarian main course with rustic torn bread.

Serves 4
Preparation 10 minutes
Cooking 20 minutes

½ butternut squash, about 600g
2 garlic cloves
2 tbsp olive oil
8 fresh thyme sprigs
2 large yellow peppers
40g whole almonds
1 tbsp honey
finely pared zest and juice of
  1 lemon

Each serving provides • 195kcal
• 6g protein • 25g carbohydrates of
which 17g sugars • 9g fat of which
1g saturates • 6g fibre

ALTERNATIVE INGREDIENTS
• When in season use 2-3 small patty
pan squashes, halved, per portion
instead of the butternut squash slices.
Add 10 minutes to the cooking time.
• Aubergine slices work well in place of
butternut squash. Allow 3 large slices
per portion or 2 large aubergines in
total. When available, use white-
skinned aubergines for a change.
• Try pistachios instead of almonds
and add 50g sliced pitted black olives.

1 Preheat the oven to 200°C (180°C fan oven), gas 4. Peel the butternut squash and scoop out the seeds. Slice the garlic. Cut the squash into 12 slices, each about 1cm thick. Transfer the slices to a shallow roasting tin. Drizzle with 1 tablespoon of the oil and add the garlic and thyme. Roast in the oven for 20 minutes or until softened and beginning to brown.

2 Meanwhile, slice the peppers into 1cm strips. When the butternut squash has just 5 minutes left of cooking time, heat the remaining 1 tablespoon of oil in a frying pan over a medium-high heat. Add the peppers and fry for 5 minutes, stirring frequently, until they are tender and beginning to brown. Transfer the peppers and squash to a warmed serving dish.

3 Add the almonds, honey and lemon zest and juice to the frying pan. Stir-fry over a high heat for a few seconds until the mixture is bubbling and the lemon juice and honey have thickened to form a glaze. Spoon over the vegetables and serve.

COOK'S TIPS

★ Butternut squash will continue to soften after it has been removed from the oven. To test if it is cooked, carefully prick with a fork – it should be tender but firm.
★ Use either set or runny honey. To measure out set honey, use a knife to fill a tablespoon measure. With runny honey, dip the spoon into the jar then scrape off the excess honey from the sides of the spoon and level the top with a knife.

SUPERFOOD

BUTTERNUT SQUASH
A source of both types of fibre –
soluble and insoluble – butternut
squash helps to promote digestive
health and lower blood cholesterol.
The nutrient-packed orange flesh is
bursting with antioxidants alpha and
beta-carotene, as well as vitamin E.

Herby **asparagus** omelettes

The delicate flavour of asparagus marries perfectly with light fluffy eggs in a nutritious dish that can be rustled up in minutes. Serve with a salad and sliced tomato drizzled with olive oil.

Serves 2
Preparation 5 minutes
Cooking 8 minutes

8 asparagus spears
4 eggs
4 tbsp chopped fresh dill
10g butter

Each serving provides • 257kcal • 20g protein • 5g carbohydrates of which 4g sugars • 18g fat of which 3g saturates • 3g fibre

ALTERNATIVE INGREDIENTS
• If you are concerned about your cholesterol levels, use 1 tablespoon of olive oil per omelette instead of butter. Heat it in the pan until hot rather than adding it to a hot pan.
• Use chopped mixed fresh herbs instead of dill – fennel, parsley, chives, thyme and tarragon are all delicious with eggs.
• For a fish and herb omelette, add 25g chopped smoked salmon per portion, sprinkling it over the egg in step 3 before adding the asparagus.

1 Trim or snap any tough ends from the asparagus (see Cook's Tips on page 47) and lay the spears in a frying pan. Add just enough boiling water to cover, bring back to the boil then reduce the heat. Cover and simmer for 5 minutes or until the asparagus is just tender. Drain.

2 Meanwhile, beat 2 eggs in a bowl with 1 tablespoon of water and 2 tablespoons of dill. Heat a frying pan or omelette pan until very hot. Add 5g of the butter and swirl it around the pan. Over a high heat, pour the beaten eggs into the pan and cook for 1-2 minutes, lifting the edge of the omelette as it cooks to allow the egg to run on to the hot pan.

3 When the egg is almost set, add 4 asparagus spears. Fold the omelette over the asparagus, turn out onto a plate and keep warm. Repeat with the remaining ingredients to cook the second omelette.

COOK'S TIPS
★ To ensure that your omelettes are hot when you eat them, prepare warm plates for serving and have accompaniments ready on the table.
★ Use a heavy pan to make the omelettes, ensuring that it is evenly coated with the butter to prevent the eggs from sticking.

SUPERFOOD

EGGS
The ultimate natural fast food, eggs are easy to cook, nutritious and versatile. Rich in vitamins A and D for eye and bone health, eggs also contain the pigments zeaxanthin and lutein, which may help to prevent degenerative eye disease.

Colourful **tofu**-stuffed **peppers**

Sweet grilled pepper shells cradle bite-size tomatoes and marinated tofu pieces for a vivid, juicy Mediterranean-style dish. Serve with nutty new potatoes.

Serves 4
Preparation 5 minutes
Marinating 1 hour
Cooking 15 minutes

3 tbsp olive oil
pinch of grated nutmeg
¼ tbsp paprika
¼ tsp dried marjoram
2 large garlic cloves, crushed
400g packet firm tofu
4 large green peppers
24 cherry tomatoes
1 tsp fennel seeds
75g herby mixed salad, such as
    rocket, watercress and basil

Each serving provides • 218kcal
• 10g protein • 8g carbohydrates of
which 7g sugars • 17g fat of which
2g saturates • 5g fibre

ALTERNATIVE INGREDIENTS
• Add a pinch of dried chilli flakes to
the tomatoes for a hint of heat.
• Use cumin seeds instead of fennel
and sprinkle the tofu with tandoori
seasoning or good-quality curry powder
rather than nutmeg.
• Ring the changes with halloumi or
Indian paneer cheese instead of tofu,
although this will increase the amount
of saturated fat per portion.
• For delicate flavours, try yellow
peppers with yellow cherry tomatoes
and basil leaves in place of garlic.

1 Mix the oil, nutmeg, paprika, marjoram and 1 crushed garlic clove in a shallow dish just large enough to hold the block of tofu. Add the tofu and turn it to coat both sides, then cover and set aside to marinate for 1 hour.

2 Preheat the grill to the hottest setting. Cut each pepper in half and remove the seeds. Grill, cut sides down, for 3-4 minutes, until blistered but not blackened. Turn them cut sides up and grill for a further 2 minutes or until juicy and just tender.

3 Cut each tomato in half and mix them with the fennel seeds and remaining 1 crushed garlic clove in a bowl. Remove the tofu from the marinade and slice it into eight strips, then cut these across in half.

4 Divide the tomatoes between the pepper halves and grill for 2 minutes. Place two pieces of tofu in each pepper half, nestling them at an angle among the tomatoes. Drizzle the remaining marinade over the tofu and grill for a further 4-5 minutes or until the tofu is just beginning to brown. Divide the salad among four plates, place the pepper halves on top and serve.

COOK'S TIPS

★ Before cutting the peppers in half, sit them on your chopping board or work surface to check the best place for slicing through so that they stand steadily.

★ As well as chilled tofu, used in this recipe, which has a relatively short shelf-life and must be stored in the fridge, look out for long-life packs of tofu, which make a good storecupboard ingredient. Smoked tofu pieces also work well in this recipe.

SUPERFOOD

TOFU
Also known as soybean curd, tofu is a low-fat, high-protein food. Soya protein helps to lower blood cholesterol levels, so tofu is good for heart health. A source of calcium, tofu can also play a role in maintaining strong bones.

Spring **greens** stir-fry with **ham** and toasted **almonds**

Simply stir-fry leeks, cucumber and mangetout with lime zest, heart-friendly toasted almonds and lean ham and you have a super-quick light dish, great with couscous.

Serves 4
Preparation 10 minutes
Cooking 12 minutes

350g mangetout
50g flaked almonds
2 leeks
½ cucumber
200g lean cooked ham
2 tbsp olive oil
grated zest of 1 lime
4 lime wedges, to garnish

Each serving provides • 300kcal • 21g protein • 7g carbohydrates of which 5g sugars • 21g fat of which 4g saturates • 5g fibre

ALTERNATIVE INGREDIENTS
• Sugarsnap peas make a good substitute for mangetout. They are more substantial and often have a fuller flavour.
• Try pastrami or smoked pork loin, chicken or turkey as an alternative to the ham.
• For a vegetarian meal, leave out the ham and add 100g frozen soya beans or shelled broad beans in step 3. Use cashew nuts instead of almonds, increasing the quantity to 75g.

1 Place the mangetout in a large frying pan and pour in just enough boiling water to cover. Bring back to the boil, cover and cook over a high heat for 1 minute until the mangetout are bright green and slightly puffed. Drain and set aside.

2 Roast the almonds in a dry frying pan over a medium-high heat for 2 minutes. Shake the pan frequently so that the nuts cook evenly and do not burn. Transfer to a plate.

3 Slice the leeks. Peel the cucumber and cut it into 1cm wide sticks. Cut the ham into 2cm strips. Add the oil to the frying pan and stir-fry the leeks over a medium-high heat for 3 minutes. Add the lime zest and cucumber and cook for a further 5 minutes, or until the leeks are reduced and the cucumber is cooked.

4 Stir in the mangetout, ham and almonds and stir-fry for 1 minute to heat through. Serve garnished with lime wedges.

COOK'S TIPS
★ Carefully zest the lime using a parer so you can use the leftover lime, minus the zest, as a garnish rather than buying two limes.
★ Do not cook the mangetout for too long or they will go soft and turn a dull-green colour. They should be bright green with a crunchy texture.
★ Air-dried, uncooked ham, such as Westphalian, prosciutto, Parma or Serrano, is not recommended for a stir-fry.

SUPERFOOD

ALMONDS
With high levels of cholesterol-lowering monounsaturated fats, almonds are especially good for keeping the heart healthy. They are also rich in essential vitamin E, an important antioxidant that may help to fight the free radical damage that can eventually lead to cancer or heart disease.

Broccoli mash with poached egg

Melt-in-the-mouth mash teamed with vitamin C-rich broccoli and tangy black olives makes a delicious alternative to plain potato. Top with a poached egg for extra protein and flavour.

Serves 4
Preparation 15 minutes
Cooking 25 minutes

Each serving provides • 341kcal
• 15g protein • 36g carbohydrates
of which 3g sugars • 16g fat of which
3g saturates • 5g fibre

1kg potatoes
2 garlic cloves
200g tender broccoli spears
40g pitted black olives
4 eggs
2 tbsp olive oil
4 tbsp semi-skimmed milk
grated zest of 1 lemon
4 tbsp chopped fresh parsley

ALTERNATIVE INGREDIENTS
• Use sweet potatoes instead of regular potatoes, or a mixture of half sweet and half regular.
• Add 200g swede and 200g carrot to the potatoes as a change to the broccoli. Cut the swede into 3cm chunks and cook for 5 minutes before adding the carrot and potatoes.

1 Peel the potatoes and cut them into 2cm cubes. Peel the garlic. Roughly chop the broccoli and slice the olives. Place the potatoes and garlic in a large saucepan and pour in just enough boiling water to cover. Bring back to the boil over a high heat, reduce the heat to low, cover and simmer for 15 minutes or until tender.

2 Meanwhile, pour an inch of boiling water into a large pan set over a medium heat. Bring back to the boil and carefully break the eggs, one at a time, into the water, keeping them separate until the white is set. Simmer for 8-10 minutes or until set.

3 Drain the potatoes in a colander. Pour the oil into the potato pan, add the broccoli and stir-fry over a medium-high heat for 2 minutes before adding the milk. Bring to the boil, cover and cook for a further 2 minutes. Remove the pan from the heat, return the potatoes and mash. Stir up the broccoli once the potatoes are thoroughly mashed.

4 Gently mix in the lemon zest, olives and parsley. Carefully remove the eggs from the pan with a slotted spoon and place one on top of each portion of mash before serving.

COOK'S TIPS
★ Use potatoes recommended for boiling, such as King Edward or Maris Piper.
★ To poach an egg successfully, keep the water at a bare simmer throughout cooking. Cook until the white is set – this will take 5-10 minutes over a low heat. Alternatively, use an egg poacher to help to give a uniform shape.

SUPERFOOD

BROCCOLI
An original superfood hero, broccoli is one of the top-scoring antioxidant vegetables. It contains sulforaphane, a phytochemical known to activate enzymes that may destroy cancer-causing chemicals. Also, it takes only one 85g serving of lightly cooked broccoli to provide up to 100 per cent of your daily vitamin C requirements.

Broccoli

SUPERFOOD

A versatile vegetable in the kitchen, broccoli is also rich in a number of nutrients. These include phytochemicals, or plant chemicals, which may help to prevent some cancers and heart disease as well as protect against the signs of ageing. Broccoli contains plenty of vitamin C, too, boosting the immune system.

Broccoli pâté

Serves 4
Preparation 15 minutes Cooking 28 minutes

Each serving provides • 157kcal • 1g protein • 3g carbohydrates of which 2g sugars • 11g fat of which 3g saturates • 3g fibre

Preheat the oven to 180°C (160°C fan oven), gas 4. Cook **350g broccoli florets** in a pan of boiling water for 3 minutes or until barely cooked. Drain and refresh under cold running water and pat dry with kitchen paper. Transfer the broccoli to a large bowl and lightly mash. Stir in **3 beaten eggs, 50ml semi-skimmed milk, 3 tablespoons grated Parmesan cheese** and then **2 finely chopped spring onions**. Season to taste. Lightly brush four ramekins with **vegetable oil** and fill each one with a quarter of the broccoli mixture. Place the ramekins on a baking sheet and bake in the oven for 25 minutes or until set and golden. Allow to cool and then serve.

COOK'S TIPS
★ Garnish with cherry tomatoes or basil leaves and serve with wholegrain bread or oatcakes.

Summer broccoli and lemon soup

Serves 4
Preparation 10 minutes Cooking 32 minutes

Each serving provides • 150kcal • 8g protein • 18g carbohydrates of which 6g sugars • 6g fat of which 1g saturates • 5g fibre

Heat **1 tablespoon olive oil** in a large frying pan. Add **1 finely chopped onion** and fry gently over a low heat for 5 minutes or until softened. Add **2 crushed garlic cloves** and stir for 1 minute before adding **500g broccoli florets**, cut in half if large, and **250g finely diced potato**. Pour in **1 litre vegetable stock**, bring to the boil, then lower the heat immediately, cover and simmer for 25 minutes. Cool a little then purée in a blender. Return the soup to the pan, add the **juice of ½ lemon** and reheat gently. Stir **1 tablespoon plain yogurt** into each bowl of soup and sprinkle each with **½ tablespoon finely snipped chives** before serving piping hot.

COOK'S TIPS
★ Do not boil the soup, except to bring the stock up to temperature, otherwise it will lose its vibrant green colour and may look unappetising.

Italian pasta with pine nuts

Serves 4
Preparation 10 minutes Cooking 15 minutes

Each serving provides • 552kcal • 20g protein • 62g carbohydrates of which 4g sugars • 27g fat of which 5g saturates • 10g fibre

Cook **300g wholewheat spaghetti** in a saucepan of boiling water for 12 minutes or until tender, or according to the packet instructions. Add **400g broccoli florets**, cut in half if large to the pan for the last 5 minutes of cooking. Meanwhile, heat **3 tablespoons olive oil** in a small frying pan and add **4 crushed garlic cloves** and **1 finely chopped red chilli**. Stir over a medium heat for 2 minutes. Drain the pasta and broccoli and transfer them to a serving dish. Pour the garlic and chilli oil over the hot pasta and toss thoroughly to coat. Mix together **4 tablespoons toasted pine nuts, 2 tablespoons grated Parmesan cheese** and **2 tablespoons breadcrumbs**. Sprinkle the topping over the pasta before serving.

COOK'S TIPS
★ To make breadcrumbs, put 1 slice of wholemeal bread into a food processor and blend until it turns to crumbs. Transfer to a baking sheet and toast under the grill for around 5 minutes, turning regularly or until golden.

Sweet potato, broccoli and lentil salad

Serves 4
Preparation 15 minutes Cooking 25 mins

Each serving provides • 472kcal • 14g protein • 43g carbohydrates of which 9g sugars • 28g fat of which 4g saturates • 9g fibre

Preheat the oven to 200°C (180°C fan oven), gas 6. Peel **400g sweet potatoes** and cut into 2.5cm cubes. Toss the cubes in **3 tablespoons olive oil** and arrange on a baking sheet. Bake for 25 minutes or until cooked through and golden. Meanwhile, cook **150g brown** or **puy lentils** for 25 minutes in a pan of boiling water or until tender, then drain. Cook **300g broccoli florets** in a pan of boiling water for 5 minutes. Transfer to a colander and refresh under cold running water, then pat dry. Halve **150g cherry tomatoes** and then chop **1 small bunch fresh coriander leaves**. Make a dressing by mixing **2 tablespoons olive oil, 2 tablespoons sesame oil, 2 tablespoons light soy sauce, ½ teaspoon chilli sauce** and **½ teaspoon finely grated fresh root ginger**.

Toss the broccoli, potato and lentils with the tomatoes, coriander and dressing. Serve warm or cold.

COOK'S TIPS
★ This salad is ideal as part of a buffet or as a starter. Alternatively, serve it as an accompaniment to grilled chicken breasts.

Broccoli, carrot and mushroom stir-fry

Serves 4
Preparation 10 mins Cooking 6 mins

Each serving provides • 201kcal • 6g protein • 15g carbohydrates of which 13g sugars • 13g fat of which 2g saturates • 4g fibre

Heat **1 tablespoon vegetable oil** in a wok or nonstick frying pan. Add **200g broccoli florets** and **150g carrots**, cut into thin julienne strips (see Cook's Tips). Stir-fry over a high heat for 2 minutes and add **8 spring onions**, sliced lengthways, and cook for a further 2 minutes. Stir in another **1 tablespoon vegetable oil**, plus **100g sliced button mushrooms** and **2 crushed garlic cloves**. Stir-fry for 1 minute and then pour in **2 tablespoons light soy sauce, 2 teaspoons runny honey** and **1 tablespoon rice vinegar**. Heat through for 1 minute and serve sprinkled with **4 tablespoons cashew nuts**.

COOK'S TIPS
★ To make julienne strips, first peel the carrots. Trim four sides of each carrot to create a rectangle. Cut the rectangle lengthways into 3mm slices then stack the slices and cut lengthways to make more 3mm strips.

Ratatouille with feta gratin

A light version of a classic dish that contains all the goodness of aubergines, courgettes and tomatoes. The topping of bread and Greek cheese turns a side dish into a vegetarian main meal.

Serves 4
Preparation 20 minutes
Cooking 20 minutes

1 aubergine, about 300g
1 onion
2 tbsp olive oil
1 garlic clove, crushed
2 courgettes
4 large tomatoes
2 tbsp tomato purée
4 tbsp chopped fresh parsley
4 fresh basil sprigs

Topping
2 slices wholemeal bread
150g feta cheese
1 tbsp olive oil

Each serving provides • 294kcal
• 10g protein • 19g carbohydrates of which 11g sugars • 20g fat of which 7g saturates • 5g fibre

ALTERNATIVE INGREDIENTS
• For a more traditional ratatouille, add 1 diced green pepper with the onion in step 1.
• Use a 400g can chopped tomatoes instead of fresh tomatoes.

1 Trim and discard the stalk end of the aubergine and cut the flesh into 1cm cubes. Chop the onion. Heat the oil in a large saucepan over a high heat, add the onion and garlic and cook for 1 minute. Add the aubergine, reduce the heat to medium and cook for 5 minutes, stirring occasionally until softened.

2 Meanwhile, cut the courgettes into 1cm cubes. Add them to the pan and continue to cook for a further 2 minutes, stirring occasionally until the vegetables start to brown.

3 Preheat the grill to the hottest setting. Dice the tomatoes then add them plus the tomato purée to the pan. Stir in 6 tablespoons of cold water. Heat the mixture until simmering, cover and cook over a medium to medium-low heat for 8-10 minutes. Stir in the parsley and transfer to a shallow ovenproof dish or gratin dish.

4 For the topping, cut the bread into 1cm cubes. Crumble the feta into a bowl, add the bread then pour over the olive oil and toss to coat. Sprinkle the topping over the ratatouille and grill for 1-2 minutes or until the cheese softens and the bread browns. Strip the leaves from the basil sprigs and sprinkle them over the ratatouille before serving.

COOK'S TIPS

★ Do not worry about salting the aubergines before use. In the past, aubergine cultivars were bitter and had to be salted (known as degorging) to draw out the sour juices, but varieties available in supermarkets today have been bred to avoid this and can therefore be added straight into the ratatouille.

SUPERFOOD

AUBERGINES
Rich in antioxodants, aubergines may help to protect against cancer and heart disease. They also contain vitamin K, needed to regulate blood clotting, some folate for heart health and a useful amount of fibre.

Healthy **mixed grill** with **tomatoes**

Ripe tomatoes have unbeatable flavour and are crammed with antioxidants to help to protect cells. Combine with green beans, mushrooms, a fried egg and bread for a delicious meat-free big breakfast.

Serves 4
Preparation 10 minutes
Cooking 20 minutes

200g green beans
4 tbsp olive oil
1 garlic clove, crushed
½ tsp dried mixed herbs
12 slices baguette
6 tomatoes
8 large open mushrooms
4 eggs
2 tbsp snipped fresh chives
2 tbsp chopped fresh parsley

Each serving provides • 423kcal • 16g protein • 37g carbohydrates of which 7g sugars • 24g fat of which 4g saturates • 5g fibre

ALTERNATIVE INGREDIENTS
• Serve two spoonfuls of baked beans instead of green beans.
• Try poached or scrambled eggs as a change to fried eggs.
• For a main meal, omit the fried bread and serve with mashed potato.
• Top each mushroom with a slice of halloumi cheese or tofu 1cm thick and leave out the egg.

1 Preheat the grill to the hottest setting and line the grill pan with foil. Trim the beans and place them in a saucepan. Pour in boiling water to cover, then bring back to the boil, reduce the heat, cover and cook for 5 minutes or until tender. Drain and keep warm.

2 Mix the oil, garlic and herbs and brush a little over one side of the baguette slices. Fry, oiled sides down, in a dry frying pan over a medium heat for 4 minutes or until browned underneath. Set aside.

3 Halve the tomatoes and place them on the grill pan, cut sides down. Place the mushrooms on the grill pan, stalk sides up. Brush everything with the flavoured oil and grill for 3 minutes. Turn over, brush with more oil and grill for another 3 minutes. Add the bread, untoasted sides up, and brush sparingly with the oil. Grill for 1-2 minutes.

4 Meanwhile, heat the remaining garlic and herb oil in the frying pan over a high heat. Break in the eggs and cook for 1-2 minutes. Transfer the eggs to four plates. Add the mushrooms, tomatoes and beans. Sprinkle with chives and parsley before serving with the bread.

COOK'S TIPS
★ Slice tomatoes in half horizontally rather than down through the stalks. This way they sit flat on the grill pan and cook evenly.

SUPERFOOD

TOMATOES
The antioxidants in tomatoes may help to combat the effects of oxygen free radicals in the body. These molecules can damage cells, which researchers think may lead to cancer and some other diseases. Antioxidants are able to 'mop up' the free radicals and so protect cells.

Creamy avocado and aubergine stacks

A topping of mellow halloumi cheese adds a taste of Cyprus to little towers of tender sun-ripened vegetables for an enticing mix of textures and flavours. Just add a tomato salad.

Serves 4
Preparation 10 minutes
Cooking 12 minutes

1 large aubergine, about 400g
2 tbsp olive oil
1 garlic clove, crushed
grated zest of 1 lemon and
   juice of ½ lemon
2 firm ripe avocados
250g halloumi cheese
25g flaked almonds

Each serving provides • 465kcal
• 16g protein • 6g carbohydrates of
which 4g sugars • 42g fat of which
15g saturates • 6g fibre

ALTERNATIVE INGREDIENTS
• Try Indian paneer or mozzarella
cheese instead of the halloumi. Paneer
retains a similarly firm texture during
cooking, but the mozzarella will melt.
• If you do not have a fresh lemon, use
2 tablespoons of bottled lemon juice.
The recipe will taste just as good but
with a slightly less zingy flavour.
• Use pine kernels instead of the
flaked almonds.
• Sliced tomatoes can be grilled on top
of aubergines – include them instead
of the almonds or in place of the
avocado slices. Use 1-2 tomato slices
for each slice of aubergine.

1 Preheat the grill to the hottest setting and line the grill pan with foil. Trim and cut the aubergine into 12 slices. Place the aubergine on the foil. Mix the olive oil and garlic and brush sparingly over the aubergine. Grill for 4 minutes until just beginning to brown in places. Turn over, brush with more oil and grill for a further 4 minutes until tender.

2 Place the lemon zest and juice in a shallow dish. Cut the avocados into quarters. Peel and cut each quarter into three slices, coating them in the lemon juice to prevent discolouration. Cut the halloumi into 12 slices.

3 Sprinkle the almonds over the aubergines and arrange three avocado slices, with the lemon zest, on each. Top each stack with a slice of halloumi and brush with any remaining oil. Grill for 4 minutes until the cheese browns.

COOK'S TIPS

★ For a balanced stack, layer up a large slice of aubergine, then a medium slice of avocado and finally a small slice of cheese. If top-heavy, the stacks will topple over.
★ If the heat is not evenly distributed under the grill, re-arrange the aubergine slices when turning them so that they brown all over.

SUPERFOOD
. . . .
AVOCADOS
Unusually for a fruit, avocado pears
are high in fat – 20g in half an avocado
– though most of the fat is the healthy,
monounsaturated kind that helps to
lower blood cholesterol and keep
hearts healthy. Avocados are also rich
in fibre. Half an avocado provides one
quarter of your total daily fibre needs.

Glazed pears with feta cheese

Salty feta offsets the sweetness of honey-glazed pears for a refreshingly different and healthy salad. Toasted pumpkin seeds add extra bite, and zinc and selenium to boost the immune system.

Serves 4
Preparation 10 minutes
Cooking 10 minutes

½ crunchy lettuce, such as cos
    or iceberg
60g rocket
juice of 2 limes and grated zest
    of 1 lime
1 tbsp honey
4 firm, just ripe pears, about 600g
4 tbsp pumpkin seeds
200g feta cheese

Each serving provides • 303kcal
• 133g protein • 23g carbohydrates
of which 21g sugars • 18g fat of which
8g saturates • 6g fibre

ALTERNATIVE INGREDIENTS
• Blue cheese, such as Stilton, is
a delicious alternative to feta here.
Or try dolcelatte for a creamy texture.
• Firm apples with a sweet-sharp
flavour can be used instead of the
pears for a crunchier salad. Use lemon
zest with apples rather than lime.
• Pine nuts make a good substitute
for pumpkin seeds.
• Peppery rocket is delicious with
the lime and feta, but watercress also
works well, as does radicchio, the
slightly bitter, red-leafed Italian chicory.

1 Coarsely shred the lettuce and divide it among four large plates together with the rocket. Stir the lime juice, honey and 4 tablespoons of water together in a frying pan.

2 Peel, core and slice the pears, removing the stalks. Add to the frying pan and bring to the boil over a high heat. Cook, turning the pear slices, for 3-5 minutes or until the liquid has evaporated and the slices are slightly golden. Remove the pan from the heat, add 2 tablespoons of water and stir to glaze the pears.

3 Toast the pumpkin seeds by sprinkling into a separate dry frying pan and cooking over a medium heat for 3-4 minutes. Stir occasionally to prevent the seeds from blackening.

4 Arrange the pears on top of the leafy salad. Crumble the feta and divide it between the plates of salad leaves. Sprinkle the lime zest and toasted pumpkin seeds over the top, then serve.

COOK'S TIPS
★ Peel the pears whole, quarter them lengthways and then you will be able to cut the core out easily. Then cut each quarter lengthways into neat slices. Have the juices ready in the pan and add the pears as they are prepared so they do not discolour.
★ Use a spatula or fish slice and fork to turn the pears in the frying pan. The cooking time will depend on the type of pan. For instance, the juices may evaporate and begin to caramelise more quickly in a thin metal pan. Take care when adding water to a hot pan as it may spit.
★ A zester is a useful kitchen tool for removing the zest from citrus fruit, such as lime, but if you don't have one use a vegetable peeler.

SUPERFOOD

PEARS
Like most fruits, pears are excellent for effective weight control. They are low in calories, yet have a good 'fullness factor', great for staving off hunger. Pears also have a low glycaemic index (GI) rating, so they help to keep blood sugars steady.

Warm **potato** and **broad bean** salad

For an elegant, flavour-drenched warm salad, take nutty new potatoes and high-fibre broad beans, drizzle them with a herby vinaigrette, then serve up on red chard leaves.

Serves 4
Preparation 15 minutes
Cooking 15 minutes

Each serving provides • 247kcal
• 7g protein • 28g carbohydrates of
which 4g sugars • 13g fat of which
2g saturates • 6g fibre

500g baby new potatoes
1kg fresh broad beans or 300g
  frozen baby broad beans
1 tsp sugar
1 tsp English mustard
1 tsp cider vinegar
3 tbsp olive oil
3 large thyme sprigs
100g red chard
4 tbsp snipped fresh chives

ALTERNATIVE INGREDIENTS
• Freshly cooked baby beetroots are delicious in this salad with the broad beans. Trim off the leaves but keep the roots and stalks in place. Wash and boil 300g beetroots for 20 minutes until tender. Drain and place in cold water until cool enough to handle, then rub off the skins under water. Cook the broad beans separately. Add the hot beetroot to the dressing and then the broad beans.

1 Place the potatoes in a large saucepan and pour in boiling water to cover. Bring back to the boil, reduce the heat, cover and cook for 10 minutes. Meanwhile, shell the broad beans, if using fresh ones. Soak the beans in a bowl of hot water for 3-4 minutes before peeling off the pale green outer skins. Add the beans to the potatoes, bring back to the boil, cover and cook for 4 minutes until tender.

2 Make a vinaigrette by whisking the sugar, mustard and vinegar in a large bowl until the sugar has dissolved. Whisk in the oil and rub the thyme leaves off the stalks and into the bowl. Season to taste.

3 Finely shred the chard and make a bed of leaves on four plates. Drain the potatoes and beans and stir them into the vinaigrette. Sprinkle with chives and mix again. Top the chard with the potato and bean salad.

COOK'S TIPS

★ Sugar does not dissolve in oil, so to avoid a grainy vinaigrette combine it with the mustard and vinegar before adding the olive oil.
★ Chard has a slightly bitter taste that is pleasant in young leaves but can be slightly too strong in older ones. Choose small, young leaves or if only older ones are available, reduce their quantity by half and mix them with 'sweeter' leaves, such as lamb's lettuce, little gem hearts or finely shredded Chinese cabbage.

SUPERFOOD

BROAD BEANS
Part of the legume family, broad beans are a good source of both soluble and insoluble fibre to keep the digestive system in good order. They also contain energy-releasing B vitamins, including folate, which helps to maintain healthy blood and circulation.

Fruity **chicory** and **apple** salad

Apples and dates add sweetness to the subtle flavours of celeriac and crisp, health-promoting chicory to conjure up a great light salad or accompaniment for grilled poultry or pork.

Serves 4
Preparation 15 minutes

1 tbsp cider vinegar
2 tbsp olive oil, plus 1 tbsp
  for serving
250g celeriac, about ¼ large
  celeriac
2-3 dessert apples, about 250g
50g pistachio nuts
150g medjool dates
3-4 heads chicory

Each serving provides • 334kcal • 5g protein • 37g carbohydrates of which 35g sugars • 20g fat of which 3g saturates • 7g fibre

ALTERNATIVE INGREDIENTS
• Try 50g of walnuts or pecans instead of the pistachio nuts.
• Any fresh dates are fine if you cannot get hold of medjool dates.
• Ready-to-eat dried apricots or dried cranberries make good alternatives to the dates.
• For a more substantial meal, top the salad with 100g crumbled feta cheese. For a meat option stir-fry 100g sliced chorizo or kabanos (Polish sausage) for 1 minute before adding to the salad.
• This salad is great served in wraps. Spread wheat tortillas with low-fat soft cheese flavoured with garlic and herbs. Top with the salad, omitting the chicory, and roll up.

1 Whisk the vinegar and 2 tablespoons of oil together in a large bowl to make a dressing. Peel and coarsely grate the celeriac, add it to the dressing and mix thoroughly.

2 Cut the apples into quarters, remove the cores, then cut each quarter into two wedges. Slice the wedges across widthways and mix with the celeriac. Shell and roughly chop the pistachios. Halve, stone and chop the dates. Stir the nuts and dates into the celeriac mixture.

3 Separate the individual chicory leaves and arrange them on a serving plate. Drizzle with the remaining olive oil. Pile the salad onto the plate and use the chicory leaves to scoop up the salad.

COOK'S TIPS
★ The coarsest disc on a food processor is ideal for grating celeriac. Alternatively, use the coarse blade on a hand-held grater and press firmly to remove good-sized shreds.
★ Prepare the salad up to 2 hours in advance of serving. Cover the serving plate with cling film and store in the fridge until needed.

SUPERFOOD

CHICORY
A herby salad leaf, chicory helps to promote digestive health because it contains naturally high levels of inulin, a type of carbohydrate that the body cannot digest. Inulin encourages the growth of 'friendly' gut bacteria in the large intestine.

SUPERFOOD

Apples

Easily available apples offer many nutritional benefits and may even help to sharpen mental alertness. They also contain plenty of soluble fibre that can help to lower blood cholesterol, and with an average calorie content of only 65kcal, an apple is the perfect healthy snack.

Baked oaty apples

Serves 4
Preparation 10 minutes, plus 15 minutes standing
Cooking 40 minutes

Each serving provides • 249kcal • 2g protein
• 48g carbohydrates of which 43g sugars • 7g fat
of which 4g saturates • 5g fibre

Preheat the oven to 180°C (160°C fan oven), gas 4.
Put **100g sultanas** in a heatproof bowl and cover with
hot water. Leave them to plump up for 15 minutes.
Meanwhile, warm **2 tablespoons runny honey** in a
small saucepan with **2 tablespoons rolled oats** and
½ teaspoon ground mixed spice. Drain the sultanas
and stir them into the oats. Core **4 cooking apples**
and score them horizontally with a sharp knife to
penetrate the skin. Place the apples in an ovenproof
dish and fill each cavity with the sultanas and oats.
Place **1 small knob of butter** on the top of each apple.
Pour **200ml of water** around the apples in the dish.
Bake for 40 minutes or until the apples are soft. Baste
the apples with the juices halfway through cooking to
keep them moist.

COOK'S TIPS

★ Try to use unblemished apples as bruises may spoil
the appearance of your dessert and may affect the
dish's nutritional content. Choose from a variety of
cooking apples, such as Bramley or Golden Noble.
★ Piping-hot custard makes a tasty accompaniment
to stuffed apples.
★ Vary the sweet filling by using chopped dried apricots
instead of sultanas and replace the oats with chopped
or flaked almonds.

Walnut and apple stuffing

Serves 4
Preparation 10 minutes Cooking 38 minutes

Each serving provides • 148kcal • 4g protein
• 24g carbohydrates of which 11g sugars • 5g fat
of which 1g saturates • 4g fibre

Preheat the oven to 180°C (160°C fan oven), gas 4.
Heat **1 tablespoon olive oil** in a frying pan and cook
1 large finely chopped onion over a medium-low heat
for 5 minutes or until softened. Meanwhile, put **125g
stale wholemeal bread** in a food processor and turn
into breadcrumbs. Finely chop **2 red apples**, leaving on
the nutritious skins, and add them to the pan. Stir for
2 minutes, take off the heat and add the wholemeal

breadcrumbs, **3 tablespoons chopped fresh parsley, 1 tablespoon chopped fresh sage, 2 tablespoons chopped walnuts** and **2 tablespoons dried cranberries**. Mix together and leave to cool for 1 minute before stirring in **1 beaten egg yolk**. Season to taste then spoon the mixture into a shallow ovenproof dish. Dissolve **1 vegetable stock cube** in **100ml of boiling water** and pour it over the stuffing. Bake in the oven for 25 minutes or until golden.

COOK'S TIPS

★ If you do not have a food processor, use a blender to make the breadcrumbs, or rub the stale bread against the coarse side of a grater until it crumbles.

Apple and ginger smoothie

Serves 4
Preparation 10 minutes

Each serving provides • 203kcal • 4g protein • 46g carbohydrates of which 46g sugars • 3g fat of which 2g saturates • 2g fibre

Roughly chop **4 dessert apples**. Place them in a blender, or in a bowl if you have a stick blender. Add **200ml apple juice** and **20g finely grated fresh root ginger**. Blend until smooth then add **500ml frozen vanilla yogurt** and an additional **300ml apple juice**. Blend again until smooth and pour the smoothie into four tall glasses.

COOK'S TIPS

★ This smoothie works well with any type of dessert apple, but the flavour is best with slightly sharp green apples, such as Granny Smith.
★ Try 1 teaspoon ground ginger or 20g finely chopped stem ginger instead of the fresh root ginger.

Carrot, apple and beetroot salad

Serves 4
Preparation 15 minutes Marinating 30 minutes

Each serving provides • 131kcal • 1g protein • 6g carbohydrates of which 6g sugars • 11g fat of which 2g saturates • 2g fibre

Grate **2 carrots** and **1 small cooked beetroot** into a large serving bowl. Make the French dressing by mixing **3 tablespoons olive oil, ½ tablespoon white wine vinegar, ½ tablespoon balsamic vinegar, ½ teaspoon French mustard, a pinch of caster sugar** and a little

seasoning. Add **3 tablespoons raisins, 2 tablespoons cashew nuts** and **4 tablespoons French dressing** to the serving bowl. Finely chop **2 red dessert apples,** leaving on the skins. Stir the apples into the salad, making sure that they are coated with the dressing to prevent discolouration. Marinate the salad for 30 minutes before serving.

COOK'S TIPS

★ To cook raw beetroot, place a small whole beetroot in a fine-meshed sieve over a pan of boiling water and steam for 15 minutes or until cooked but still firm. Drain the beetroot and run it under cold water before peeling the skin. Leave it to cool before grating. Do not over-cook the beetroot because it will not grate easily when soft and the crunchy texture of the salad will be lost.

Fig, apple and cinnamon compote

Serves 4
Preparation 5 minutes Cooking 22 minutes

Each serving provides • 143kcal • 2g protein • 22g carbohydrates of which 22g sugars • 6g fat (no saturates) • 4g fibre

Slice **2 dessert apples** and **1 cooking apple**. Put them in a saucepan with **125ml orange juice, 4 chopped ready-to-eat dried figs** and **1 level teaspoon ground cinnamon**. Bring to the boil, then turn down the heat and simmer, uncovered, for 20 minutes or until the apples are tender when gently pressed with the back of a spoon. Sprinkle over **2 tablespoons toasted pine nuts** before dividing between four bowls to serve.

COOK'S TIPS

★ Cinnamon is a sweet spice and using it in this fruity dish means that there is no need for added sweeteners, such as sugar. Add half a cinnamon stick to the compote instead of ground cinnamon, but remember to remove it before serving.
★ Vanilla or butterscotch ice cream, or a spoonful of crème fraîche, taste great with the compote.

Lightly spiced **vegetable** medley

An imaginative combination of flavours that will really lift a simple fish, meat or poultry dish. The warm and aromatic cardamom seeds add a delicate hint of spice to the tender vegetables.

Serves 4
Preparation 20 minutes
Cooking 25 minutes

Each serving provides • 286kcal
• 13g protein • 36g carbohydrates of which 15g sugars • 13g fat of which 3g saturates • 7g fibre

1 onion
2 celery sticks
1 large carrot
1 aubergine
450g potatoes
250g cauliflower florets
10 green cardamom pods
2 tbsp vegetable oil
4 garlic cloves, crushed
2 tbsp ground coriander
250g spinach
20g chopped fresh coriander
finely grated zest of 1 lemon
300g plain yogurt

ALTERNATIVE INGREDIENTS
• Try sweet potatoes or yams instead of regular potatoes.
• Leave out the aubergine and add 2 chopped parsnips at the same time as the cauliflower.
• For a different take on spiced vegetables, add 1 finely chopped fresh green chilli to the onion mixture in step 2, then add a 400g can chopped tomatoes in step 3 and reduce the water to 100ml.

1 Thinly slice the onion and celery. Halve and slice the carrot. Chop the aubergine into small chunks. Dice the potatoes. Break any larger cauliflower florets in half or into quarters. Scrape out the seeds from the cardamom pods.

2 Heat the oil in a large pan over a medium-high heat. Add the onion, celery, carrot, garlic and cardamom seeds. Stir, cover and cook for 3 minutes. Stir in the aubergine and sprinkle in the ground coriander without stirring. Cover and cook for another 3 minutes.

3 Add the potatoes. Stir in 200ml of boiling water, cover and bring back to the boil. Reduce the heat so that the mixture simmers steadily and then cook for 10 minutes. Stir in the cauliflower and cook for another 8 minutes or until all the vegetables are tender.

4 Shred the spinach and stir it thoroughly into the vegetable mixture. Cook, stirring, for 1 minute or until the spinach has wilted. Stir in the fresh coriander and lemon zest. Divide the vegetables among four plates or bowls and serve with plain yogurt.

COOK'S TIPS
★ To remove the little brown seeds from cardamom pods, slit the papery pods with the point of a knife and scrape out the small black or beige seeds with the blade.

SUPERFOOD

SPINACH
A superstar among green vegetables, spinach is bursting with the colourful carotenoids named lutein, zeaxanthin and beta-carotene. These natural chemicals are great for eye health and cancer protection. Rich in folate, spinach is also good for the heart.

Wilted **greens**, crispy **bacon** and **pine nuts** on **polenta**

Savour tender, iron-rich spinach and cabbage with crispy bacon on a bed of golden polenta. Garlic, fennel seeds, juicy sultanas and pine nuts inject tempting colours and textures.

Serves 4
Preparation 10 minutes
Cooking 15 minutes

100g smoked bacon or pancetta
300g cabbage
3 tbsp olive oil
2 garlic cloves, crushed
1 tsp fennel seeds
50g sultanas
50g pine nuts
200g baby spinach
500g readymade polenta

Each serving provides • 403kcal • 1g protein • 32g carbohydrates of which 13g sugars • 26g fat of which 4g saturates • 4g fibre

ALTERNATIVE INGREDIENTS
• Cavolo nero, a dark-leafed Italian cabbage, is ideal for this recipe, but any green cabbage, such as savoy, works well.

1 Preheat the grill to the hottest setting and cover the grill pan with foil. Dice the smoked bacon. Finely shred the cabbage. Heat 2 tablespoons of the olive oil in a large frying pan over a high heat. Add the smoked bacon or pancetta to the pan with the garlic and fennel seeds. Reduce the heat to medium and cook for 3 minutes until the bacon begins to crisp.

2 Add the sultanas, pine nuts and cabbage to the frying pan. Mix well, cover and cook for 3 minutes until the cabbage has softened slightly. Stir in the spinach. Cover and cook for a further 2 minutes until the spinach has wilted and the cabbage is tender.

3 Meanwhile, cut the polenta into 1cm slices and position them on the grill pan. Brush with ½ tablespoon of the remaining oil and grill for 5 minutes until golden. Turn over, brush with the remaining ½ tablespoon of oil and grill for a further 5 minutes. Allow 2-3 slices of polenta per portion and spoon the cabbage and spinach mixture over the top.

COOK'S TIPS

★ To cook your own polenta (ground cornmeal), pour 1.5 litres of water into a saucepan and bring to the boil. Gradually stir in 350g polenta. Bring back to the boil, reduce the heat and simmer for 35-40 minutes, stirring continuously until the polenta is thick and smooth. Brush a baking sheet with olive oil and turn the polenta out onto it. Spread evenly with a palette knife and leave to set. When cold, use a sharp, wet knife to cut the polenta into blocks or slices.

SUPERFOOD

PINE NUTS
Like most nuts, pine nuts are a good source of both polyunsaturated and monounsaturated fats, which help to lower harmful cholesterol in the blood. Pine nuts also contain vitamin E and folate, which help to protect the heart.

Sweet potato medallions with minted pea purée

Colourful petit pois puréed with lively mint make a delicious topping for roasted sweet potato slices. Brimming with carotenoids and other antioxidants, this dish is a powerhouse of goodness.

Serves 4
Preparation 10 minutes
Cooking 32 minutes

2 tbsp vegetable oil
1 large sweet potato
250g frozen petit pois
100g low-fat soft cheese
8 large shredded fresh mint leaves
2 tbsp snipped fresh chives
4 marjoram sprigs

Each serving provides • 215kcal
• 6g protein • 23g carbohydrates
of which 8g sugars • 11g fat of which
3g saturates • 6g fibre

ALTERNATIVE INGREDIENTS
• Use ordinary potatoes instead of
sweet potatoes.
• Try slices of celeriac instead of
sweet potato. Omit the mint from the
pea purée.
• Substitute 100g ricotta or firm cream
cheese for the low-fat soft cheese.
• For a delicious lunch dish, top the
potatoes with sliced mozzarella or thin
slices of chevre goat's cheese for the
final 3 minutes of cooking. Add the
pea purée and heat for 1-2 minutes.

1 Preheat the oven to 200°C (180°C fan oven), gas 6. Brush a baking sheet with a little of the oil or line it with a sheet of nonstick paper. Peel and cut the potato into slices, 1cm thick, and place them on the baking sheet. Carefully brush the potato slices with oil, season to taste and bake for 30 minutes, or until beginning to brown.

2 Meanwhile, put the petit pois in a saucepan. Pour over boiling water, bring back to the boil, cover and cook for 2 minutes. Drain and purée in a blender or food processor. Mix the peas with the soft cheese, mint and chives. Season to taste.

3 Remove the roasted potato circles from the oven. Strip the leaves from the marjoram, sprinkle them over the potatoes and top with the pea purée. Warm through in the oven for 2 minutes, then grind a little black pepper over each medallion before serving.

COOK'S TIPS
★ Petit pois, or fresh young peas, are better than ordinary peas for this recipe because they have tender skins. Standard frozen peas or mature fresh peas do not produce a fine purée.
★ If you do not have a blender or food processor, mash the petit pois with a potato masher

SUPERFOOD

SWEET POTATOES
Antioxidant carotenes give nutrient-packed sweet potatoes their orange colour. The potatoes also contain vitamin E, which helps to protect against heart disease, and are a good source of fibre, especially if you eat the skins.

Fish & seafood

Your heart, joints and brain will reap the benefits if you eat more fresh fish and seafood. Here are some great new ways to savour their succulence and delicate, clean tastes.

One-pot **fish** casserole with spicy **yogurt**

This chunky vegetable-laden fish casserole has a Continental touch – toasty croutons spread with a piquant yogurt topping to give a tangy crunch to every delicious mouthful.

Serves 4
Preparation 15 minutes
Cooking 20 minutes

1 leek
2 celery sticks
1 carrot
700g potatoes
2 tbsp olive oil
100g button mushrooms
600ml hot fish stock
250g skinless white fish fillet
250g skinless salmon fillet
1 tbsp chopped fresh tarragon
2 tbsp chopped fresh parsley

Spicy yogurt
40g mayonnaise
40g plain yogurt
1 garlic clove, crushed
½ tsp paprika
pinch of chilli powder
1 baguette

Each serving provides • 565kcal
• 34g protein • 26g carbohydrates
of which 6g sugars • 24g fat of which
4g saturates • 6g fibre

ALTERNATIVE INGREDIENTS
• Make this casserole with mixed
fresh or frozen seafood instead of,
or in addition to, the fish.
• Try fresh mackerel fillets instead
of the salmon.

1 Preheat the grill to the hottest setting. Slice and rinse the leek. Slice the celery, dice the carrot and cut the potatoes into 4cm chunks. Heat the oil in a large saucepan over a high heat. Add the leek, celery and carrot, reduce the heat to medium, cover and cook for 3 minutes.

2 Add the potatoes and mushrooms to the pan and stir in the hot fish stock. Bring to the boil, cover and simmer for 10 minutes or until the potatoes are tender. Cut the white fish and salmon into 3cm pieces and stir them into the casserole. Bring back to simmering point, re-cover the pan and cook for a further 5 minutes or until the fish is cooked.

3 Meanwhile, mix the mayonnaise, yogurt, garlic, paprika and chilli powder. Slice the baguette and grill both sides for 2-3 minutes or until golden. Stir the tarragon and parsley into the casserole before transferring it to four large bowls. Serve with the spicy yogurt and toasted baguette slices.

COOK'S TIPS
★ Select boiling potatoes rather than baking potatoes as the pieces will hold their shape within the casserole rather than break down.

SUPERFOOD

YOGURT
With an ideal combination of protein and carbohydrate, low-fat plain yogurt can help to fight fatigue and keep hunger at bay – good news for weight control. Yogurt is also a good source of calcium – one pot provides almost one third of daily calcium needs – important to help prevent osteoporosis.

Seared **tuna steaks** in a warm **herb** dressing

A punchy dill and horseradish sauce adds bite to the delicate combination of fresh vegetables and lightly seared tuna. It is a great way to raise energy levels and safeguard your heart.

Serves 4
Preparation 10 minutes
Cooking 8 minutes

Each serving provides • 266kcal
• 28g protein • 11g carbohydrates of which 10g sugars • 14g fat of which 3g saturates • 3g fibre

160g oyster mushrooms
250g baby corn
250g sugarsnap peas
2 tbsp vegetable oil
4 fresh tuna steaks
2 tbsp horseradish sauce
6 tbsp plain yogurt
4 tbsp snipped fresh chives
2 tbsp chopped fresh dill

ALTERNATIVE INGREDIENTS
• Try enoki or other mushrooms instead of oyster, stir-frying them over a high heat for 1 minute until softened.
• Fresh mackerel fillets taste terrific as an alternative to tuna when flash-fried. Use 4 mackerel fillets and cook them skin-side up for 1 minute, then turn them over and cook for another 2 minutes until the skin is crisp.

1 Slice the mushrooms. Place the baby corn in a saucepan and cover with boiling water. Bring back to the boil over a high heat, cover and cook for 1 minute. Add the sugarsnap peas, cover and bring back to the boil then drain immediately.

2 Heat a large frying pan and swirl 1 tablespoon of the oil around the pan. Add the tuna steaks and cook over a high heat for 2 minutes on each side, or until just firm and browned. The fish should feel slightly springy, not hard, and still be pink in the middle. Transfer the tuna to a dish, cover and keep warm.

3 Add the remaining 1 tablespoon of oil to the frying pan and stir-fry the corn and sugarsnap peas for 1 minute. Divide the vegetables between four warmed plates. Add the mushrooms to the pan and stir-fry over a high heat for 30 seconds. Transfer to the plates.

4 Add the horseradish, yogurt, chives and dill to the pan. Stir to combine then instantly take off the heat. Slice the tuna steaks and put them on the plates. Add a spoonful of sauce and serve.

COOK'S TIPS
★ Tuna is an oily fish that quickly goes past its best. When buying tuna, choose steaks that have been neatly trimmed, with firm, dense red flesh. Avoid steaks with a strong meaty smell or ones that look a dull brown.

SUPERFOOD

TUNA
Fresh tuna is packed with essential omega-3 oils. Proven to help to protect against heart disease, these oils are also good for joint and brain health. Tuna contains iodine, needed for a healthy metabolism, plus vitamins D and B12 to help to fight fatigue.

Trout with almonds and vibrant peppers

Tuck into succulent grilled trout fillets, combined with vitamin-packed sweet peppers and toasted almonds, and savour the anti-ageing benefits of this dish. Serve with a frisée salad.

Serves 4
Preparation 5 minutes
Cooking 6 minutes

1½ tbsp vegetable oil
4 trout fillets, about 175g each
2 large peppers (1 red, 1 yellow)
50g flaked almonds
4 lemon wedges, to garnish

Each serving provides • 369kcal • 38g protein • 6g carbohydrates of which 5g sugars • 22g fat of which 3g saturates • 4g fibre

ALTERNATIVE INGREDIENTS
• Add a chopped mild or medium-hot fresh green chilli to the peppers and garnish the dish with a lime instead of the lemon.
• Green peppers work just as well as yellow peppers. Sprinkle with plenty of chopped fresh parsley before serving.
• Fresh mackerel fillets are a good alternative to the trout.

1 Preheat the grill to the hottest setting. Line a grill pan with a layer of foil and brush with a little of the oil. Lay the trout fillets in the middle of the pan, skin-side down. Cut the peppers into 1cm-wide slices and arrange them around the edges of the fish.

2 Brush the trout and peppers with a little more oil and then grill for 2-3 minutes or until the fish is firm and opaque on top. Turn the fish fillets over and brush the skin with the remaining oil. Grill for a further 2 minutes or until the skin is bubbling and beginning to crisp.

3 Sprinkle the almonds over the fish and grill for 30-60 seconds until browned. Transfer to plates and serve the fish skin-side up, so the skin can be savoured or discarded, and garnish with lemon wedges.

COOK'S TIPS
★ Watch the flaked almonds closely as they cook – they brown quickly and will then taste bitter. Take the fish from under the grill as soon as the nuts are golden.

SUPERFOOD

TROUT
The freshwater trout is a good source of high-quality protein and vitamins A and D. As with other oil-rich fish, it is an excellent source of omega-3 oils, which help to lower the risk of heart disease and stroke. These oils can also help to alleviate symptoms of rheumatoid arthritis and help to maintain mental alertness.

Crispy coriander **mackerel** with zesty **beans**

Lemon and rosemary transform a dish of floury butter beans into the perfect foil for robustly flavoured grilled mackerel. Ready in under half an hour, this brain-power booster is the smart choice for a quick, tasty meal.

Serves 4
Preparation 10 minutes
Cooking 10 minutes

Each serving provides • 394kcal
• 29g protein • 15g carbohydrates
of which 2g sugars • 25g fat of which
5g saturates • 5g fibre

1 leek
1 tbsp olive oil
2 finely chopped rosemary sprigs
400g can butter beans, drained
finely grated zest of 1 lemon
4 large or 8 small mackerel fillets,
  about 500g
1 tbsp vegetable oil
1 tbsp crushed coriander seeds
  (see Cook's Tips)
8 lemon wedges, to garnish

ALTERNATIVE INGREDIENTS
• Flageolet beans make an excellent substitute for butter beans.
• To serve the bean and leek mixture as a base for grilled sausages, steaks or burgers, use canned mixed beans instead of butter beans.
• Sardines work well in this recipe. Buy gutted and cleaned fish and open them out flat for grilling.

1 Preheat the grill to the hottest setting and line the grill pan with foil. Slice the leek. Heat the olive oil in a large frying pan over a high heat. Add the rosemary and leek to the pan, reduce the heat and cook for 5 minutes or until the leek is tender. Stir in the butter beans and lemon zest. Set aside and keep warm.

2 Place the mackerel fillets, skin sides down, on the grill pan then brush each one with a little vegetable oil. Sprinkle with ½ tablespoon crushed coriander seeds and grill for 2 minutes or until just firm.

3 Turn over the mackerel and brush the skin with the rest of the oil. Grill for 1 minute and sprinkle with the remaining ½ tablespoon crushed coriander seeds. Cook for a further 2 minutes to crisp the skin.

4 Transfer the butter bean and leek mixture to a serving plate. Top with the mackerel fillets and pour over the juices from the foil. Garnish with lemon wedges and serve.

COOK'S TIPS
★ Use a pestle and mortar to crush the coriander seeds. Put the mortar in a plastic bag, gather the edges around the pestle to prevent the seeds from escaping and pound the seeds. If you do not have a pestle and mortar, put the coriander seeds into a bowl and crush them with the end of a rolling pin.

SUPERFOOD

MACKEREL
The omega-3 fatty acids found in oil-rich fish such as mackerel have many health benefits beyond keeping the heart healthy. Evidence is emerging about their role in maintaining mental alertness and helping to prevent the onset of dementia.

Pan-fried **salmon** on a bed of baby **spinach**

The heat from the cooked salmon is all that it takes to soften fresh spinach leaves and enhance their flavour. Serve with tagliatelle for a warm, vitamin-rich, multi-textured salad.

Serves 4
Preparation 10 minutes
Cooking 5 minutes

Each serving provides • 321kcal
• 27g protein • 2g carbohydrates
of which 2g sugars • 23g fat of which
4g saturates • 2g fibre

500g skinless salmon fillet
40g green pimento-stuffed olives
2 spring onions
200g cherry tomatoes
100g baby spinach
20 fresh basil leaves
2 tbsp olive oil
grated zest and juice of 1 lemon

1 Cut the salmon fillet into 4cm-square chunks. Slice the stuffed olives in half, finely chop the spring onions and cut the cherry tomatoes in half. Divide the spinach between four plates and sprinkle each portion with 5 basil leaves.

2 Heat the oil in a large frying pan over a high heat. Add the salmon chunks and cook for 4 minutes, turning occasionally until they are opaque but soft. Add the olives, lemon zest and juice, and spring onions to the pan. Leave to bubble for a few seconds, then spoon the salmon and its juices over each bed of spinach and basil.

3 Add the tomatoes to the pan and stir them around for 30 seconds to warm through and to pick up any cooking sediments from the pan. Spoon the tomatoes over the salmon and serve.

COOK'S TIPS

★ If baby spinach leaves are not available, choose small maincrop spinach leaves for maximum flavour. Avoid mature spinach leaves as these are too large and firm to eat raw as a salad.

ALTERNATIVE INGREDIENTS
• Use a mixed leaf base instead of spinach – try rocket, lamb's lettuce, mizuna or watercress.
• Use scallops and pancetta instead of the salmon. Dry-fry 100g diced smoked bacon or pancetta before adding the oil and cooking 300g small queen scallops, without the roes, for about 1 minute or until opaque.
• Cook 450-500g squid rings instead of salmon. You can buy squid from the fishmonger's counter and ask to have it sliced into rings. Cook as for the salmon in step 2.

SUPERFOOD

SALMON
A rich source of protein, salmon is also high in vitamin A (great for healthy eyes and skin) and vitamin D (needed to make bones strong and guard against osteoporosis). Salmon is a beneficial source of selenium, too, which helps to boost the immune system and regulate the thyroid gland.

SUPERFOOD

Salmon

Brimming with omega-3, a type of oil beneficial for your heart, brain and joints, salmon is one of the healthiest fish you can buy. High in protein and an excellent source of heart-protective vitamin E, salmon is also one of the few dietary sources of vitamin D, a crucial nutrient for keeping your bones strong.

Salmon niçoise

Serves 4
Preparation 10 minutes Cooking 6 minutes

Each serving provides • 326kcal • 28g protein • 6g carbohydrates of which 5g sugars • 21g fat of which 4g saturates • 2g fibre

Cook **3 eggs** in a pan of boiling water for 6 minutes or until hard boiled. Meanwhile, steam **400g skinless salmon tail** and **75g green beans** for 5 minutes or until the salmon is just cooked but still moist and the green beans are tender. Leave to cool. Drain the eggs, remove the shells and cut into quarters. Cut **8 stoned black olives** in half and halve **4 drained anchovy fillets**. Wash the outer leaves from **1 cos or little gem lettuce** and place them in a large salad bowl. Cut the lettuce heart into 8 segments and add to the bowl. Add **3 roughly chopped tomatoes, 6 finely chopped spring onions** and the green beans. Make a French dressing by mixing **4 tablespoons virgin olive oil, 1 tablespoon red wine vinegar, ½ teaspoon French mustard, ½ teaspoon caster sugar** and **1 crushed garlic clove**. Season to taste and pour over the salad. Divide the salmon tail into 12 large pieces and place them on the salad. Add the olives and anchovy fillets. Arrange the eggs on top of the salad before serving.

COOK'S TIPS

★ If you do not have a steamer, microwave the salmon and beans in a microwave-proof dish with a tight-fitting lid. Pour in 2 tablespoons of water, cover with the lid and cook on high for 3-4 minutes or until the fish is opaque and the beans are cooked but still crunchy.

Salmon and broccoli risotto

Serves 4
Preparation 10 minutes Cooking 35 minutes

Each serving provides • 566kcal • 26g protein • 64g carbohydrates of which 3g sugars • 25g fat of which 5g saturates • 3g fibre

Heat **3 tablespoons olive oil** in a large frying pan. Add **1 finely chopped onion** and fry over a medium-low heat for 5 minutes or until softened. Add **3 crushed garlic cloves** and **275g risotto rice**. Stir for 1 minute and add **1.3 litres fish stock** in 200ml amounts, stirring regularly. Allow each ladleful of stock to be absorbed by the rice before adding the next one. This will take around 25 minutes. Meanwhile, cut **300g skinless salmon fillet** into bite-size pieces. Stir the salmon into the rice after 12 minutes of cooking time. Continue to cook the risotto for another 6 minutes, then stir in **250g broccoli florets,** cut in half if large. Cook for 5 minutes or until the salmon and broccoli are cooked through and the rice is creamy but still slightly nutty in the centres. Stir in **2 tablespoons grated Parmesan cheese** and transfer to four plates. Garnish with **1 tablespoon chopped fresh parsley** before serving.

COOK'S TIPS
★ For a change, replace the broccoli with cooked peas, or asparagus tips when in season.

Crunchy baked salmon

Serves 4
Preparation 10 minutes Cooking 15 minutes

Each serving provides • 415kcal • 28g protein
• 8g carbohydrates of which 1g sugars • 30g fat
of which 4g saturates • 1g fibre

Preheat the oven to 180°C (160°C fan oven), gas 4. Place **3 crushed garlic cloves, 2 tablespoons pine nuts** and **4-5 sprigs fresh basil leaves** in a bowl and pound them together to release the aroma of the basil. Stir in **3 tablespoons olive oil** and **60g fresh breadcrumbs**. Season to taste. Place **4 salmon fillets, about 125g each**, skin-side down, on a baking sheet and cover each one with a quarter of the topping, spreading it evenly over the fish. Bake for 15 minutes or until cooked through and the topping is slightly browned and crisp.

COOK'S TIPS
★ Serve with a mixed leaf and avocado salad, or cherry tomatoes on the vine baked in the oven at the same time as the fish.

Ginger salmon kebabs

Serves 4
Preparation 10 minutes Marinating 30 minutes
Cooking 5 minutes

Each serving provides • 272kcal • 21g protein
• 5g carbohydrates of which 4g sugars • 19g fat
of which 3g saturates • 2g fibre

Preheat the grill to hot. Cut **400g skinless salmon fillets** into bite-size cubes and place in a non-metallic shallow bowl. Cut **2 yellow peppers** into squares and add them to the dish. In a bowl, combine **2 tablespoons olive oil**, **3 teaspoons finely grated fresh root ginger**, **2 crushed garlic cloves, 1 finely chopped green chilli (optional)** and the **juice of ½ lemon**. Gradually spoon

the marinade over the salmon and peppers then turn to coat. Cover and marinate for 30 minutes. Thread the marinated salmon and peppers alternately onto four skewers. Grill the kebabs for about 3 minutes, and then turn, brush with the remaining marinade and grill for a further 2 minutes. Garnish with **2 tablespoons fresh chopped coriander** and serve.

COOK'S TIPS
★ Make this dish as hot or mild as you prefer. Choose the chilli according to its strength – mild, medium or very hot – or omit the chilli altogether for a non-spicy meal.

Tropical mango and salmon salad

Serves 4
Preparation 10 minutes Marinating 30 minutes
Cooking 5 minutes

Each serving provides • 271kcal • 23g protein
• 20g carbohydrates of which 8g sugars • 12g fat
of which 2g saturates • 2g fibre

Preheat the grill to high. Place **400g skinless salmon fillets,** cut into 50g pieces, in a non-metallic dish. Make a marinade by combining **4 tablespoons light coconut milk, 2 teaspoons fish sauce, 1 finely chopped red chilli** and **1 teaspoon ground coriander seeds**. Pour the marinade over the salmon and gently turn to coat. Cover and marinate for 30 minutes. Meanwhile, slice **½ cucumber** and **1 fresh ripe mango**. Arrange **100g mixed green salad** on four plates and add the cucumber slices. In a bowl, make a dressing by mixing **4 tablespoons light coconut milk, 1 tablespoon fish sauce,** the **juice of ½ lime, 1 crushed garlic clove, 1 teaspoon Thai chilli sauce** and **½ teaspoon caster sugar**. Remove the salmon from the marinade and grill for 5 minutes or until cooked through in the centre. Arrange the salmon on the salad, drizzle with dressing and garnish each plate with **2 fresh basil leaves**.

COOK'S TIPS
★ Marinate the salmon for up to an hour if you have time, but avoid leaving it for any longer as the fish will begin to 'cook' in the marinade.

Succulent **salmon** with tangy **pomegranate** glaze

Jewel-like pomegranate seeds add colour and zing to salmon fillets soaked in a deliciously fruity marinade. A quick dish to prepare and one that is guaranteed to impress.

Serves 4
Preparation 10 minutes
Marinating 15 minutes
Cooking 12 minutes

Each serving provides • 354kcal • 31g protein • 4g carbohydrates of which 4g sugars • 24g fat of which 4g saturates • no fibre

100ml pomegranate juice drink
2 tbsp soy sauce
1 garlic clove, sliced
4 salmon fillets, about 150g each
2 tbsp vegetable oil
seeds from ½ pomegranate
  (see Cook's Tips)

ALTERNATIVE INGREDIENTS
• Use tuna steaks instead of salmon, allowing around 100g per portion.
• If you have a juicer, use it to make fresh pomegranate juice for the marinade. Juice the seeds from 1-2 fresh pomegranates to get 100ml juice.

1 To make the marinade, pour the pomegranate juice drink and soy sauce into a large, shallow non-metallic dish. Stir the garlic into the juice. Place the salmon in the marinade and turn to coat. Cover and set aside to marinate for 15 minutes.

2 Preheat the grill to the hottest setting. Line the grill pan with foil and brush with a little of the oil. Drain the salmon, place on the foil, skin-side down, and brush with oil. Pour the marinade into a small saucepan over a high heat and boil for 2-3 minutes or until thick and syrupy.

3 Spoon a little of the reduced marinade over the salmon portions and grill for 3 minutes. Turn, baste with more marinade and grill for a further 4-6 minutes, basting once more, until glazed and cooked through. Transfer the salmon to four plates, pour any glaze from the grill pan over the fish and sprinkle with pomegranate seeds before serving.

COOK'S TIPS

★ To prepare a pomegranate, use a sharp knife to score the skin into quarters, top to bottom, without piercing deeply into the fruit. Hold the pomegranate over a large bowl and pull it apart. The membranes and seeds will separate into uneven sections. Remove the seeds from the sections with your fingers, taking care to remove all the membrane and any pith, which both taste bitter.
★ Serve the salmon with 100g mixed salad leaves divided between the four portions.

SUPERFOOD

POMEGRANATES

There is some evidence that links pomegranate juice with slowing down the effects of ageing. The natural phytochemicals found in pomegranates may have anti-inflammatory properties that can help to relieve some of the symptoms of rheumatoid arthritis.

Oat-crunch **fish**
with **avocado** salsa

Wholegrain rolled – or porridge – oats make a fibre-rich, golden crispy coating for melt-in-the-mouth pan-fried fish. Serve a tomato and avocado salsa for just the right amount of palate-cleansing bite.

Serves 4
Preparation 10 minutes
Cooking 12 minutes

Each serving provides • 352kcal • 27g protein • 18g carbohydrates of which 3g sugars • 20g fat (no saturates) • 4g fibre

1 large ripe tomato
1 small green pepper
1 spring onion
1 garlic clove, crushed
dash of Tabasco sauce
1 ripe avocado
4 tbsp semi-skimmed milk
8 tbsp rolled oats
4 skinless white fish fillets,
    such as hoki, haddock or hake
2 tbsp olive oil
lemon wedges, to garnish

ALTERNATIVE INGREDIENTS
• Try thick pieces of skinned plaice or skinned lemon sole fillets. Mackerel and trout are also delicious served in this way.
• Use a pinch of dried chilli flakes or 1 finely chopped fresh chilli instead of Tabasco.
• For a Mediterranean slant on the salsa, add 4-6 shredded basil leaves in step 1, plus the grated zest of 1 lime.

1 Dice the tomato and pepper and finely chop the spring onion. Mix them together with the garlic in a small bowl. Stir in the Tabasco sauce. Dice the avocado and mix it with the other salsa ingredients.

2 Place the milk in a large shallow dish and spread half the oats over a large plate. Place the fish fillets in the milk and turn to coat them thoroughly. Transfer one fish fillet from the milk to the oats. Sprinkle 1 tablespoon of oats on top of the fillet and press them on gently to form a crust on both sides.

3 Heat a large frying pan over a medium-high heat. Add 1 tablespoon oil then transfer the oat-coated fillet to the pan. Coat a second fillet and add it to the pan. Cook the fish for 3 minutes or until the underneath is crisp. Turn the fillets and cook the second side for another 3 minutes until crisp and golden.

4 Transfer the cooked fillets to a plate and keep them warm. Cook the remaining two fillets in the same way. Put the fish on four plates, add the salsa and garnish with lemon wedges.

COOK'S TIPS
★ Use a fish slice and fork to turn the fillets. Be gentle but firm, sliding the slice under each fillet in one movement to avoid breaking the fish.
★ Rolled oats, or porridge oats, are the most successful variety for the oat crunch because they are slightly flaky and broken, which helps them to coat the fish. Avoid 'whole rolled' oats or superior-quality oats.

SUPERFOOD

OATS
With a low glycaemic index (GI) value, oats provide sustained energy, helping to regulate blood sugar levels. Rolled oats and oatmeal are wholegrain foods that are packed with fibre for heart and digestive health. Oats are also plentiful in B vitamins, which are vital for maintaining a healthy metabolism.

Citrus **fish** with sautéed **leeks** and **courgettes**

Spoon a zesty orange sauce over moist white fish nestling on a bed of vegetables, gently infused with garlic – and enjoy. Wholesome fish has never been more delectable.

Serves 4
Preparation 15 minutes
Cooking 15 minutes

2 leeks
2 celery sticks
4 courgettes
450g thick skinless white fish fillets,
  such as hake, hoki or pollock
3 tbsp olive oil
2 garlic cloves, sliced
finely pared zest and juice of
  1 orange

Each serving provides • 242kcal
• 24g protein • 7g carbohydrates
of which 6g sugars • 13g fat of which
2g saturates • 4g fibre

ALTERNATIVE INGREDIENTS

• Use 200g mixed stir-fry vegetables (sold in fresh or frozen packs) instead of the courgettes.
• Try salmon fillets with lemon zest and juice instead of white fish with orange zest and juice.
• Serve firm bean curd (tofu) instead of fish. Cook 350g plain or smoked bean curd in the same way as the fish in step 3. Turn over once to brown both sides, then slice the bean curd and serve it with the vegetables.

1 Thinly slice the leeks and rinse them in a colander. Slice the celery and courgettes. Cut the fish into 4cm chunks. Heat a large frying pan over a high heat and pour in 2 tablespoons oil. Add the leeks, celery and garlic. Reduce the heat to medium and cook, stirring, for 4 minutes or until the leeks are softened.

2 Stir in the courgettes and cook for another 3 minutes or until the courgettes begin to soften. Do not overcook them as they will soften further when removed from the heat. Divide the vegetables between four warmed plates, set aside and keep warm.

3 Heat the remaining 1 tablespoon oil in the frying pan over a high heat. Add the fish and orange zest. Reduce the heat to medium and cook for 3 minutes. Pour in the orange juice and simmer for a further 3 minutes or until the chunks of fish are firm and opaque.

4 Use a slotted spoon to transfer the fish to the plates. Boil the pan juices over a high heat for about 30 seconds, season to taste and spoon them over the fish before serving.

COOK'S TIPS

★ If you do not have a parer, peel the orange zest using a potato peeler, then cut the zest into fine strips using a small, sharp knife.
★ Serve the dish with a jacket potato baked in the oven for 1 hour at 190°C (170°C fan oven), gas 5.

SUPERFOOD

ORANGES

Famous for their vitamin C content, oranges also contain more than 170 different beneficial plant compounds. The nutrients and natural chemicals in oranges are thought to help to boost the immune system, regulate blood pressure and promote healthy skin.

Herb and walnut crusted fish fillets

Chopped walnuts, herbs and breadcrumbs make a satisfying, mineral-rich topping for lightly baked fish. Partner with simple buttered veg – these elegant fillets should be the star of the show.

Serves 4
Preparation 10 minutes
Cooking 20 minutes

Each serving provides • 330kcal
• 27g protein • 8g carbohydrates
of which 1g sugars • 21g fat of which
3g saturates • 2g fibre

2 tbsp olive oil, plus 1 tsp for
  greasing
4 thick portions skinless white fish
  fillets, about 125g each
50g walnuts
75g fresh wholemeal breadcrumbs
4 tbsp chopped fresh parsley
2 tbsp snipped fresh chives
4 lemon wedges, to garnish

SUPERFOOD

WALNUTS
Nuts are high in fat, but most of this
is the monounsaturated kind that helps
to guard against heart disease and
lowers blood cholesterol. Walnuts also
contain health-promoting omega-3 oils,
plus copper and magnesium to help to
maintain strong bones, plus nerve and
muscle function.

ALTERNATIVE INGREDIENTS
• Use swordfish or shark steaks
instead of white fish. Top each portion
with 1-2 thick slices of tomato before
adding the breadcrumb topping.
Sprinkle 1 chopped garlic clove over
the tomatoes for a punchy flavour.

• Try cashew nuts instead of walnuts
and 1 tablespoon chopped fresh
tarragon instead of parsley.
• Add the grated zest of 1 lemon and
1 finely chopped fresh green chilli to
the breadcrumb mix for a citrus topping
with a hint of heat.

1 Preheat the oven to 190°C (170°C fan oven), gas 4. Grease a large
ovenproof dish with oil and place the fish fillets in it.

2 Chop the walnuts and add them to a bowl with the breadcrumbs,
parsley and chives. Stir in 2 tablespoons olive oil, then scatter the
breadcrumb topping over each portion of fish, gently pressing it down.

3 Bake in the oven for 20 minutes, or until the topping is browned and
the fish is cooked through. Serve garnished with lemon wedges.

COOK'S TIPS
★ Hake, hoki and pollock are all suitable fish for this recipe. If the fillets
are thin, or have thin tail ends, fold them in half and tuck the tail ends
underneath to make a thick, neat portion.
★ To make 75g fresh breadcrumbs, whizz 2 medium slices wholemeal
bread in a food processor or blender. Alternatively, use a 75g chunk of
bread and rub it over the coarse blade of a grater into a large bowl. Fresh
breadcrumbs freeze well, so make a large batch if you want extra for
another time. The crumbs can be used from frozen.

Delicate **sole** wraps with **grapes** and savoury white sauce

Try this more substantial variation of a French classic, sole véronique. The generous sprinkling of green grapes marries perfectly with mild fish and a light, creamy sauce.

Serves 4
Preparation 10 minutes
Cooking 18 minutes

40g lean rindless bacon
1 celery stick
1 small leek
1 tbsp olive oil
400ml dry white wine
8 skinless lemon sole fillets,
    about 65g each
2 tsp cornflour
200g seedless green grapes
120g low-fat soft cheese

Each serving provides • 250kcal
• 28g protein • 12g carbohydrates of
which 10g sugars • 10g fat of which
3g saturates • 1g fibre

ALTERNATIVE INGREDIENTS
• For a non-alcoholic meal, use 400ml
grape juice instead of wine.
• Make a fennel sauce to serve with
the fish. Trim and chop 1 small fennel
bulb and add it to the sauce instead
of the celery.
• Parsley, thyme and lemon make a
good combination of ingredients for
flavouring white sauce. For a herby
flavoured sole recipe, add 2 fresh
thyme sprigs and the grated zest
of ½ lemon with the wine in step 2.
Stir in 2 tablespoons chopped fresh
parsley just before serving.

1 Dice the bacon and celery and then chop the leek. Heat the oil in a large frying pan over a high heat. Add the bacon to the pan, reduce the heat to medium and cook for 1 minute. Add the celery and leek and cook for 2 minutes or until the leek is softened.

2 Pour the wine into the pan, turn up the heat and bring to the boil. Reduce the heat to low, cover and simmer for 3 minutes. Roll up the sole fillets, from head to tail end, and secure with wooden cocktail sticks.

3 Mix the cornflour to a smooth paste with 1 tablespoon cold water, then stir this into the pan. Continue to stir the sauce until it begins to thicken. Add the fish rolls to the pan, bring back to the boil, reduce the heat, cover and simmer for 10 minutes or until the fish is cooked through. Stir once or twice during cooking.

4 Slice the grapes in half and place half of them on a serving plate. Add the fish rolls and remove the cocktail sticks. Whisk the soft cheese into the sauce and cook until just beginning to boil. Season to taste and spoon the sauce over the fish. Top with the remaining half of the grapes and a sprinkling of black pepper before serving.

COOK'S TIPS
★ Select a white wine for cooking that you would be happy to drink with the meal, otherwise your sauce may taste acidic.
★ Look for firm, creamy-coloured fish fillets. Avoid any that look old, grey or slightly discoloured. Ask the fishmonger to skin the fish.

SUPERFOOD

GRAPES
The skins of grapes contain large quantities of flavonoids (the pigments that give grapes their colour), which have beneficial antioxidant properties. Despite being higher in natural sugars than many other fruit, grapes have a low glycaemic index (GI) rating and so can help with appetite control.

Mediterranean **seafood** pie

For low-fuss healthy eating, it is hard to beat a delicious mix of prawns, squid and mussels. Here, oregano, tomatoes and leeks nestle temptingly among the seafood under a cheesy potato crust.

Serves 4
Preparation 10 minutes
Cooking 25 minutes

1kg potatoes
1 large leek
1 tbsp olive oil
1 garlic clove, crushed
400g can chopped tomatoes
¼ tsp dried oregano
350g frozen cooked mixed
  seafood, including mussels,
  prawns and squid
25g grated Parmesan cheese

Each serving provides • 378kcal • 29g protein • 50g carbohydrates of which 6g sugars • 8g fat of which 2g saturates • 6g fibre

ALTERNATIVE INGREDIENTS
• Add 50g sliced pitted black olives to the seafood mixture and the grated zest of 1 lemon to the potatoes.
• For a 'meatier' dish, include 200g white fish, cut into chunks, and only half the seafood. Cook for 2-3 minutes at step 3 before adding the seafood.
• Mussels and boiled eggs are a good alternative to mixed seafood. Use 350g cooked mussels and 4 hard-boiled eggs. Shell the eggs then cut into quarters. Arrange in the dish before pouring in the mussel mixture.

1 Peel the potatoes and cut into 3-5cm chunks. Transfer them to a large saucepan. Add boiling water, cover and bring back to the boil. Simmer for 10 minutes or until they are tender.

2 Meanwhile, preheat the grill to the hottest setting. Slice the leek. Heat the oil in a saucepan and cook the leek and garlic over a high heat for 2-3 minutes, stirring regularly, until the leek has reduced and softened. Stir in the tomatoes, rinsing out the can with 1 tablespoon of water. Add the oregano and bring to the boil. Reduce the heat, cover and simmer for 2 minutes.

3 Add the frozen cooked seafood to the pan with the tomatoes and bring back to the boil. Stir, then re-cover the pan and simmer for a further 2 minutes or until the seafood is thoroughly heated through. Season to taste. Pour into a 1.4 litre, or 25cm diameter, ovenproof dish.

4 Drain the potatoes and mash them. Spoon the potatoes evenly over the seafood, forking them up to the edge of the dish. Sprinkle with the Parmesan and grill for 12-13 minutes or until the topping is golden.

COOK'S TIPS
★ Cutting root vegetables into chunks and using boiling water from a kettle reduces cooking time and saves energy. Pour in just enough water to cover the vegetables and use a large pan that covers the ring.
★ The green parts of leeks add colour, flavour and nutritional value. Thinly slice the leek and separate into rings so that any grit can be washed away when rinsed in a colander under cold-running water.
★ Baking potatoes are ideal for this recipe as they tend to break down quickly when boiled, making them easy to mash.

SUPERFOOD

SEAFOOD
Low in fat, especially saturated fat, seafood is a good source of high-quality protein. It is also full of vital minerals and trace elements, including iron, zinc and selenium, so eating seafood can help to maintain a healthy immune system.

Chilli prawn
and **pea** stir-fry

Rustle up a health-boosting meal in no time using prawns and frozen peas, which are often higher in nutrients than some shop-bought 'fresh' ones. Noodles make an Asian-inspired accompaniment.

Serves 4
Preparation 10 minutes
Cooking 6 minutes

25g fresh root ginger
1 fresh red chilli
300g white cabbage
1 tbsp vegetable oil
1 tsp sesame oil
300g frozen peas
350g peeled cooked large prawns
4 tbsp chopped fresh coriander

Each serving provides • 178kcal
• 19g protein • 11g carbohydrates
of which 6g sugars • 6g fat of which
1g saturates • 6g fibre

ALTERNATIVE INGREDIENTS

• If fresh prawns are not available, use frozen ones instead. Add them to the pan at the end of step 1 and allow an additional 1-2 minutes cooking time for them to thaw and heat through.
• Substitute small fresh scallops for the prawns. Use them whole or slice larger ones. Other cooked shellfish, such as cockles, baby clams or squid rings, work well in this dish.

1 Peel and finely grate the root ginger. Chop the chilli into thin slivers, discarding the seeds. Slice the cabbage into thin strips, 2-3mm wide.

2 Heat the two oils in a large frying pan over a high heat. Stir-fry the ginger and chilli for a few seconds, then add the peas and stir-fry for 2 minutes or until they turn bright green and are completely thawed.

3 Add the cabbage to the pan. Stir-fry for a further 3 minutes, then add the prawns and cook for another 1 minute to heat them through. Toss in the coriander and stir, then serve immediately.

COOK'S TIPS

★ Select chillies according to how hot you want the food to taste – their strength is usually stated on the packaging. Mild to medium are good with light ingredients. Remember that starchy accompaniments will 'absorb' the heat.
★ When you are preparing chillies be careful to avoid rubbing your eyes by accident. Wash your hands immediately to get rid of the chilli stains, or wear a pair of rubber washing-up gloves for the task.
★ Use whichever frozen peas you prefer – petit pois are small and sweet, but this recipe also works well with ordinary peas.

SUPERFOOD

PEAS

Frozen peas are frozen within hours of harvesting, locking in the nutrients, unlike some fresh peas that may have spent days in transit. Peas are an excellent source of fibre, which promotes a healthy digestive system.

SUPERFOOD

Peas

Rich in a range of vitamins and minerals, peas are an excellent source of vitamin C to boost the immune system, and potassium for healthy muscle and nerve function. Peas are also high in fibre, which is good for digestion and for the heart, and in lutein, a natural plant pigment that helps to protect eyesight.

Peas à la française

Serves 4
Preparation 10 minutes Cooking 25 minutes

Each serving provides • 168kcal • 10g protein • 19g carbohydrates of which 8g sugars • 7g fat of which 2g saturates • 12g fibre

Melt a **small knob of butter** in a saucepan over a medium heat with **1 tablespoon olive oil**. Add **16 small peeled shallots** and cook, stirring occasionally, for 5 minutes or until lightly golden. Cut **1 soft round-headed lettuce** into eight pieces and add them to the pan with **600g frozen peas, 200ml hot vegetable stock** and **1 teaspoon caster sugar**. Bring to the boil, cover and simmer over a low heat for 20 minutes. Season to taste before serving.

COOK'S TIPS

★ Use 2 sliced onions if you cannot buy shallots, and substitute fresh peas for frozen ones when in season. Note that shelling the fresh peas will increase your preparation time by 15 minutes.
★ Succulent chicken or lamb are ideal served with peas à la française.
★ To add a minty twist, 5 minutes before the end of cooking sprinkle a few fresh mint leaves, or spearmint if available, and a handful of chopped fresh chervil into the pan. Remove the mint leaves before serving.

Spicy Punjabi peas with lamb

Serves 4
Preparation 10 minutes Cooking 30 minutes

Each serving provides • 361kcal • 27g protein • 18g carbohydrates of which 11g sugars • 21g fat of which 7g saturates • 6g fibre

Put **1 large chopped onion, 3cm grated fresh root ginger, 2 finely chopped chillies** and **2 garlic cloves** in a blender, or in a bowl if you have a stick blender, and whizz to a coarse paste. Heat **2 tablespoons vegetable oil** in a large frying pan over a medium heat. Add the paste and stir until the fragrant aromas begin to rise. Add **400g minced lamb, 1 tablespoon garam masala** and **2 teaspoons turmeric** and cook, stirring, for 5 minutes or until the meat is lightly browned. Add **250g chopped peeled tomatoes** and cook, with a lid on the pan, over a medium-low heat for 20 minutes. Add **250g frozen peas** and continue cooking for another 5 minutes. Season to taste. Stir a handful of **chopped fresh coriander** into **200g plain yogurt** and serve it with the lamb.

COOK'S TIPS
★ Serve with plain rice or chapatis – Indian flatbread.

Lemon and pea sauce

Serves 4
Preparation 5 minutos Cooking 4 minutes

Each serving provides • 197kcal • 9g protein • 12g carbohydrates of which 3g sugars • 13g fat of which 2g saturates • 10g fibre

Put **500g frozen peas** in a saucepan of boiling water to cover. Bring back to the boil, cover with a lid and simmer over a low heat for 4 minutes or until tender. Drain and refresh under cold running water. Put the cooked peas in a blender, or in a bowl if you have a stick blender, with **1 large garlic clove, 1 tablespoon tahini paste, juice of ½ lemon, 1 teaspoon ground cumin, 1 teaspoon ground coriander, 2 tablespoons olive oil** and **1 teaspoon ground black pepper**. Blend for about 20 seconds or until smooth. Season, spoon into a serving bowl and garnish with **1 tablespoon finely chopped fresh parsley**.

COOK'S TIPS
★ Use this pea sauce as a dip, transforming it into a refreshing starter or party dish when served with batons of crunchy raw vegetables.
★ Serve as a refreshing accompaniment to grilled meats or fish.

Creamy Italian mangetout with pasta

Serves 4
Preparation 5 minutes Cooking 10 minutes

Each serving provides • 376kcal • 17g protein • 62g carbohydrates of which 7g sugars • 8g fat of which 5g saturates • 8g fibre

Add **300g dried pasta shapes** such as penne or fusilli to a saucepan filled with boiling water. Cook the pasta for 10 minutes or until tender but with some bite. Meanwhile, cook **300g mangetout** in a pan of boiling water for 3 minutes or until cooked. Drain and return the mangetout to the pan. Stir in **200ml low-fat soft cheese, 1 tablespoon snipped chives, 2 teaspoons finely chopped fresh mint** and **4 chopped spring onions**. Stir gently until the cream cheese melts. Drain the pasta and transfer it to the pan with the

sauce and mangetout. Mix it together and serve with **2 teaspoons grated Parmesan cheese** scattered over each portion.

COOK'S TIPS
★ For a contrasting flavour, add 100g broad beans to this dish, cooked with the mangetout.

Minted pesto with leeks and peas

Serves 4
Preparation 5 minutes Cooking 9 minutes

Each serving provides • 167kcal • 5g protein • 10g carbohydrates of which 4g sugars • 12g fat of which 2g saturates • 7g fibre

First make the pesto by mixing **1 small handful finely chopped fresh mint leaves, 1 tablespoon extra virgin olive oil, 2 teaspoons balsamic vinegar, ½ teaspoon caster sugar** and seasoning in a small bowl. Thinly slice **2 small leeks**. Heat **2 tablespoons olive oil** over a medium-low heat and add the leeks. Fry for 5 minutes or until softened. Meanwhile, simmer **300g frozen peas** in a pan of boiling water for 4 minutes or until cooked. Add the cooked peas to the leeks in the pan then stir in the minted pesto.

COOK'S TIPS
★ Try this recipe as a side dish with lamb steaks.
★ Mix the pesto, leeks and peas with wholewheat pasta and top with grated Parmesan cheese for a tasty supper.

Potato and courgette medley with pickled herring

Toss hot new potatoes, crunchy courgettes and gherkins in a dill and yogurt dressing, then heap on a plate with tangy pickled herring. Here is a meal that will help to keep your body in shape.

Serves 4
Preparation 15 minutes
Cooking 15 minutes

420g new potatoes or waxy
   salad potatoes
4 small courgettes
4 large gherkins
2 tbsp chopped fresh dill
2 tbsp snipped fresh chives
1 tbsp olive oil
6 tbsp plain yogurt
2 tbsp wholegrain mustard
260g pickled herrings or
   rollmops, drained
1 large head of red or white chicory

Each serving provides • 326kcal
• 19g protein • 32g carbohydrates of
which 15g sugars • 15g fat of which
2g saturates • 3g fibre

ALTERNATIVE INGREDIENTS
• Use smoked mackerel, salmon or
trout instead of herring.
• If new potatoes are out of season,
use tinned or small maincrop potatoes.
Dice them and simmer in boiling water
for 5-7 minutes until just tender.
• Substitute a little gem lettuce
instead of the head of chicory. Little
gems have a slightly less bitter flavour
than chicory, while still providing a
crunchy texture.

1 Cut the potatoes in half, place them in a saucepan and cover with boiling water. Bring back to the boil over a high heat, cover and simmer for 15 minutes until tender.

2 Trim and slice the courgettes and slice the gherkins. Mix the raw courgettes and gherkins in a large bowl with the dill, chives and olive oil. Drain the potatoes and add them to the bowl, tossing them to coat in the herbs and oil.

3 Mix together the yogurt and mustard to make a dressing. Slice the herrings in half or thirds. Arrange the chicory leaves on four plates. Divide the potato salad between the plates, arrange the herrings on top and spoon over a little dressing.

COOK'S TIPS
★ Scissors are ideal for snipping chives. They are also great for finely shredding soft-leaved herbs, such as dill, fennel, mint and sage.
★ Pickled herrings are sold canned or in jars, or in tubs in supermarket chiller cabinets. The name 'rollmops' refers to the way the fillets are rolled up and packed in a sweetened vinegar marinade.

SUPERFOOD

HERRING
Oily fish, such as herring, is one of the few foods naturally high in vitamin D, which is great for bone health. Emerging evidence suggests that a lack of vitamin D may be linked to an increase in the risk of developing diabetes, osteoporosis, multiple sclerosis and cancer.

Prawn goulash with cauliflower and beans

Smoky paprika and the aniseed taste of caraway seeds transform juicy prawns in a twist on a Hungarian classic. Cool yogurt and rice perfectly complement the rich spices.

Serves 4
Preparation 5 minutes
Cooking 13 minutes

Each serving provides • 232kcal • 19g protein • 11g carbohydrates of which 8g sugars • 13g fat of which 4g saturates • 3g fibre

1 onion
2 tbsp olive oil
1 garlic clove, crushed
350g cauliflower
1 tbsp paprika
1 tsp caraway seeds
2 bay leaves
400g can chopped tomatoes
300g frozen green beans
300g peeled cooked large prawns
150g plain yogurt

ALTERNATIVE INGREDIENTS
• Use frozen cooked prawns if fresh prawns are not available. Bring the sauce to the boil, add the frozen prawns and simmer for 2-3 minutes until they have thawed. Do not boil the prawns or they will toughen.
• Try skinless fresh salmon instead of prawns. Cut 350-400g salmon fillet into bite-size chunks and add them to the pan in step 4. Simmer for 3-4 minutes until cooked but still firm.

1 Finely chop the onion. Place the oil, onion and garlic in a large saucepan over a medium-high heat. Cook for 5 minutes or until the onion is beginning to soften.

2 Break the cauliflower into bite-size florets and add them to the pan. Stir in the paprika, caraway seeds and bay leaves. Cover and cook for 2 minutes.

3 Stir in the chopped tomatoes and 4 tablespoons of boiling water. Bring back to the boil, reduce the heat slightly, cover and simmer for 3 minutes until the cauliflower is just tender.

4 Stir in the frozen beans. Bring back to the boil, re-cover and cook for 2 minutes. Finally, add the prawns and gently heat through for 1 minute. Serve topped with a large spoonful of yogurt.

COOK'S TIPS

★ Tender young cauliflower leaves and stalks are deliciously mild and sweet, and are just as nutritious as the florets. Although not used in this recipe, reserve leftover leaves and stalks for stir-fries.
★ This dish also works well served with potato gnocchi, which are small dumplings sold fresh or in long-life vacuum packs.

SUPERFOOD

CAULIFLOWER

A member of the brassica family of vegetables, along with sprouts, broccoli and cabbage, cauliflower contains a range of antioxidants that can disarm potentially harmful free radicals and help to protect the body against cancer and heart disease.

Sesame squid
with Oriental vegetables

Seasonings of chilli, garlic and sesame seeds lend tempting aromas of the Far East to protein-packed squid. A serving of soft noodles makes a great texture contrast to the crunchy vegetables.

Serves 4
Preparation 15 minutes
Cooking 6 minutes

Each serving provides • 294kcal • 22g protein • 5g carbohydrates of which 3g sugars • 21g fat of which 3g saturates • 4g fibre

450g squid tubes
1 red chilli
2 garlic cloves, crushed
grated zest of 1 lemon
1 leek
2 celery sticks
1 large yellow pepper
1 large courgette
250g pak choi
3 tbsp vegetable oil
4 tbsp toasted sesame seeds
4 lemon wedges, to garnish

ALTERNATIVE INGREDIENTS
• Instead of toasted sesame seeds, use 4 tablespoons pine nuts.
• For a stronger vegetable flavour, use red instead of yellow pepper and choi sum (mustard greens).

1 Slice the squid tubes into 2cm wide rings and place them in a bowl. Finely chop the chilli and mix it with the squid. Stir in the garlic and lemon zest. Thinly slice the leek, celery, pepper and courgettes. Slice the pak choi, discarding the tough base.

2 Heat 2 tablespoons of the oil in a large frying pan over a high heat. Add the leek and celery and stir-fry for 2 minutes. Add the pepper and courgettes and continue to stir-fry for 1 minute. Add the pak choi and cook for 2 minutes or until it has wilted.

3 Heat another pan over a high heat. Add the remaining 1 tablespoon of oil. Add the squid and chilli flavouring. Fry for 1 minute, turning once, until the squid is firm. Divide the vegetables between four plates. Place the squid on top of the vegetables and sprinkle with sesame seeds. Garnish each portion with a lemon wedge and serve.

COOK'S TIPS
★ Heat the pan before adding the oil to cook the squid – the pan will retain the heat and the squid will cook quickly. Cook it too slowly and the squid will be chewy.
★ Marinating the squid with garlic and chilli at the end of step 1 will intensify the flavour. Use a mild chilli for a hint of heat or a tiny bird's eye chilli for a fiery flavour. If marinating the squid, mix 1 tablespoon oil with the seasoning, then cover and chill until needed.
★ If you buy sesame seeds that are not already toasted, heat them in a large frying pan on a medium heat for approximately 3-5 minutes until they begin to brown.

SUPERFOOD

SESAME SEEDS
Even eaten in small amounts, sesame seeds are still highly nutritious. They are rich in unsaturated fats, particularly polyunsaturated fats, which help to lower harmful cholesterol and so are good for heart health. The seeds also contain fibre to boost digestive health and calcium to protect bones.

Poultry & game

Low-fat protein-packed poultry and game have a natural affinity for healthy herbs and fruits, and for simple cooking methods such as grilling and stir-frying. So explore the flavours – and enjoy.

Aromatic **chicken** with zesty grilled **vegetables**

An infusion of cardamom and lemon lends exotic flavour and irresistible Indian fragrance to simple low-fat ingredients. The courgettes are filling yet low in calories, so you can tuck into this tastebud-tingling dish with gusto.

Serves 4
Preparation 10 minutes
Cooking 15 minutes

8 green whole cardamom pods
grated zest of 2 lemons
2 tbsp olive oil
12 baby courgettes
½ cucumber
4 skinless chicken breast fillets,
  about 120g each
4 shredded fresh mint leaves

Each serving provides • 268kcal
• 34g protein • 3g carbohydrates
of which 3g sugars • 13g fat of which
3g saturates • 2g fibre

ALTERNATIVE INGREDIENTS
• Use any white meat, such as
turkey or pork, instead of chicken.
• The seasonings and vegetables
in this recipe work well with fish, too.
Grill mackerel or salmon fillets for
3-5 minutes on each side depending
on the thickness of the fish.
• Substitute 2 teaspoons fennel seeds
for the cardamom pods.
• Leave out the cardamom and add
1 tablespoon chopped rosemary
and 2 finely chopped garlic cloves.

1 Preheat the grill to the hottest setting and line the grill pan with foil. Scrape the small seeds from the cardamom pods into a small dish. Add the zest from 1 lemon and stir in the oil. Cut the courgettes in half lengthways. Cut the cucumber in half widthways, then in half lengthways and into batons about the same size as the courgettes.

2 Place the chicken in the centre of the grill pan and lay the courgettes and cucumber around the edges. Brush the chicken, courgettes and cucumber with the cardamom and lemon oil.

3 Grill everything for 5 minutes, then turn the chicken and vegetables over and grill for a further 10 minutes or until the chicken is cooked through and the vegetables begin to brown. Divide the chicken between four plates and sprinkle over the mint and remaining lemon zest. Transfer the courgettes and cucumber batons to the plates and pour over any cooking juices.

COOK'S TIPS
★ To check that the chicken is cooked, turn one piece over and pierce the thickest part with the tip of a sharp knife. The meat should be white, not pink, and the juices should run clear. If necessary cook for a few minutes longer. Turn the fillet over to conceal the slit when serving.
★ Serve the chicken and vegetables with brown rice or new potatoes.

SUPERFOOD

COURGETTES
A water content of over 90 per cent makes the courgette a low-energy (or low-calorie) food. With potassium to help to regulate blood pressure, folate for heart health and carotenes with antioxidant benefits, courgettes add plenty of health boosters to a balanced diet.

Oriental **chicken** stir-fry with **cashew nuts**

Mildly sweet and crunchy, cashew nuts are crammed with fibre, antioxidants, vitamins and minerals. Even better, tossed in with chicken and vegetables, they make an easy, delicious stir-fry.

Serves 4
Preparation 20 minutes
Cooking 10 minutes

2 tsp cornflour
100ml dry sherry
2 tbsp soy sauce
2 tsp sesame oil
180g mangetout
1 onion
4 celery sticks
100g shiitake mushrooms
2 carrots
100g unsalted cashew nuts
2 tbsp vegetable oil
300g stir-fry chicken strips
1 garlic clove, crushed
200g beansprouts

Each serving provides • 257kcal
• 23g protein • 17g carbohydrates
of which 9g sugars • 11g fat of which
2g saturates • 4g fibre

ALTERNATIVE INGREDIENTS
• Try beef stir-fry strips (or frying steak cut into 2cm strips) instead of the chicken. Use 300g shiitake mushrooms and omit the beansprouts.
• This is a good recipe for using 500g ready-prepared mixed stir-fry vegetables. Add them in step 3 and stir-fry together instead of adding them in stages.
• Use oyster or chestnut mushrooms instead of the shiitake variety.

1 In a small bowl, mix the cornflour with 1 tablespoon of cold water to form a smooth paste. Stir in the sherry, soy sauce and sesame oil. Place the mangetout in a large saucepan. Add just enough boiling water to cover, bring back to the boil then immediately drain and set aside. Thinly slice the onion, celery and mushrooms. Cut the carrots into 5mm sticks.

2 Dry-fry the cashew nuts in a large frying pan over a medium-high heat for 2 minutes, shaking the pan until they begin to brown. Transfer to a plate. Add the oil and chicken strips to the pan. Stir-fry for 1 minute, increasing the heat to high, if necessary, so the chicken begins to brown. Add the onion, celery, carrots and garlic and stir-fry for 2 minutes.

3 Return the nuts to the pan, add the mushrooms and stir-fry for 2 minutes. Pour in 120ml of boiling water and stir in the cornflour paste. Bring to the boil and add the mangetout and beansprouts. Simmer for 2 minutes, stirring, until the sauce thickens and the beansprouts are thoroughly cooked. Season to taste and serve with rice or noodles.

COOK'S TIPS
★ There are many kinds of soy sauce, but the choice in supermarkets will usually be between dark and light varieties. Dark soy sauce is richer and thicker than light, with a lower salt content. If the amount of salt is a concern, look out for bottles of reduced-salt soy.

SUPERFOOD

CASHEW NUTS
High in nutritional value, cashew nuts are a good source of fibre, vitamin E, B vitamins and folate. Like other nuts, they satisfy hunger more readily than many other foods. Studies suggest nuts can help with weight management when eaten as part of a balanced diet.

Tarragon **chicken** with tangy **apricot** sauce

An energising dish, where dried fruit, pine nuts and fresh orange juice complement superbly the more traditional tarragon seasoning. It is perfect with green beans and crushed new potatoes.

Serves 4
Preparation 5 minutes
Cooking 20 minutes

4 chicken breast fillets,
   about 120g each
4 tbsp Dijon mustard
1 tbsp vegetable oil
120g ready-to-eat dried apricots
6 fresh tarragon sprigs
juice of 2 oranges
4 tbsp pine nuts

Each serving provides • 350kcal • 34g protein • 16g carbohydrates of which 16g sugars • 17g fat of which 2g saturates • 2g fibre

ALTERNATIVE INGREDIENTS
• Use 1-2 rosemary sprigs instead of the fresh tarragon, or try 1 teaspoon dried tarragon if fresh is not available.
• Substitute chopped walnuts or pecans for the pine nuts.
• Try pork chops or steaks instead of the chicken breasts.

1 Preheat the grill to the hottest setting. Spread 2 tablespoons of the mustard over one side of the chicken breasts. Turn and spread with the remaining 2 tablespoons of mustard. Place the chicken, skin-side down, in a flameproof casserole dish and drizzle with the oil. Grill on one side for 10 minutes.

2 Slice the dried apricots. Turn over the chicken and grill for a further 5 minutes. Sprinkle with the apricots and tarragon. Pour over the orange juice and grill for a further 5 minutes until the chicken is browned and cooked through.

3 Sprinkle the pine nuts over the chicken and grill for 30 seconds to warm through. Serve the chicken with the apricots, pine nuts and juices spooned over.

COOK'S TIPS

★ Salt and pepper is not included in this recipe because the mustard sufficiently seasons the chicken. The apricot and orange bring a sweet-tangy balance that would be spoilt by additional saltiness.
★ As an alternative to crushed potatoes, serve the chicken with grilled polenta slices. Buy readymade polenta and follow the packet instructions or make your own (see page 95).

SUPERFOOD

DRIED APRICOTS

As a concentrated source of energy-boosting carbohydrate, dried apricots make great snacks. They are also rich in the antioxidant beta-carotene, and just a handful of apricots provides up to one-sixth of your daily vitamin A needs – good news for eye health.

Herbed **chicken** with **cranberry** coleslaw

Dried cranberries lend a rich intensity to a yogurty coleslaw, turning it into a light but distinctive accompaniment for thyme and sage-flavoured chicken. Team it with golden roast potatoes.

Serves 4
Preparation 15 minutes
Cooking 12 minutes

Each serving provides • 412kcal • 31g protein • 15g carbohydrates of which 14g sugars • 25g fat of which 4g saturates • 5g fibre

8 fresh thyme sprigs
6 large fresh sage leaves
2 tbsp vegetable oil
450g skinless, boneless chicken breasts
300g white cabbage
1 carrot
1 onion
4 tbsp mayonnaise
4 tbsp plain yogurt
50g dried cranberries

ALTERNATIVE INGREDIENTS
• This recipe is great for using up leftovers from a roast chicken. Remove the meat from the bones and sprinkle with 2 tablespoons fresh thyme before serving with the coleslaw.
• Try raisins, diced dried apricots or chopped apple with its skin still on instead of cranberries.

1 Rub the leaves off the thyme sprigs into a large, shallow dish. Shred the sage leaves and add them to the dish with 1 tablespoon oil. Add the chicken breasts and turn them in the herb mixture to coat.

2 Shred the cabbage, coarsely grate the carrot and finely chop the onion, then mix them together in a large bowl. Blend the mayonnaise and yogurt and stir them into the vegetables. Season to taste and stir in the cranberries.

3 Heat a frying pan over a high heat. Add the remaining 1 tablespoon oil and add the chicken, including any herb mixture from the dish. Reduce the heat to medium and cook for 2 minutes on each side or until browned. Reduce the heat to low and cook for 8 minutes, turning once or twice, until the chicken is cooked through (see Cook's Tips).

4 Divide the cranberry coleslaw between four plates. Slice the chicken and divide the pieces evenly over the salad.

COOK'S TIPS
★ Chicken breast sizes vary and the cooking time will depend on how large and thick they are. Make a small slit in the side of one of the chicken breasts using a sharp knife to see if the centre is cooked. If the meat is slightly pink, then continue to cook for a few more minutes.

SUPERFOOD

CRANBERRIES
Dried cranberries, like other dried fruit, have more concentrated nutritional goodness than the fresh variety. There is some evidence that cranberries (as cranberry juice) can lower the risk for women of developing recurrent urinary tract infections.

Spanish **chicken** with **peppers** and **olives**

Here is a complete meal-in-a-pan that makes the most of the flavour-drenched ingredients that give Mediterranean cooking its healthy reputation. For contrasting texture, serve with a crisp salad.

Serves 4
Preparation 15 minutes
Cooking 23 minutes

4 skinless chicken breast fillets, about 120g each
1 large onion
3 peppers (2 red, 1 green)
2 tbsp olive oil
2 large garlic cloves, crushed
225g long-grain rice
600ml hot chicken stock
400g can chopped tomatoes
60g pitted black olives
1 tbsp chopped fresh parsley

Each serving provides • 466kcal
• 35g protein • 59g carbohydrates
of which 8g sugars • 12g fat of which
2g saturates • 3g fibre

ALTERNATIVE INGREDIENTS
• Use stir-fry strips of lamb or beef as
a change to chicken. Allow 400-450g
of meat for four people and stir-fry it
for just 1 minute in step 1.
• When there is slightly more time to
spare, use brown rice instead of white.
Cook the rice for an extra 10 minutes
in step 2.

1 Cut each piece of chicken lengthways into three thick strips. Chop the onion and dice the peppers. Heat the oil in a large lidded frying pan and cook the chicken for 3 minutes over a medium heat or until browned and part cooked. Transfer the chicken to a plate.

2 Fry the onion, peppers and garlic for 5 minutes over a medium heat, stirring until slightly softened. Return the chicken to the pan with any juices and sprinkle in the rice. Add the hot stock, then pour in the tomatoes. Bring back to the boil over a high heat. Stir, cover and simmer for 15 minutes or until the rice is tender. Stir once again to prevent the rice from sticking to the base of the pan.

3 Roughly chop the olives and sprinkle them over the dish together with the parsley. Remove the pan from the heat, season to taste, re-cover and leave to stand for 1-2 minutes before serving.

COOK'S TIPS
★ If pitted olives are not available, buy olives with their stones still in place and use a cherry pitter to remove the stones quickly and efficiently before chopping.

SUPERFOOD

CHICKEN
Lean chicken is a good source of the amino acid tyrosine, which can help to promote mental alertness. It also contains the energy-releasing B vitamin niacin, which can help to boost energy levels, especially when you eat chicken with starchy foods such as rice.

SUPERFOOD

Chicken

High in protein and low in cholesterol-raising saturated fat, succulent chicken is a good meat to eat regularly. It contains all the essential amino acids, including tryptophan, which boosts levels of serotonin in the body, helping to combat emotional fatigue.

Sophisticated chicken salad

Serves 4
Preparation 35 minutes Marinating 30 minutes
Cooking 15 minutes

Each serving provides • 333kcal • 25g protein • 8g carbohydrates of which 6g sugars • 22g fat of which 3g saturates • 1g fibre

Preheat the grill to medium-high. In a large bowl, mix **3 tablespoons olive oil, juice of ½ lemon, 2 crushed garlic cloves** and seasoning. Add **3 skinless chicken breast fillets,** with each fillet cut into three diagonal slices. Turn the chicken in the oil mixture and leave to marinate for around 30 minutes. Meanwhile, make a dressing by mixing **2 tablespoons olive oil, 1 tablespoon balsamic vinegar, 1 tablespoon oil from a jar of sun-dried tomatoes, pinch of caster sugar** and **ground black pepper.** Transfer the chicken pieces to a nonstick baking sheet and grill for 8 minutes. Turn, baste with the marinade and cook for 7 minutes or until the juices run clear when the chicken is pierced with the tip of a sharp knife. In another large bowl, mix together **80g watercress, 40g rocket leaves, 10 halved cherry tomatoes, 6 chopped sun-dried tomatoes** and **¼ sliced cucumber.** Divide the salad between four plates and arrange the grilled chicken on top. Drizzle with the dressing and scatter **1 teaspoon finely chopped sun-dried tomatoes** over each serving.

COOK'S TIPS
★ Serve with warmed focaccia or olive bread.

Lazy days bake

Serves 4
Preparation 10 minutes Cooking 45 minutes

Each serving provides • 359kcal • 22g protein • 37g carbohydrates of which 14g sugars • 15g fat of which 2g saturates • 5g fibre

Preheat the oven to 180°C (160°C fan oven), gas 4. Heat **1 tablespoon olive oil** in a frying pan over a medium heat. Add **8 skinless chicken thigh fillets** and pan-fry for 10 minutes to brown all over. Cut **500g sweet potatoes** into 1.5cm slices and put them in a large bowl. Add **3 large red onions,** cut into quarters, and **2 tablespoons olive oil.** Coat the vegetables with the oil, then transfer them to a large roasting tin. Place the browned chicken in the roasting tin then add **8 unpeeled whole garlic cloves, 1 tablespoon finely chopped fresh thyme, 1 teaspoon finely chopped** fresh rosemary and seasoning. Roast in the oven for 15 minutes, then turn and sprinkle with the **juice of 1 lemon** and **200ml hot chicken stock**. Roast for a further 20 minutes or until the chicken is cooked through and the vegetables are tender. Serve with the pan juices poured over.

COOK'S TIPS

★ If the pan juices in the roasting tin begin to look dry near the end of cooking, pour in 4 tablespoons hot chicken stock or water.

★ Steamed kale or spring greens add bite and plenty of beneficial iron as a side vegetable with this dish.

Tex-Mex chicken wraps

Serves 4
Preparation 10 minutes Cooking 8 minutes

Each serving provides • 574kcal • 35g protein • 75g carbohydrates of which 3g sugars • 17g fat of which 3g saturates • 5g fibre

Cook **130g frozen sweetcorn** in a saucepan of boiling water for 3 minutes, then drain and set aside. Slice **4 skinless chicken breast fillets**, about 120g each, into 1cm strips. Heat **1 tablespoon olive oil** in a frying pan over a medium heat. Add the chicken fillets, **1 crushed garlic clove, 1 teaspoon paprika** and seasoning. Stir-fry for 5 minutes or until the chicken is cooked through. In a bowl, mash **1 sliced large ripe avocado** with **4 tablespoons readymade tomato salsa**. Stir in the sweetcorn and chicken, divide the mixture between **8 warmed wholemeal flour tortillas** (see Cook's Tips) and top with **1 heaped teaspoon reduced-fat crème fraîche**. Fold each tortilla up at the bottom and in at each side to make a handy parcel.

COOK'S TIPS

★ Warm the tortillas in a microwave or oven, following the packet instructions.

Gorgeous pasta salad

Serves 4
Preparation 5 minutes Cooking 13 minutes

Each serving provides • 363kcal • 30g protein • 50g carbohydrates of which 18g sugars • 6g fat of which 1g saturates • 2g fibre

Cook **175g wholewheat pasta spirals** in a saucepan of boiling water for 10 minutes or according to the manufacturer's instructions. In a small bowl, make

the dressing by combining **5 tablespoons plain yogurt, 1 tablespoon lemon juice, ½ teaspoon French mustard, a pinch of caster sugar** and seasoning. Chop **250g broccoli florets** into 2-3cm lengths. Add them to the pasta and cook for 3 minutes then drain and leave to cool for 5 minutes. Transfer the broccoli and pasta to a serving bowl, add 4 tablespoons of the dressing and toss to coat. Cut **300g cooked skinless chicken breast fillets** into 2-3cm chunks and add them to the pasta with **1 chopped green pepper, 1 chopped red dessert apple**, with the skin left on, **3 tablespoons sultanas** and **2 tablespoons walnut pieces**. Mix the salad together and serve.

COOK'S TIPS

★ Replace the broccoli with green beans – cook them for 3 minutes or until tender but still with some bite.

★ Add flaked almonds instead of walnut pieces for a slightly sweeter, more delicate flavour.

Winter barley soup

Serves 4
Preparation 10 minutes Cooking 43 minutes

Each serving provides • 321kcal • 26g protein • 31g carbohydrates of which 7g sugars • 12g fat of which 1g saturates • 6g fibre

Heat **2 tablespoons vegetable oil** in a large saucepan over a medium-low heat. Add **1 large chopped onion, 2 sliced celery sticks** and **2 sliced carrots**. Cook for 10 minutes, stirring occasionally. Slice **150g mushrooms** and add them to the pan with **2 crushed garlic cloves**, then stir-fry for 1 minute. Slice **350g skinless chicken breast fillets** into 1cm strips and add them to the pan with **100g pearl barley**. Pour in **1 litre hot chicken stock**, cover and bring to the boil. Reduce the heat to low and simmer for 30 minutes or until the barley is tender. Season to taste. Just before serving, toast **4 teaspoons flaked almonds** by dry-frying them over a medium heat for 2 minutes. Ladle the soup into bowls and garnish with **1 teaspoon chopped fresh parsley** and 1 teaspoon of the toasted flaked almonds per portion.

COOK'S TIPS

★ Use leftover roast chicken instead of raw chicken and reduce the cooking time by 10 minutes.

Sherry-infused **chicken livers** with **mushrooms** and **beans**

Rich chicken livers are invigorated with a splash of sherry, soft mushrooms and crisp green beans in this iron-rich dish. Velvety mash makes the perfect accompaniment.

Serves 4
Preparation 10 minutes
Cooking 15 minutes

Each serving provides • 211kcal • 14g protein • 6g carbohydrates of which 4g sugars • 14g fat of which 2g saturates • 4g fibre

250g chicken livers
1 onion
3 tbsp olive oil
2 garlic cloves, crushed
5 shredded sage leaves
300g small mushrooms,
300g frozen green beans
2 tbsp dry or medium sherry
grated zest of 1 lemon
4 tbsp chopped fresh parsley
4 lemon wedges, to garnish

ALTERNATIVE INGREDIENTS
• To use fresh green beans instead of frozen, trim the ends and cook in a pan of boiling water for 3-4 minutes or until tender. Drain and mix into the chicken livers in step 3 just before serving.
• For fans of liver and bacon, add 50g diced smoked bacon or pancetta to the onion, garlic and sage in step 1.
• For a non-alcoholic meal, substitute white wine vinegar for the sherry.

1 Remove any tough white parts from the chicken livers and cut them into bite-size pieces. Slice the onion. Heat 1 tablespoon of the oil in a large frying pan over a high heat. Add the onion, garlic and sage, reduce the heat to medium and cook for 5 minutes until softened.

2 Cut the mushrooms in half and add them to the frying pan. Cook for 3 minutes then add the frozen beans and cook, stirring, for another 3 minutes until the beans are hot and most of the juice from the mushrooms has evaporated.

3 Push the vegetables to one side of the pan and pour in the remaining 2 tablespoons of oil. Add the chicken livers and cook over a medium heat for 2-3 minutes, turning until they are firm and cooked. Stir in the sherry and lemon zest and simmer for 1 minute. Sprinkle with parsley and garnish with lemon wedges.

COOK'S TIPS

★ The best way to prepare chicken livers is to place them on a plate and snip away the tough white sinews with a pair of scissors.

SUPERFOOD

CHICKEN LIVER

A rich source of easily absorbed iron and low in fat, chicken livers are packed with vitamin A, needed for healthy skin and to promote good vision. In addition, they contain some zinc and B vitamins, including B12, and heart-protecting folate.

Sweet **pepper** and **turkey** grill with glazed **mango**

The classic combo of turkey, ham and cheese is made lighter and healthier by adding grilled fruit and vegetables. High levels of protein and fibre will satisfy your hunger and help to keep you lean.

Serves 4
Preparation 10 minutes
Cooking 15 minutes

Each serving provides • 278kcal • 27g protein • 12g carbohydrates of which 11g sugars • 13g fat of which 4g saturates • 2g fibre

4 turkey breast steaks, about
   100g each
2 tbsp vegetable oil
1 ripe mango
2 red peppers
1 tsp granulated sugar
1 tbsp cider vinegar
4 thin slices cooked ham
4 large fresh sage leaves
50g grated mature Cheddar cheese

ALTERNATIVE INGREDIENTS
• Chicken fillets or pork escalopes make delicious alternatives to turkey.
• Thinly sliced pears work just as well as mango. Use green pepper strips instead of red and swap blue cheese for the Cheddar cheese.

1 Preheat the grill to the hottest setting. Lay the turkey steaks on the grill pan and sprinkle with 1 tablespoon of the oil. Grill for 6 minutes until lightly browned. Peel and thinly slice the mango. Cut the peppers into 1cm strips.

2 Turn over the turkey steaks. Lay the mango around the turkey, then top the steaks with the pepper strips and sprinkle with the remaining oil. Grill for a further 6 minutes until the turkey is cooked – pierce it with a knife and if the juices run clear, then it is done.

3 Stir the sugar and cider vinegar together until the sugar dissolves, then sprinkle it over the peppers and mango. Top each turkey steak with a folded ham slice, 1 sage leaf and cheese. Grill for 3 minutes, or until the cheese has melted to a golden crispness. Serve drizzled with any cooking juices.

COOK'S TIPS
★ Reduce the total fat content of this recipe by using half-fat Cheddar cheese and lean slices of ham with any excess fat trimmed off.
★ Serve the turkey grills with couscous or bulgur wheat for added fibre and B vitamins, or turn it into a turkey melt sandwich on multigrain bread.

SUPERFOOD

TURKEY
As a white meat, turkey is a naturally lower-fat alternative to red meat. It is a good source of niacin, a B vitamin that helps to convert carbohydrates to energy in the body. Turkey also contains zinc, which helps to boost the immune system.

Light and spicy **turkey chilli**

Cholesterol-lowering turkey guarantees the feel-good factor in this variation on a traditional chilli, while mushrooms and kidney beans add low-fat flavour. Serve with rice and salad for a main meal.

Serves 4
Preparation 10 minutes
Cooking 30 minutes

Each serving provides • 325kcal • 39g protein • 29g carbohydrates of which 14g sugars • 7g fat of which 1g saturates • 15g fibre

ALTERNATIVE INGREDIENTS
• For a vegetarian chilli replace the turkey with 500g minced Quorn.
• An equal quantity of minced pork makes a tasty alternative, especially if minced turkey is not available.
• Replace the peas with 250g sliced courgettes and cook for 2-3 minutes more or until the courgettes are tender.
• Try cannellini beans or chickpeas instead of red kidney beans, and add frozen sweetcorn instead of peas.
• Okra is a good addition in this recipe. Thickly slice 250g okra, discarding the stalk ends. Add to the chilli 5 minutes before the end of cooking in step 3.

SUPERFOOD

MUSHROOMS
Low in fat and calories, mushrooms make an ideal addition to any weight-control dietary plan. They provide some B vitamins that encourage energy release from foods and are a useful source of selenium, an important antioxidant.

1 tbsp vegetable oil
500g minced turkey
2 tsp cumin seeds
½-2 tsp dried chilli flakes
  (see Cook's Tips)
1 large onion
1 red pepper
2 carrots
100g small mushrooms
2 garlic cloves, crushed
400g can chopped tomatoes
420g can red kidney beans, drained
200g frozen peas

1 Heat the oil in a large saucepan over a medium-high heat for a few seconds. Add the minced turkey, cumin seeds and chilli flakes and cook for 5 minutes, stirring occasionally, until the mince is lightly browned. If necessary, increase the heat to high for the final minute to boil off any excess juices from the turkey.

2 Prepare the vegetables – coarsely chop the onion, seed and dice the pepper, coarsely dice the carrots and chop the mushrooms into quarters. Add the garlic, onion, pepper, carrots and mushrooms to the pan. Continue to cook over a medium-high heat for a further 5 minutes, stirring frequently, until the vegetables are softened.

3 Stir in the tomatoes and 100ml of boiling water. Bring back to the boil, reduce the heat slightly and cover the pan. Cook at a fairly rapid simmer for 15 minutes, stirring once or twice. Stir in the kidney beans and peas. Simmer for 1 minute or until the beans and peas are heated through.

COOK'S TIPS
★ If you cannot buy minced turkey in your local supermarket, make your own by placing 500g lean turkey meat in a mincer or food processor and processing it until the turkey has an even consistency.
★ Add chilli flakes according to taste – ½ teaspoon will give a slight piquancy, 1 teaspoon will create a medium-hot chilli, while 2 teaspoons will produce a hot result.

Turkey souvlaki with grilled **vegetables**

Take a popular Greek fast food, combine it with sweet red peppers, punchy garlic and onions and you have a mouthwatering easy-to-prepare meal. Serve with brown rice instead of pitta bread.

Serves 4
Preparation 10 minutes
Cooking 10 minutes

Each serving provides • 495kcal • 34g protein • 61g carbohydrates of which 12g sugars • 15g fat of which 2g saturates • 5g fibre

225g quick-cook brown rice
½ tsp dried chilli flakes
3 tsp dried oregano
½ tsp ground mace
4 garlic cloves, crushed
3 tbsp vegetable oil
4 thin turkey breast fillets, about 450g
3 onions
2 red peppers
½ cucumber
200g plain yogurt
8-10 large shredded fresh mint leaves, to garnish
4 lemon wedges, to garnish

ALTERNATIVE INGREDIENTS
• Use chopped fresh green or red chillies instead of dried chilli flakes, selecting the variety according to your taste for fiery food – most supermarkets have a rating system to indicate whether chillies are mild, medium or hot.
• For a meat-free alternative, use 2 large aubergines instead of the turkey. Trim the ends and slice the aubergines lengthways before grilling.
• Serve a large bowl of mixed salad instead of the cucumber and yogurt. Allow 1 large tomato, 1 spring onion and a wedge of lettuce per portion.

1 Put the rice in a pan of boiling water, cover, bring back to the boil and cook for 10 minutes or refer to the packet instructions. Preheat the grill to the hottest setting.

2 Meanwhile, cover the grill pan with foil. Mix the chilli flakes, oregano, mace, garlic and oil in a large shallow dish. Add the turkey, turning it in the mixture to coat.

3 Cut the onions into wedges then cut the peppers into thick strips. Transfer the turkey to the foil. Put the onions and peppers in the shallow dish. Using a spatula, scrape the remaining herb mixture over the vegetables and transfer them to the foil. Grill the turkey and vegetables for 8 minutes, turning to make sure they do not burn.

4 Slice the cucumber and cut each slice in half. Drain the rice when cooked and divide it between four plates. Top with the vegetables and turkey and add a spoonful of yogurt to each portion. Sprinkle with mint and garnish with lemon wedges to serve.

COOK'S TIPS
★ Thin turkey breast fillets are often labelled as quick-cook turkey breast steaks. Thicker portions, or packs that contain unevenly cut breast meat, are more economical and suitable for this recipe. To ensure even cooking, slice the turkey into similar thicknesses before grilling.

SUPERFOOD

TURKEY
Lower in fat than red meats, turkey is a healthy choice when watching your weight. Rich in high-quality protein, needed for the growth and repair of body tissues, turkey makes a nutritious contribution to a well-balanced diet.

Succulent **duck** with **chestnuts** and **prunes**

Red wine and prunes bring out the richness of duck, seasoned with robust rosemary and juniper, while chestnuts and a hint of orange add extra flavour dimensions. Divine served with courgette batons and mash.

Serves 4
Preparation 10 minutes
Cooking 15 minutes

Each serving provides • 338kcal • 26g protein • 32g carbohydrates of which 20g sugars • 13g fat of which 3g saturates • 5g fibre

1 onion
6 juniper berries
1 tbsp vegetable oil
4 skinless, boneless duck breast
   fillets, about 120g each
2 fresh rosemary sprigs
16 ready-to-eat prunes
150g peeled cooked chestnuts
pared zest of 1 orange
400ml red wine
8 orange slices, to garnish

ALTERNATIVE INGREDIENTS
• Try venison leg steaks or pork loin steaks instead of duck.
• Use dried peaches as a change to prunes. Cut the peaches in half and again widthways to form chunks.
• Substitute cranberry juice or pomegranate juice drink for the red wine. Pomegranate juice drinks tend to be very sweet, so mix it with the juice of 1 orange before adding it to the pan.
• Replace the chestnuts with small button mushrooms.

1 Slice the onion and crush the juniper berries. Heat a frying pan over a high heat. Add the vegetable oil and the duck breasts and pan-fry for 1 minute on each side, pressing the duck onto the hot pan to brown evenly. Reduce the heat to medium, add the onion and rosemary and cook for 2 minutes. Turn the duck and onions, cover with a lid and cook for 2 minutes more. Transfer them to a plate.

2 Add the crushed juniper berries, prunes, chestnuts and orange zest to the pan. Pour in the wine and bring to the boil over a high heat. Boil for 3 minutes to reduce the wine a little.

3 Return the duck and onions to the pan with any juices and turn down the heat to low. Cover and simmer for 3 minutes, stirring now and then. Divide the duck, chestnuts and prunes between four plates. Spoon over the sauce and garnish with orange slices.

COOK'S TIPS
★ Juniper berries are one of the flavouring ingredients in gin. They are dark purple-black, tender and easily crushed into small pieces with a pestle and mortar. You will find them in the herb and spice aisle in most large supermarkets.
★ Cooked chestnuts are usually sold vacuum-packed or in cans.

SUPERFOOD

PRUNES
Prunes have the highest antioxidant score of all fruit, helping to protect the body against cancer. They also provide a concentrated source of valuable nutrients, including fibre, carbohydrate, vitamins, minerals and phytonutrients (essential nutrients found in plants that help to keep us healthy).

Chinese **duck** with **pancakes**

A lower-fat version of crispy duck, this recipe uses skinless duck breasts and balances the richness of the hoisin sauce with green peppers and a zingy ginger marinade.

Serves 4
Preparation 15 minutes
Marinating 30-60 minutes
Cooking 8 minutes

Each serving provides • 459kcal • 29g protein • 37g carbohydrates of which 9g sugars • 18g fat of which 4g saturates • 3g fibre

60g fresh ginger
1 garlic clove, crushed
1 tbsp soy sauce
1 tsp sesame oil
6 tbsp dry sherry
4 skinless duck breast fillets, about 120g each
1 green pepper
½ cucumber
8 spring onions
2 tbsp vegetable oil
20 Chinese pancakes
4 tbsp hoisin sauce

ALTERNATIVE INGREDIENTS

• Instead of using whole duck breast fillets, try more economical stir-fry duck fillets. Stir-fry in hot oil for 3-5 minutes, then pour in the marinade and stir in the hoisin sauce. Bring to the boil, reduce the heat and simmer for 1 minute.
• Pork or lamb steaks make a delicious alternative to duck.
• As a change to Chinese pancakes, serve 2 large wholemeal tortillas for each portion.

1 Grate the ginger into a large shallow dish. Stir in the garlic, soy sauce, sesame oil and sherry. Add the duck and turn to coat in the marinade. Cover and marinate for 30-60 minutes. Cut the pepper and cucumber into batons. Trim and slice the spring onions into fine strips. Arrange the vegetables on a serving dish.

2 Heat the vegetable oil in a frying pan over a high heat. Transfer the duck to the pan, reserving the marinade. Fry the duck for 1 minute on each side. Reduce the heat to low, cover and cook for 5 minutes, turning twice, until the duck is browned but still pink inside. Warm the pancakes according to the packet instructions.

3 Slice the duck and transfer it to a warmed serving dish. Add the marinade to the pan and boil it with the pan juices for 1 minute to thicken. Scrape the sediment off the base of the pan and stir in the hoisin sauce before removing from the heat. Serve each pancake with the vegetable batons, onion strips, a few slices of duck and the sauce.

COOK'S TIPS

★ Marinate the duck breast fillets in an airtight container in the fridge for up to 24 hours to intensify the garlic flavour.
★ To check whether the duck is cooked, pierce one fillet with a small knife – if the meat is bloody, it needs further cooking, but if pink but firm it is cooked. If you prefer your meat well done, cook the duck for 9-10 minutes until the inside is brown.

SUPERFOOD

GINGER
Some studies have linked ginger to relief from arthritis and joint pain. Compounds in ginger called gingerols may have antioxidant properties, helping to protect against heart disease and some cancers.

Pan-fried **venison** with **nectarine** chutney

Venison has about one-third the fat of beef, and is lower in saturated fat and calories, too. Dress with a fruity chutney, rich in potassium, and accompany with crushed potatoes and watercress for a delicious, guilt-free steak dinner.

Serves 4
Preparation 15 minutes
Cooking 10 minutes

Each serving provides • 282kcal • 30g protein • 20g carbohydrates of which 19g sugars • 11g fat of which 2g saturates • 2g fibre

2 red onions
4 ripe nectarines
2 tbsp vegetable oil
2 tbsp light soft brown sugar
2 tbsp red wine vinegar
¼ tsp ground allspice
4 venison steaks, about 125g each

ALTERNATIVE INGREDIENTS
• Duck breasts taste excellent with this fruit chutney instead of venison.
• A pinch each of ground cinnamon and mace, instead of allspice, gives warmth to the chutney.
• Try peaches, plums or firm mangos as a change to nectarines.

1 Thinly slice the onions and cut the nectarines into 1cm slices. Heat 1 tablespoon of the oil in a saucepan over a medium heat. Add the onions and cook for 5 minutes until beginning to brown. Stir in the sugar and vinegar then reduce the heat to low. Stir in the allspice and nectarines. Cook for 3 minutes until the onions and nectarines are softened.

2 Meanwhile, use scissors to snip off any membrane around the edge of the venison steaks as this will shrink rapidly during cooking and cause the steaks to curl. Heat a large frying pan over a high heat until very hot. Pour in the remaining 1 tablespoon of oil and add the steaks. Cook for 2 minutes on each side until browned. Use a spatula to press them gently onto the pan so that they cook evenly.

3 Reduce the heat to medium-low and cook the steaks for 2 minutes more, turning once, until the meat is cooked to your liking (see Cook's Tips). Transfer the steaks to four warmed plates, season with freshly ground black pepper and serve with the chutney.

COOK'S TIPS

★ Cook the venison for 5 minutes, turning once, for a steak that is pink in the middle or up to 8 minutes, turning twice, for a steak that is well done and brown throughout.
★ Venison steaks vary in thickness, which will affect their cooking times. Lay the steaks well apart on a sheet of greaseproof paper or cling film, cover with a second sheet, then beat the steaks with a rolling pin or meat tenderiser until they are an even thickness. For this recipe, a steak 1.5-2cm thick is best.

SUPERFOOD

NECTARINES

As a good source of potassium, which lowers blood pressure, nectarines may help to protect against strokes. They also contain some insoluble fibre for keeping the digestive system healthy, plus soluble fibre to help to lower blood cholesterol.

Gamy **venison** sausages with **sweetcorn** relish

A honey and vinegar relish full of colourful vegetables makes an eye-catching accompaniment to meaty sausages. Serve with green salad and crispy roast potatoes for a satisfying meal.

Serves 4
Preparation 10 minutes
Cooking 20 minutes

2 peppers (1 red, 1 orange)
1 carrot
1 onion
8 venison sausages
2 tbsp vegetable oil
1 garlic clove, crushed
150g frozen sweetcorn
1 tsp cornflour
3 tbsp cider vinegar
3 tbsp honey
1 tbsp wholegrain mustard

Each serving provides • 474kcal
• 28g protein • 34g carbohydrates of which 24g sugars • 26g fat of which 7g saturates • 5g fibre

ALTERNATIVE INGREDIENTS
• Transform the relish into a cold accompaniment by reducing the vinegar and honey to 1 tablespoon each. Add 100g frozen broad beans with the sweetcorn. Stir in the vinegar and honey but leave out the cornflour and mustard. Allow the relish to cool before serving.
• Serve the sausages sliced on top of large baked potatoes with the relish. Add a spoonful of crème fraîche or Greek yogurt.
• Try any good-quality sausages, such as bratwurst, pork with leek and apple, Toulouse or Italian-style.

1 Preheat the grill to high. Finely dice the peppers and carrot, and chop the onion. Grill the sausages for 20 minutes, turning, until they are evenly browned.

2 Meanwhile, heat the oil in a saucepan over a high heat. Add the peppers, carrot, onion and garlic. Mix well, reduce the heat to medium and cook for 5 minutes, stirring occasionally until the vegetables have softened. Stir in the sweetcorn, cover and cook for 1 minute or until the corn has thawed.

3 Mix the cornflour with the vinegar to form a paste. Stir the honey, mustard and vinegar paste into the pan. Bring the relish to the boil and simmer for 1 minute. Transfer the cooked sausages to four plates then serve with the relish.

COOK'S TIPS
★ If your oven is on for the roast potato accompaniment, place the sausages in a shallow ovenproof dish or in a roasting tin. Allow about 30 minutes at 180°C (160°C fan oven), gas 5, until the skins are browned and the sausages cooked. Turn them halfway through cooking.

SUPERFOOD

SWEETCORN
The distinctive yellow colour of corn is due to the pigment lutein, a compound with an important role in eye health. Lutein can help to protect eyes from age-related macular degeneration, which is one of the most common forms of blindness in the UK.

Meat

You do not have to give up red meat to stay healthy. Just choose lean cuts, use smaller amounts and pair with superfood superstars for lighter old favourites and exciting new discoveries.

Lamb medallions with redcurrant jus

Try a quick, lower-fat version of a slow-roasted country classic that has lost none of its flavour or goodness. Team it with crushed new potatoes for a hearty, sustaining meal.

Serves 4
Preparation 10 minutes
Cooking 15 minutes

Each serving provides • 437kcal • 26g protein • 20g carbohydrates of which 12g sugars • 28g fat of which 9g saturates • 2g fibre

200g new potatoes
2 leeks
450g lamb loin fillet
3 tbsp olive oil
250g small broccoli florets
400g can flageolet beans, drained
2 chopped fresh rosemary sprigs
6 tbsp balsamic vinegar
2 tbsp redcurrant jelly

SUPERFOOD

FLAGEOLET BEANS
As with other beans, the flageolet scores low on the glycaemic index (GI) scale, which makes it a longer-lasting energy source than many other foods. These beans also contain high levels of fibre – good news for heart and digestive health.

ALTERNATIVE INGREDIENTS
• As a less expensive alternative to fillet, slice lean lamb steaks into wide strips at an acute angle across the grain of the meat.
• Sliced pork tenderloin or stir-fry pork strips make good alternatives to lamb.

• Try chickpeas or borlotti beans instead of flageolet beans.
• Redcurrant jelly has a sharp-sweet flavour. Other suitable fruit preserves include crabapple or rowan jelly and orange marmalade.

1 Boil the potatoes in a pan of boiling water for 15 minutes or until cooked. Meanwhile, slice the leeks, cut each slice in half and rinse in a colander. Cut the lamb fillet into 2cm thick slices. Heat 2 tablespoons oil in a large frying pan over a high heat. Add the leeks, reduce the heat to medium and cook, stirring, for 3 minutes or until tender.

2 Add the broccoli and cook, stirring, for another 3 minutes. Stir in the flageolet beans and heat through for 1 minute. Put the vegetables and beans in a dish, cover and keep warm.

3 Add the remaining 1 tablespoon oil, lamb slices and rosemary to the pan. Cook over a medium-high heat for 2 minutes, pressing the lamb slices onto the pan so that they brown quickly and evenly. Turn the slices and cook for a further 3 minutes or until browned. Transfer the lamb to the dish with the vegetables and keep warm.

4 Replace the pan over a high heat. Pour in 4 tablespoons of water and the balsamic vinegar. Add the redcurrant jelly, stirring until melted. Boil the redcurrant sauce rapidly, stirring continuously, for 1 minute. Drain the potatoes and gently crush them with a fork. Divide the lamb, beans and potatoes between four plates and spoon over the sauce.

COOK'S TIPS
★ Fillet of lamb is a lean section of meat cut from the neck or loin of the animal. It is sometimes sold as tenderloin, or ready sliced as medallions. This recipe uses loin fillet as it can be cooked reasonably quickly without becoming tough.

Indian **lamb** with **apricots**

Everyone enjoys a no-fuss meal at the weekend and this korma-style curry is both quick and nutritious. Serve the tender strips of lamb and succulent apricots with warmed naans.

Serves 4
Preparation 15 minutes
Cooking 12 minutes

4 tbsp flaked almonds
350g lean lamb
1 onion
100g dried apricots
1 tbsp vegetable oil
1 large garlic clove, crushed
4 tbsp ground almonds
1 tbsp tandoori spice mix
200ml plain yogurt
25g fresh coriander leaves, chopped

Each serving provides • 294kcal
• 23g protein • 17g carbohydrates of which 15g sugars • 15g fat of which 4g saturates • 7g fibre

ALTERNATIVE INGREDIENTS
• Ring the changes by using pork or chicken instead of lamb.
• For a full-flavoured alternative, kangaroo and ostrich, sometimes found at farmers' markets, are both lean meats that are great for stir-frying.
• If you cannot find tandoori spice mix, good-quality curry powder works well.
• Try pistachio nuts instead of flaked almonds, toasting them very lightly.
• Reduce the apricots to 75g and add 25g dried cranberries.

1 Toast the flaked almonds in a large, dry frying pan over a medium heat, shaking the pan occasionally until they are browned. Remove from the pan and set aside. Cut the lamb into bite-size strips, halve and thinly slice the onion and slice the dried apricots.

2 Increase the heat to high, add the oil and stir-fry the lamb for around 4 minutes or until the meat is browned. Add the onion and the garlic to the pan. Stir-fry for 2 minutes until the onion begins to soften.

3 Stir the apricots, ground almonds and spice mix into the lamb and continue to fry for 2-3 minutes, reducing the heat slightly if needed to prevent the mixture from burning.

4 Stir in the yogurt, taking care as the hot liquid may spit. Let the sauce bubble for 1-2 minutes, turning and stirring until it is thick and creamy. Stir in the coriander leaves and toasted almonds before serving.

COOK'S TIPS
★ Scissors are more effective than a knife for cutting apricots into strips.
★ Leg steaks or fillet are the best cuts of lamb for this recipe. Look out for ready-cut stir-fry strips, too.
★ Getting the pan hot before adding the meat is important for a tasty result. This way, the meat browns and cooks quickly to become tender and succulent, instead of stewing and toughening in its own juices.

SUPERFOOD

DRIED APRICOTS
Good for eye, heart and digestive health, just three dried apricots count as one of your 5-a-day servings of fruit and vegetables. Unusually for a fruit, dried apricots are a useful source of calcium, which is good for keeping bones strong.

Sautéed **lamb** and **green beans** with creamy **caper** sauce

A seemingly self-indulgent dish cleverly deceives your taste buds by using low-fat soft cheese instead of cream. Salty capers work brilliantly with lamb and administer a real flavour kick. Serve with boiled new potatoes.

Serves 4
Preparation 10 minutes
Cooking 20 minutes

Each serving provides • 314kcal • 23g protein • 9g carbohydrates of which 5g sugars • 21g fat of which 9g saturates • 4g fibre

1 onion
400g lamb fillet
2 tbsp capers
1 tbsp vegetable oil
250g frozen green beans
1 tsp cornflour
2 tbsp semi-skimmed milk
100g low-fat soft cheese
3 tbsp chopped fresh parsley

ALTERNATIVE INGREDIENTS
• Fresh green beans work just as well as frozen ones. Trim and cook them in boiling water for around 2-3 minutes until just tender. Drain and continue as for the frozen beans.
• Use frozen broad beans instead of green beans.
• Try veal or pork escalopes instead of lamb. Cook the meat whole and fried on either side or cut into thin strips and stir-fry.

1 Slice the onion, then slice the lamb into 1cm thick pieces. Drain and rinse the capers. Heat the oil in a large frying pan over a high heat. Add the onion, reduce the heat to medium and cook for 5 minutes or until the onion begins to soften and brown.

2 Push the onion to one side of the pan and add the lamb. Cook for 6 minutes, turning the meat occasionally and pressing the pieces onto the bottom of the hot pan to ensure they brown evenly. Add the green beans and cook, stirring in the onion, for a further 2 minutes. In a small dish, stir the cornflour and milk together to form a smooth paste. Use tongs or a slotted spoon to transfer the meat, beans and onion to a dish and keep warm.

3 Add 6 tablespoons of boiling water to the pan and boil over a high heat, stirring with a whisk. Reduce the heat to low, whisk in the milk and cornflour paste and bring back to the boil. Beat the soft cheese lightly with a fork to soften it then gradually whisk it into the sauce until smooth and hot. Stir in the capers and parsley. Transfer the lamb and beans to four plates and spoon a little sauce over each portion.

COOK'S TIPS
★ When adding the boiling water to the empty pan in step 3, run the whisk over the bottom of the pan to remove any meat and vegetable sediment. This will add extra flavour to the creamy caper sauce.

SUPERFOOD

GREEN BEANS
This versatile vegetable is a good source of both vitamins and minerals, including some calcium and folate. Just 4 tablespoons of green beans count as one of your 5-a-day, and with virtually no fat they are a low-calorie bonus to any weight-management programme.

Devilled **steak** with **pepper** batons

A hot tomato and mustard coating gives plenty of 'devilish' flavour to lean beef. Then sun-ripened sweet peppers and onions soak up all the delicious pan juices. Serve with oven-baked potato wedges.

Serves 4
Preparation 15 minutes
Cooking 10 minutes

1 tbsp tomato purée
2 tbsp wholegrain mustard
4 thin beef escalopes, about
　75g each
4 tbsp rolled oats
4 peppers (2 red, 2 yellow)
2 onions
2 tbsp vegetable oil

Each serving provides • 260kcal
• 21g protein • 16g carbohydrates of
which 14g sugars • 13g fat of which
3g saturates • 5g fibre

ALTERNATIVE INGREDIENTS
• When time is short, serve the steaks in burger buns with a side salad.
• For a spicier topping, add 1 crushed garlic clove and a pinch of dried chilli flakes to the tomato mixture.
• Use pork, veal, chicken or turkey escalopes instead of beef.
• To make a rich, mushroom glaze for this dish, fry 250g sliced or button mushrooms in the pan after cooking the meat for 2-3 minutes. Add 2 tablespoons brandy and boil rapidly to reduce the alcohol to a thick consistency. Remove from the heat and pour over the steak.

1 Mix together the tomato purée and wholegrain mustard. Place the beef escalopes on a board and spread a thin layer of the mixture over them. Sprinkle the escalopes with oats and pat to make a neat coating. Turn and repeat for the other sides. Slice the peppers and onions into long strips.

2 Heat a large nonstick frying pan over a high heat. Add 1 tablespoon oil, reduce the heat to medium and add the steaks. Press down the tops of the steaks gently but firmly with a slice or spatula for 3 minutes or until the oat base is crisp and golden. Turn the steaks and cook for 2 minutes or until browned. Transfer to four plates and keep warm.

3 Replace the pan over a high heat, add the remaining 1 tablespoon oil, plus the peppers and onions. Cook for 2 minutes, stirring up the juices from the pan. Reduce the heat and cook for another 3 minutes or until the vegetables slightly soften. Transfer the peppers and onions to the plates of steak and serve.

COOK'S TIPS
★ Make sure that you buy beef escalopes and not thin frying steaks. Unlike thin frying steaks, escalopes are lean and not marbled with fat, making them ideal for coating. In addition, they do not have the fine line of chewy connective tissue that some thin steaks have, which needs to be removed before cooking.

SUPERFOOD

OATS
Because they help to stabilise blood sugar levels, oats, if eaten regularly, can lower the risk of developing Type 2 diabetes. As part of a low-fat diet, oats can also help to lower blood cholesterol levels, which may lessen the risk of developing heart disease.

SUPERFOOD

Beef

Lean beef is an excellent source of high-quality protein – one 50g serving will provide up to one-third of your daily needs. It also contains only around 5 per cent fat, almost half of which is the healthier monounsaturated type. Rich in iron, zinc and B vitamins, beef helps to boost the immune system and improves the health of your blood.

Italian summer casserole

Serves 4
Preparation 10 minutes Cooking 30 minutes

Each serving provides •243kcal • 27g protein • 8g carbohydrates of which 7g sugars • 12g fat of which 3g saturates • 2g fibre

Heat **1 tablespoon vegetable oil** in a flameproof casserole dish over a medium heat. Slice **1 onion** and **1 yellow pepper** and add them to the dish. Cook for 5 minutes, stirring occasionally. Add **1 chopped garlic clove** and **400g thinly sliced lean beef steak**. Stir-fry for 2 minutes or until the meat is lightly browned. Add **400g can chopped tomatoes, 1 tablespoon red pesto, 1 beef stock cube, 100ml of boiling water** and then **2 tablespoons chopped fresh parsley**. Bring to the boil, turn down the heat to low, cover and simmer for 20 minutes, stirring halfway through. Remove the lid and cook for a further 5-10 minutes or until the liquid has reduced to give a moist but not watery result. Scatter over **40g sliced pitted green olives** and serve.

COOK'S TIPS
★ For quick cooking, a cut of beef such as rump or sirloin is best, but less expensive braising steak is also fine. Trim off any excess fat and increase the cooking time to 1 hour, adding more water to the pan halfway through to prevent the meat from drying out.
★ Serve the casserole with new potatoes and a green vegetable, or with wholewheat penne pasta.

Beef and vegetable bolognese sauce

Serves 4
Preparation 10 minutes Cooking 1 hour 10 minutes

Each serving provides • 201kcal • 23g protein • 10g carbohydrates of which 8g sugars • 8g fat of which 2g saturates • 3g fibre

Heat **1 tablespoon olive oil** in a large frying pan and add **1 large onion, 1 large carrot** and **1 large celery stick**, all finely chopped. Fry over a medium-high heat, stirring occasionally, for 5 minutes or until the onion softens. Push the vegetables to the edge of the pan and add **350g lean minced beef**. Turn the heat up and stir-fry the meat for 2 minutes to brown slightly. Stir in **227g can chopped tomatoes, 1 tablespoon tomato purée, 1 beef stock cube, 200ml of boiling water** and **2 teaspoons dried Mediterranean herbs**. Season to taste. Bring to the boil, turn down the heat to low, cover and simmer for 1 hour, adding a little water towards the end of cooking if the dish looks dry.

COOK'S TIPS
★ Serve the bolognese sauce over wholewheat spaghetti or brown rice and top with grated Parmesan cheese and some extra ground black pepper.

Spinach, beef and beansprout stir-fry

Serves 4
Preparation 10 minutes Cooking 7 minutes

Each serving provides • 192kcal • 26g protein • 3g carbohydrates of which 2g sugars • 9g fat of which 3g saturates • 2g fibre

Heat **1 tablespoon vegetable oil** in a wok or large frying pan over a high heat. Add **400g lean beef steak strips** and cook, stirring occasionally, for 1-2 minutes or until browned. Turn the heat down to medium-high and stir in **1 finely chopped red chilli** and **2 teaspoons grated fresh root ginger**. Add **6 chopped spring onions, 150g baby leaf spinach** and **100g fresh beansprouts**. Stir-fry for 2 minutes or until the spinach has wilted and the beansprouts are thoroughly cooked. Stir in **2 teaspoons soy sauce, 1 beef stock cube** and **100ml of boiling water** and cook for 1-2 minutes. Transfer the stir-fry to four plates and garnish with **2 tablespoons chopped fresh coriander**.

Sweet potato and mushroom cottage pie

Serves 4
Preparation 10 minutes Cooking 1 hour 10 minutes

Each serving provides • 408kcal • 26g protein • 43g carbohydrates of which 17g sugars • 17g fat of which 4g saturates • 7g fibre

Preheat the oven to 180°C (160°C fan oven), gas 4. Bake **600g sweet potatoes**, in their skins, for around 45 minutes until tender. Meanwhile, heat **1 tablespoon vegetable oil** in a large saucepan and add **1 finely chopped onion** and **1 diced carrot**. Cook over a medium heat, stirring, for 5 minutes, then add **350g lean minced beef**. Fry for 2-3 minutes until lightly browned. Stir in **150g roughly chopped large flat mushrooms, 400g can chopped tomatoes, 2 teaspoons dried mixed herbs** and **2 tablespoons tomato purée**. Add **200ml of hot beef**

stock. Bring to the boil, turn down the heat to low, cover and simmer for 30 minutes, stirring occasionally. When the potatoes are cooked, remove from the oven and turn the oven temperature up to 190°C (170°C fan oven), gas 5. Carefully scoop the sweet potato flesh into a bowl and mash with **2 tablespoons olive oil** and **50ml semi-skimmed milk**. Season to taste. Transfer the beef mixture to an ovenproof dish and spread the potato over the top. Bake for 25 minutes and serve.

COOK'S TIPS
★ Instead of baking the sweet potato in the oven, microwave on high for 8 minutes or until cooked.

Paprika beef fajitas

Serves 4
Preparation 5 minutes Cooking 8 minutes

Each serving provides • 192kcal • 26g protein • 3g carbohydrates of which 2g sugars • 9g fat of which 3g saturates • 2g fibre

Thinly cut **350g lean beef steak** into 2cm wide strips and place in a shallow bowl. Sprinkle over **2 teaspoons paprika** and toss well to coat. Thinly slice **1 red onion** and **2 red peppers**. Heat **1 tablespoon vegetable oil** in a large frying pan over a medium-high heat and fry the onion and peppers for 5 minutes, stirring regularly, until softened. Add **2 finely chopped jalapeño peppers** or other **mild chillies** for the last 2 minutes of cooking. Season to taste, transfer the vegetables to a plate and keep warm. Heat **1 tablespoon vegetable oil** in the pan, then add the beef strips. Stir-fry over a high heat for 2 minutes. Gently warm **4 flour tortillas** in the microwave for 30 seconds on high. Divide the stir-fried beef and cooked vegetables between the tortillas. Add **1 tablespoon mild tomato salsa** and **1 tablespoon half-fat soured cream** to each fajita then roll up and serve.

COOK'S TIPS
★ Look for ready-sliced stir-fry strips of beef in your local supermarket, which speeds up the preparation.
★ Add slices of peeled ripe avocado to the tortillas, before rolling up, for a creamy texture.
★ Serve with shredded lettuce.

Sizzling **beef** and **sweet pepper** burgers

Crammed with Mediterranean herbs and vegetables, these juicy and delicious burgers are not just full of flavour but nutritional value to boot. Serve in toasted buns with your favourite garnishes.

Serves 4
Preparation 15 minutes
Cooking 14 minutes

Each serving provides • 243kcal • 20g protein • 20g carbohydrates of which 6g sugars • 10g fat of which 2g saturates • 3g fibre

2 large carrots
2 spring onions
1 small red pepper
1 egg
1 medium slice wholemeal bread
2 garlic cloves, crushed
1 tsp dried oregano
2 tbsp tomato purée
50g rolled oats
250g lean minced beef
1 tablespoon sunflower oil

ALTERNATIVE INGREDIENTS
• Use minced pork or lamb instead of beef, although lamb has a much higher fat content.
• Try skinned venison sausages instead of minced beef for a richly flavoured low-fat alternative.

1 Preheat the grill to medium-high. Finely grate the carrots, thinly slice the spring onions and finely chop the pepper. Beat the egg in a large bowl. Add the bread and turn the slice in the egg a couple of times. Add the carrots, spring onions, pepper and garlic but do not mix them in.

2 Stir in the oregano and tomato purée, breaking up the bread. Mix in the oats, minced beef and a little seasoning. Use your hands to squeeze, knead and thoroughly bind the ingredients.

3 Line the grill pan with foil. Shape four 20cm burgers by first rolling balls, then patting them flat. Place the burgers on the foil and brush with ½ tablespoon oil. Grill for 7 minutes until sizzling and browned.

4 Carefully turn the burgers using a large fish slice or spatula, brush with the remaining ½ tablespoon oil and cook for a further 7 minutes. Allow to stand for 2-3 minutes before serving.

COOK'S TIPS
★ Make a large batch of burgers and freeze them ready for future use. They will keep for at least 6 months in an airtight container and can be cooked from frozen by grilling slowly for 20-25 minutes, or longer if not completely cooked through.
★ To make minced beef, put 250g lean steak into a mincer or food processor and whizz until crumbly.

SUPERFOOD

RED MEAT
Lean cuts are the healthiest choice for red meat, with any visible fat removed before cooking. It is a key source of haem iron – the iron within the blood pigment haemoglobin – that is easily absorbed by the body and essential for healthy blood. Red meat also contains zinc to boost the immune system.

Steak and beetroot stroganoff

A clever way to lighten classic stroganoff is to use another Russian favourite – ruby red beetroot – while yogurt in place of sour cream cuts fat and adds calcium. Mouth-watering with noodles or rice.

Serves 4
Preparation 15 minutes
Cooking 17 minutes

1 large onion
350g button mushrooms
400g lean frying steak
250g cooked beetroot
2 tbsp sunflower oil
1 tbsp wholegrain mustard
120g plain yogurt
2 tbsp fresh thyme or oregano leaves

Each serving provides • 290kcal • 29g protein • 13g carbohydrates of which 10g sugars • 14g fat of which 4g saturates • 4g fibre

ALTERNATIVE INGREDIENTS
• Lamb is delicious cooked this way as an alternative to beef. Select fillet or thin leg steaks.
• Lightly cooked carrot strips are tasty with beef in place of beetroot.
• Add tarragon as an alternative to thyme or oregano.

1 Finely slice the onion and mushrooms and cut the steak and beetroot into 2cm strips. Heat 1 tablespoon oil in a large frying pan over a high heat. Fry the onion for 5 minutes until beginning to brown. Add the mushrooms and fry for a further 5 minutes until softened. Transfer the onion and mushrooms to a bowl and stir in the mustard.

2 Add the remaining 1 tablespoon oil to the pan and fry the steak over a high heat for 3 minutes. Reduce the heat slightly, if beginning to burn, and continue to cook for 3 minutes until browned. Any juices should have evaporated, leaving the meat moist.

3 Stir in the beetroot and cook for 1 minute. Season to taste and gently stir in the onions and mushrooms. Add 60g of the yogurt then take the pan off the heat. Stir the mixture, sprinkle with thyme or oregano leaves and divide between four plates. Drizzle each portion with a little yogurt before serving.

COOK'S TIPS
★ Ready-prepared stir-fry beef strips are available in supermarkets if you are short on time.
★ When buying cooked beetroot, make sure that you choose beetroot in their natural juices and not preserved in vinegar or your meal will have an unpleasant sour taste. See Cook's Tips on page 22 for more on ready-cooked beetroot and how to cook beetroot from fresh.

SUPERFOOD

BEETROOT
Fat-free, low-calorie and a fibre provider, beetroot is good for maintaining a healthy digestive system. It also contains plenty of folate for heart, circulation and pregnancy benefits, plus some potassium to help to regulate blood pressure.

Veal escalopes in brandy sauce with sour **cherries**

The bittersweet flavours of dried sour cherries are superb with lean, tender veal. Add a tantalising brandy sauce to satisfy even the most discerning palate and serve with mashed potatoes.

Serves 4
Preparation 10 minutes
Cooking 10 minutes

1 onion
2 tbsp vegetable oil
1 garlic clove, crushed
240g small chestnut mushrooms
4 veal escalopes, about 140g each
100g dried sour cherries
4 tbsp brandy
5 tbsp hot chicken or vegetable stock
4 tbsp chopped fresh parsley,
   to garnish

Each serving provides • 252kcal • 34g protein • 23g carbohydrates of which 22g sugars • 3g fat of which 1g saturates • 3g fibre

ALTERNATIVE INGREDIENTS
• Use beef or pork escalopes instead of veal. Alternatively, lamb steaks or cutlets are delicious with mushrooms. Cook the lamb for 2-4 minutes on each side after browning, depending on how well done you like meat cooked.
• Try sliced ready-to-eat prunes instead of dried sour cherries.
• Unsweetened apple juice can be used instead of brandy.

1 Thinly slice the onion. Heat the vegetable oil in a large frying pan over a high heat. Add the sliced onion and garlic and cook, stirring frequently, for 2 minutes or until softened.

2 Stir in the mushrooms and continue to cook for 2 minutes or until the onions begin to turn golden. Use a slotted spoon to transfer the mushroom and onion mixture to a dish and set aside.

3 Add the veal to the pan and cook over a high heat for 1 minute on each side, pressing the meat gently against the bottom of the pan to brown both sides evenly. Reduce the heat to medium or medium-low and cook for a further 2 minutes or until the meat is cooked.

4 Transfer the veal to four warmed plates. Return the mushroom and onion mixture to the pan and add the cherries and brandy. Increase the heat to high and boil, stirring, for 1 minute. Add the hot stock and boil for a further 1 minute. Divide between the plates. Garnish each serving with 1 tablespoon of parsley.

COOK'S TIPS

★ Veal escalopes are thin, tender and quick to cook in a frying pan. Browning the meat, as here, enhances the flavour and minimises the amount of oil used in cooking.
★ Dried sour cherries are usually stocked in the baking section or dried fruit aisle at the supermarket.

SUPERFOOD

DRIED CHERRIES
Rich in the plant-based antioxidants known as anthocyanins, dried cherries are good for protecting against heart disease. They are also fat free, a good source of fibre and provide an energy boost at any time of the day.

Ham and sweet potato
bubble and squeak

Transform a family suppertime favourite with generous helpings of moist ham and creamy-textured sweet potato, all spiked by the punchy flavour of aromatic fresh sage.

Serves 4
Preparation 15 minutes
Cooking 15 minutes

Each serving provides • 267kcal • 15g protein • 22g carbohydrates of which 8g sugars • 14g fat of which 3g saturates • 5g fibre

1 leek
350g sweet potatoes
200g lean cooked ham
200g cabbage, such as savoy
2 tbsp olive oil
4 large shredded fresh sage leaves

ALTERNATIVE INGREDIENTS
• Try a mixture of parsnip, turnip or white potato instead of sweet potato.
• As a change to ham, use any cooked poultry or meat, such as corned beef, chicken or leftover roast pork.
• Add diced chorizo in step 2 with the sweet potatoes for a spicy flavour. Alternatively, try diced salami, garlic sausage or frankfurter.
• Bubble and squeak is a great recipe if you want to use up any leftover cooked vegetables, such as carrot, beans, broccoli or cauliflower. Dice the vegetables and add them with, or instead of, the cabbage.

1 Thinly slice the leek, then dice the sweet potatoes and the ham into 1.5cm pieces and finely shred the cabbage. Heat the oil in a large frying pan over a high heat. Add the leek and stir-fry the mixture for 2 minutes or until softened.

2 Stir in the sweet potatoes and sage leaves. Reduce the heat to medium, add 3 tablespoons of boiling water and cover the pan. Cook for 8 minutes, shaking the pan occasionally or until the potatoes are tender and cooked through.

3 Stir in the shredded cabbage and ham. Re-cover the pan and cook for 5 minutes over a medium heat, stirring occasionally and reducing the heat to medium-low if the ingredients stick to the base of the pan. Season to taste and serve.

COOK'S TIPS
★ When buying sweet potatoes, make sure that they are smooth, plump, dry and clean.

SUPERFOOD

SWEET POTATO
This colourful root vegetable is nutrient-packed with alpha and beta-carotene – the antioxidant pigments that give the sweet potato its bright orange flesh and help to protect against cancer. It also contains vitamin E for heart health and fibre to promote digestive well-being.

Indonesian satay pork with peppers

Guarantee a juicy mouthful in every bite with a tempting combination of minced pork, crisp lettuce and peanut sauce. Peppers and onions help to boost mental alertness – perfect for a pitstop.

Serves 4
Preparation 15 minutes
Cooking 12 minutes

2 large peppers (1 red, 1 yellow)
2 tbsp vegetable oil
400g lean minced pork
2 onions
3 garlic cloves, crushed
1 tbsp ground coriander
2 tbsp soy sauce
4 spring onions
1 crunchy lettuce, such as cos, separated into leaves, to serve

For the satay sauce
4 tbsp smooth peanut butter
1 garlic clove, crushed
1 tsp sesame oil
1 tsp soy sauce

Each serving provides • 414kcal • 31g protein • 18g carbohydrates of which 14g sugars • 25g fat of which 5g saturates • 6g fibre

ALTERNATIVE INGREDIENTS
• Use 1 green pepper instead of the red pepper. Shred a quarter of a Chinese cabbage and add to the mince mixture in step 3 after stir-frying the pepper for 2 minutes. Finish as above.
• Shred the lettuce instead of using the leaves whole and serve with 2 warmed wraps per portion. Spread the sauce over the wraps, divide the pork and peppers among them, then roll up and serve with the lettuce and spring onions on the side.

1 Start by making the satay sauce. Place the peanut butter, 1 crushed garlic clove and sesame oil in a small bowl. Gradually whisk in 4 tablespoons of boiling water. The mixture will start thick and glossy, then soften after about 1 minute to become pale. Stir in the soy sauce and set aside.

2 Halve and slice the onions, then quarter and slice the peppers. Heat 1 tablespoon of vegetable oil in a large frying pan over a high heat. Add the minced pork and fry, stirring occasionally, for about 5 minutes until the meat is crumbly and browned, and the excess cooking liquor has evaporated.

3 Add the remaining 1 tablespoon of vegetable oil, the onions and the remaining 2 crushed garlic cloves to the frying pan and stir-fry them for 2 minutes. Stir in the peppers and coriander and stir-fry for a further 4-5 minutes or until the peppers are tender. Remove from the heat and stir in the soy sauce.

4 Trim and slice the spring onions diagonally. Arrange 2-3 lettuce leaves on each plate and divide the pork mixture between them. Spoon over the satay sauce and sprinkle with the spring onion slices.

COOK'S TIPS
★ To prepare large peppers, hold them upright by the stalk end on a board, then slice down to remove the flesh off the core. Slice off three sides, then cut the stalk and remaining seeds away from the fourth side.
★ If minced pork is not available at your supermarket or local butcher, put 400g pork meat, for example a shoulder joint or steak, in a food processor or mincer and grind it until it has an even consistency.

SUPERFOOD

ONIONS
Rich in plant-based substances called phytochemicals that help to prevent and protect against disease, onions are also a great source of the flavonoid quercetin, a strong antioxidant. Some studies have linked quercetin with a lower risk of developing lung cancer.

Aromatic **pork** kebabs

Juicy pieces of pork flavoured with orange zest and coriander make a brilliant match with grilled peppers and a crunchy carrot salad – two of your 5-a-day. Delicious served with warmed pitta bread.

Serves 4
Preparation 10 minutes
Cooking 10 minutes

Each serving provides • 285kcal • 25g protein • 24g carbohydrates of which 20g sugars • 11g fat of which 2g saturates • 6g fibre

400g lean pork cubes
2 large red peppers
2 large onions
2 tbsp vegetable oil
grated zest and juice of 1 orange
1 tbsp finely crushed coriander seeds
9 carrots

ALTERNATIVE INGREDIENTS
• Lamb, turkey or chicken breast all work well instead of pork.
• A meaty fish, such as swordfish or tuna, is another good alternative to the pork.
• Coarsely grated courgettes make a quick and easy salad accompaniment. Toss them with a little olive oil and a handful of shredded basil leaves.

1 Preheat the grill to the hottest setting. Line the grill pan with foil. Thread the pork onto metal skewers, without pushing the cubes of meat together tightly, and place them on the grill pan. Cut the peppers into 2cm-wide strips and thinly slice the onions. Arrange the vegetables around the edge of the kebabs.

2 Brush the pork and vegetables with oil. Sprinkle the orange zest and crushed coriander seeds over the pork. Grill for 5 minutes. Grate the carrots, then add the orange juice and mix well.

3 Using an oven glove, carefully turn the pork skewers. Then turn and rearrange the vegetables so that they cook evenly. Grill for a further 5 minutes, until the meat is browned and cooked through and the vegetables are tender.

4 Transfer the kebabs to warmed plates, add a portion of grilled vegetables to each and serve with bowls of carrot salad.

COOK'S TIPS
★ If using wooden skewers, soak them in water for 15 minutes before threading on the pork to prevent them from burning under the grill.
★ Use a pestle and mortar to crush the coriander seeds. To prevent the seeds escaping, put the mortar in a plastic bag, gather the edges around the pestle and hold onto the bag as you pound the seeds. If you do not have a pestle and mortar, put the seeds into a bowl and crush with the end of a rolling pin.

SUPERFOOD

RED PEPPERS
Half a fresh red pepper will provide your total daily vitamin C requirement. Like all vegetables, peppers are low in calories so are good for weight control.

SUPERFOOD

Citrus fruit

You need vitamin C for healthy bones and skin, and few foods give you more of that vital nutrient than citrus fruits such as limes, lemons, oranges, grapefruit and tangerines. Vitamin C also acts as an antioxidant, which helps to prevent cell damage, reducing the risk of cancer and other chronic diseases.

Sunrise fruit salad

Serves 4
Preparation 20 minutes

Each serving provides • 172kcal • 3g protein • 41g carbohydrates of which 41g sugars • 1g fat (no saturates) • 4g fibre

Peel **2 blood oranges** and **1 ruby grapefruit**, cut them into segments and place them in a bowl with any juice poured over. Peel **200g watermelon**, removing all the pips, and cut into 2-3cm cubes. Add the watermelon to the bowl, together with **100g seedless red grapes**. Cut large grapes in half if necessary. Sprinkle **4 teaspoons caster sugar** over the citrus fruit and pour in **800ml unsweetened ruby breakfast juice** or **orange and raspberry juice**. Stir and chill in the fridge until needed.

COOK'S TIPS

★ The easiest way to peel citrus fruit is to remove the top and base with a serrated knife then place the flat base on a board with a channel around the edge to catch the juices. Hold the fruit at the top while slicing down between peel and flesh, from top to bottom. Move the fruit round a little and continue slicing down until all peel is removed.

★ This fruit salad makes a refreshing starter to a fish main course.

Citrus pancakes

Serves 4
Preparation 10 minutes Cooking 12 minutes

Each serving provides • 228kcal • 9g protein • 40g carbohydrates of which 20g sugars • 5g fat of which 1g saturates • 5g fibre

Peel **2 large oranges** and slice them into segments, removing all the pith. Put the segments and any juice into a small saucepan with the **juice of 1 lemon** and **2 tablespoons runny honey**. Place the pan over a low heat, stir the mixture and warm through. Put **125g plain wholemeal flour** and a pinch of salt in a bowl. Add **1 egg** and **250ml semi-skimmed milk** and beat until the mixture becomes a smooth batter. Brush a nonstick frying pan with **a little vegetable oil** and place over a high heat. When the pan is very hot, spoon one-eighth of the batter into the centre of the pan. Swirl it around to coat the base of the pan and cook for 1 minute or until the underside is flecked brown. Turn the pancake with a spatula and cook for another 30 seconds. Transfer to a plate and keep warm. Repeat with the remaining mixture to make another seven pancakes. Serve with the warm orange mixture spooned over each pancake.

COOK'S TIPS

★ For a slightly sweeter pancake dish, use 200g tinned mandarins instead of the segmented oranges and add a light dusting of icing sugar just before serving.

Pink grapefruit and pomegranate salad

Serves 4
Preparation 10 minutes

Each serving provides • 238kcal • 1g protein • 7g carbohydrates of which 7g sugars • 23g fat of which 3g saturates • 2g fibre

Arrange **200g frisée lettuce leaves**, washed and torn if large, in a salad bowl. Peel and segment **1 large pink grapefruit**, then halve the segments and arrange them over the frisée leaves. Remove the colourful seeds from **1 pomegranate** using a small spoon to prise them out. Make a dressing by combining **6 tablespoons olive oil** with **1 tablespoon red wine vinegar**, **1 teaspoon balsamic vinegar** and any juice that has run out of the grapefruit. Drizzle the dressing over the salad and toss to combine. Sprinkle the pomegranate seeds over the salad and serve.

COOK'S TIPS

★ Frisée lettuce (also known as curly endive) has thin, green, curly leaves that look really decorative. Other attractive salad leaves include sweet lamb's lettuce or peppery rocket.

★ Use raspberry vinegar instead of red wine vinegar for a fruitier flavour.

Pork fillets with lime gremolata

Serves 4
Preparation 10 minutes Marinating 30 minutes
Cooking 10 minutes

Each serving provides • 235kcal • 27g protein • 1g carbohydrates (no sugars) • 13g fat of which 3g saturates • no fibre

In a non-metallic shallow dish, mix **2 tablespoons olive oil, juice of 1 lime, 2 tablespoons dry white wine** and **2 crushed garlic cloves**. Cut **4 pork fillets, 125g each**, diagonally in half. Coat with the marinade and leave to

marinate for 30 minutes. To make the gremolata, first zest **1 unwaxed lime**. Peel and remove the pith, then cut the lime into small chunks. Combine the lime zest with **1 tablespoon finely chopped fresh parsley** and **2 large finely chopped garlic cloves**. Cook the pieces of pork together with the marinade in a large frying pan over a medium heat for 10 minutes or until golden and cooked through. Stir in the lime chunks and then add **2 tablespoons half-fat crème fraîche** and allow to warm through. Serve the pork with the creamy lime sauce and gremolata sprinkled over the top.

COOK'S TIPS

★ Serve the pork with pan-fried potato slices and boiled green beans for a taste of summer.

★ Other white meats, such as chicken and turkey, also taste great sprinkled with gremolata. Substitute a lemon for the lime for a sharper flavour.

Clementine and red onion chutney

Serves 4
Preparation 10 minutes Cooking 10 minutes

Each serving provides • 131kcal • 1g protein • 12g carbohydrates of which 11g sugars • 9g fat of which 1g saturates • 2g fibre

Preheat the oven to 180°C (160°C fan oven), gas 4. Peel **6 clementines** and cut each fruit across the grain into 4 slices. Transfer the slices to an ovenproof dish, lightly brushed with **1 teaspoon olive oil**. Finely chop **1 red onion** and sprinkle it over the clementines. Drizzle **2 tablespoons olive oil** and **3 teaspoons red wine vinegar** over the mixture, then sprinkle in **1 teaspoon soft dark brown sugar**. Bake for 10 minutes and serve warm with a little extra olive oil drizzled over the top.

COOK'S TIPS

★ This chutney goes well with grilled chicken, venison sausages or duck breast fillets. Serve with a hearty green salad, as well.

Tender **pork** steaks with **blueberry** and **apple** sauce

Brimming with protective antioxidants, blueberries also bring colour and sweetness to a family favourite. Serve the pork with stir-fried cabbage and leeks, plus tender baby carrots.

Serves 4
Preparation 10 minutes
Cooking 18 minutes

Each serving provides • 308kcal • 30g protein • 18g carbohydrates of which 18g sugars • 13g fat of which 3g saturates • 6g fibre

2 cooking apples, about 250g
1 large leek
400g cabbage
1 tbsp granulated sugar
150g blueberries
2 tbsp vegetable oil
4 lean pork steaks

ALTERNATIVE INGREDIENTS
• Blackberries or sliced plums also taste great with pork. Halve, stone and slice the plums then cook with the apples for 1 minute.
• For a cranberry and apple sauce, cook the cranberries and apples with 3 tablespoons of water until the cranberries have softened. Then add 2 tablespoons granulated sugar and cook gently for 1 minute.
• Venison, lamb, turkey steaks and pheasant breast all taste delicious accompanied by this fruity sauce.

1 Peel and coarsely grate the apples. Trim, thinly slice and rinse the leeks then finely shred the cabbage. Place the apples in a saucepan over a high heat. Add the sugar and 1 tablespoon of water and bring to the boil, stirring. Reduce the heat to low, cover and cook for 1-2 minutes or until the apples soften. Stir in the blueberries to warm through and transfer to a serving bowl.

2 Heat a large frying pan over a high heat until really hot. Pour in 1 tablespoon of the oil and add the pork steaks. Brown for 1 minute on each side, reduce the heat to medium-low and fry for 4 minutes on each side. Transfer the pork to a plate and keep warm.

3 Add the remaining tablespoon of oil to the frying pan, increase the heat to high and stir-fry the leeks for 3 minutes or until softened. Add the cabbage and stir-fry for a further 2 minutes until the cabbage is tender. Transfer the pork and vegetables to four warmed plates and add a large spoonful of blueberry and apple sauce before serving.

COOK'S TIPS
★ Make light work of preparing the apples by peeling them whole, then hold them by the core ends and grate directly into the pan.
★ The leeks and cabbage reduce rapidly as they soften and cook, so add the cabbage in batches if your pan is small.

SUPERFOOD

CABBAGES
Bursting with nourishment, cabbages of all colours contain high levels of antioxidants that work to protect cell membranes from damage by free radicals. As a result, there are studies that link eating cabbages with a lower risk of developing cancer, especially of the digestive tract.

Sausages and supermash
with onion relish

Creamy mashed potato hits new heights with an injection of vitamin-packed carrot and courgette. Add an easy onion relish and you have the perfect matches for moist poached sausages. Serve with peas for a dash of colour.

Serves 4
Preparation 15 minutes
Cooking 35 minutes

8 good-quality pork sausages,
   about 450g
1kg potatoes
1 courgette
1 large carrot
4 onions
4 tbsp vegetable oil
2 tbsp demerara sugar
2 tbsp cider vinegar
4 tbsp semi-skimmed milk

Each serving provides • 630kcal
• 21g protein • 63g carbohydrates of
which 22g sugars • 34g fat of which
9g saturates • 6g fibre

ALTERNATIVE INGREDIENTS
• Grated celeriac or butternut squash
make good alternatives to courgette.
• Chopped celery, grated carrot and
chopped walnuts are another brilliant
mixture of complementary flavours for
livening up mashed potato.
• Serve grilled. sliced black pudding,
good-quality burgers or grilled chicken
instead of the sausages.

1 Place the sausages in a saucepan, cover with water and put on a lid. Bring the water to the boil, then reduce the heat and poach the sausages for 30 minutes. Meanwhile, peel the potatoes and cut into 3cm chunks. Transfer to a saucepan, cover with boiling water and simmer for 10 minutes or until tender. Coarsely grate the courgettes and carrots. Thinly slice the onions.

2 Heat 2 tablespoons of the oil in a saucepan over a medium heat. Add the onions and cook for 5 minutes, stirring once or twice, until softened. Add the sugar and cook for 5-6 minutes, reducing the heat if the onions begin to burn. When the sausages are cooked, carefully remove them with a slotted spoon and dry on kitchen paper. Dry-fry them in a nonstick frying pan for 3-5 minutes or until browned all over.

3 Stir the cider vinegar into the onions, turn up the heat and boil for 1 minute. Reduce the heat to low and simmer for 3-5 minutes until the liquid has virtually evaporated and the onions are glazed.

4 Drain the potatoes in a colander. Add the remaining 2 tablespoons of oil, plus the courgette and carrot, to the empty potato pan and cook over a low heat for 1 minute. Remove from the heat, replace the potatoes, pour in the milk and mash until smooth. Stir up the courgette and carrots, season and serve with the sausages and onion relish.

COOK'S TIPS
★ Make the onion relish when you have a spare moment, up to several hours in advance, then transfer it to a dish and cover until required.
★ Alternatively, cook the sausages by grilling them under a high heat for 20 minutes, turning until browned all over and cooked through.

SUPERFOOD

ONIONS
Research indicates that onions, along with other members of the allium family, may protect against stomach cancer. This is because natural phytochemicals in the onions may stimulate enzymes that get rid of harmful chemicals in the body.

Fruity **pork steaks** with glazed **plums** and **red cabbage**

Delectable sweet-and-sour flavours of ripe plums and red wine vinegar work so well with pork and cabbage. Serve with fibre-rich mixed swede and carrot mash for a real treat.

Serves 4
Preparation 10 minutes
Cooking 25 minutes

2 red onions
400g red cabbage
8 ripe plums
2 tbsp vegetable oil
4 lean boneless pork loin chops, about 130g each
pinch of ground cloves or allspice
100ml pomegranate juice drink
3 tbsp demerara sugar
3 tbsp red wine vinegar

Each serving provides • 405kcal • 31g protein • 34g carbohydrates of which 32g sugars • 17g fat of which 4g saturates • 6g fibre

ALTERNATIVE INGREDIENTS
• Grind 6 juniper berries in a pestle and mortar and use instead of the ground cloves or allspice.
• This recipe also works well with venison or lamb steaks.
• Instead of using fresh fruit, add 150g thickly sliced ready-to-eat prunes or apricots in step 2. Stir the dried fruit into the cabbage before replacing the meat. Omit the additional 1 tablespoon sugar and vinegar used to glaze the fruit in step 5.

1 Slice the onions, shred the red cabbage and cut the plums in half. Heat the oil in a large frying pan over a high heat. Add the pork steaks and cook for 3 minutes on each side until browned. Reduce the heat to medium, add the onions and cook for a further 5 minutes, stirring occasionally, until the meat is cooked through. Transfer the steaks to a shallow dish, leaving the onions in the pan.

2 Add the cabbage and cloves or allspice to the pan and fry, stirring, for 5 minutes. Pour in the pomegranate juice drink and bring to the boil. Return the pork to the pan with any juices from the dish. Reduce the heat to medium, cover and cook for 3 minutes. Transfer the pork to four plates. Add 1 tablespoon each of sugar and vinegar to the cabbage and boil for 30 seconds, stirring, to glaze the cabbage. Divide between the plates of pork.

3 Add the plums to the pan, cut sides down. Sprinkle in the remaining 2 tablespoons each of sugar and vinegar and cook over a high heat for 4 minutes, shaking the pan so that the sugar dissolves. Season to taste and divide the plums and their glaze between the plates and serve.

COOK'S TIPS
★ To halve plums, cut around the dimple in the fruit and twist the halves. They will come apart, leaving the stone on one half. Use a small pointed knife to cut out the stone.

SUPERFOOD

PLUMS

The goodness of plums, as with most fruit, is found in or around the skin – so do not peel them. Their nutritional benefits include potassium to help to regulate blood pressure and fibre for keeping the digestive system healthy. Plums also contain antioxidants to help to fight the signs of ageing.

Pasta, pulses & grains

Full of energy-giving carbohydrates, protein, fibre and vitamins, tasty wholegrains and pulses are mainstays of a healthy diet – and the key to some of the world's great dishes.

Italian spirals with **watercress** and **olive** dressing

Fiery watercress is a great foil for spirali pasta tossed in a gremolata dressing, while crunchy pistachio nuts and a little Parmesan enrich the flavour. Serve with cherry tomatoes.

Serves 4
Preparation 10 minutes
Cooking 10 minutes

Each serving provides • 588kcal • 20g protein • 61g carbohydrates of which 5g sugars • 31g fat of which 7g saturates • 7g fibre

300g pasta shapes, such as spirali
2 small leeks
150g watercress
50g shelled pistachio nuts
100g pimento stuffed olives
4 tbsp olive oil
3 garlic cloves, crushed
30g fresh chopped parsley
grated zest of 1 lemon
60g grated Parmesan cheese

ALTERNATIVE INGREDIENTS
• Enhance the nutty flavour by using a mixture of olive oil and walnut oil. Cook the leeks in 2 tablespoons olive oil, then add 2 tablespoons walnut oil to the pan once the leeks are cooked. Add walnuts instead of pistachio nuts.
• For herb-flavoured pasta, add tarragon or basil to the recipe in addition to the parsley. Chop 2 fresh tarragon sprigs with the parsley. Basil loses its flavour when chopped, so it is best to shred 2-3 large tender sprigs into the pan just before mixing in the olives in step 3.
• Try other cheese, such as Gruyère, Manchego, pecorino or a strong Cheddar, instead of Parmesan.

1 Cook the pasta in a large pan of boiling water for 10 minutes or until the pasta is tender but not soft. Alternatively, refer to the packet instructions for cooking times. Slice the leeks into rings, cut the rings into quarters and rinse. Chop the watercress and pistachio nuts. Halve the stuffed olives.

2 Halfway through cooking the pasta, heat the oil in a saucepan over a high heat. Add the garlic and leeks then reduce the heat to medium-low. Cover and cook for 5 minutes, stirring once, until the leeks soften.

3 Tip the pasta into a colander and quickly return it to the hot pan without shaking off all the cooking liquid – this way the pasta should be slightly moist and will stay hot. Add the leeks, watercress, parsley, pistachio nuts, lemon zest and stuffed olives. Stir together and divide between four plates. Serve topped with grated Parmesan cheese.

COOK'S TIPS
★ For speed, though the final dish does not look quite as attractive, blend the watercress, parsley and pistachio nuts together in a food processor until finely chopped.

SUPERFOOD

WATERCRESS
Brimming with essential nutrients, watercress contains calcium to help to maintain bone strength, iron for preventing anaemia and folate to promote heart health. It is also a good source of antioxidants, which may have anti-cancer effects as they protect the body against harmful free radicals.

Creamy **mushroom** feast with **tagliatelle**

An indulgent but nutritious sauce coats a fusion of succulent, earthy mushrooms and antioxidant-packed walnuts. They turn a simple bowl of pasta into a hearty meal.

Serves 4
Preparation 10 minutes
Cooking 15 minutes

Each serving provides • 576kcal
• 19g protein • 59g carbohydrates
of which 8g sugars • 31g fat of which
6g saturates • 5g fibre

250g tagliatelle
300g chestnut mushrooms
100g walnuts
2 tbsp olive oil
3 tsp cornflour
400ml semi-skimmed milk
100g low-fat soft cheese
4 tbsp finely chopped fresh parsley
250g oyster mushrooms
3 tbsp snipped fresh chives

ALTERNATIVE INGREDIENTS
• Replace the oyster mushrooms with exotic mushrooms such as shiitake or chanterelle. These can be found in the vegetable or salad section in most large supermarkets.
• Use 300ml semi-skimmed milk and 100ml dry sherry instead of all milk. Boil the milk sauce first, then stir in the sherry and simmer.
• Cook 2 sliced spring onions and 1 crushed garlic clove with the mushrooms in step 2.

1 Bring a large saucepan of water to the boil. Add the tagliatelle, bring back to the boil and part cover the pan. Reduce the heat and cook for 12 minutes, or according to the packet instructions, until the pasta is tender but with some bite in the centre. Meanwhile, slice the chestnut mushrooms. Roughly chop the walnuts and set aside 1 tablespoon. Heat 1 tablespoon of oil in another pan and add the chestnut mushrooms. Cook over a high heat for 5 minutes or until softened.

2 Whisk the cornflour with the milk and pour it into the mushroom mixture in the pan. Bring to the boil, stirring, then reduce the heat and simmer for 3 minutes. Stir in the soft cheese, walnuts and parsley then season to taste.

3 Drain the tagliatelle and stir it into the sauce. Cover and remove from the heat without mixing. Add the remaining 1 tablespoon of oil and oyster mushrooms to the pan you used for the pasta. Fry over a high heat for 1 minute or until hot and beginning to tinge with brown. Divide the pasta between four bowls and top with the shitake mushrooms and reserved walnuts. Sprinkle with chives and serve.

COOK'S TIPS

★ If you are using fresh tagliatelle, you will need to reduce the cooking time as fresh pasta cooks much faster than dried – usually 2-4 minutes. Check the packet for cooking instructions.

SUPERFOOD

SEMI-SKIMMED MILK
Studies show that a diet rich in low-fat dairy foods, alongside other healthy lifestyle choices such as lowering salt intake and exercising regularly, can lower blood pressure in people with hypertension. Semi-skimmed milk may also offer protection against the onset of colon cancer.

Fiery Italian vegetable pasta

Pasta is wonderful at absorbing and enhancing flavours. Combine pasta shapes with colourful sun-kissed vegetables – and some feisty chilli – for an energising lunch.

Serves 4
Preparation 10 minutes
Cooking 20 minutes

300g pasta shapes, such as shells,
    bows, spirals or tubes
1 onion
1 red chilli
2 garlic cloves
40g pitted black olives
6 sun-dried tomato halves
2 celery sticks
600g ripe tomatoes
3 tbsp olive oil
25g chopped fresh parsley
finely grated zest of 1 lemon
50g Parmesan cheese, shaved

Each serving provides • 486kcal
• 17g protein • 68g carbohydrates of
which 11g sugars • 18g fat of which
5g saturates • 7g fibre

ALTERNATIVE INGREDIENTS
• Add sun-dried tomato purée to boost
the flavour of the fresh tomatoes
instead of using chopped sun-dried
tomatoes. Add 1-2 tablespoons purée
in step 2, stirring it into the cooked
onion mixture before adding the
chopped fresh tomatoes.
• Add 50g anchovy fillets in olive oil,
chopped, with the tomatoes and then
reduce the oil for cooking the onion to
1 tablespoon.

1 Bring a large saucepan of water to the boil. Add the pasta, bring back to the boil and stir once. Reduce the heat and part cover the pan. Boil for 12 minutes, or according to the packet instructions, until tender but with some bite in the centre. Drain the pasta in a colander.

2 Meanwhile, finely chop the onion, chilli and garlic. Halve the olives, quarter the sun-dried tomatoes and dice the celery. Chop the fresh tomatoes. Heat the olive oil in a pan and add the onion, chilli, half of the garlic and celery. Cook over a high heat for 5 minutes, stirring frequently.

3 Stir in the fresh tomatoes, sun-dried tomatoes and olives. Cook the sauce for 3 minutes, then return the pasta to the pan. Stir together and season to taste.

4 Mix the remaining chopped garlic with the parsley and lemon zest. Divide the pasta between four bowls and serve topped with the parsley mixture and shaved Parmesan cheese.

COOK'S TIPS
★ Plum tomatoes are ideal for this recipe because they have firm flesh with fewer seeds in the middle than other varieties.
★ Whether this dish is piquant with a slight heat or fiery in flavour depends on your choice of chilli. A mild chilli will give a gentle warmth to the pasta and vegetables, but if you like it hot then use 2 hot chillies.

SUPERFOOD

CELERY
Crunchy celery helps to maintain a
healthy digestive system thanks to the
soluble and insoluble fibre it contains.
With its folate and potassium, celery
is also great for heart health and for
regulating blood pressure.

Pepper shells with cheesy pasta

Enjoy delicious macaroni with a twist – serve it in lightly grilled red peppers. They not only look and taste fabulous but their sweetness cuts through the full-bodied savoury sauce.

Serves 4
Preparation 15 minutes
Cooking 17 minutes

Each serving provides • 351kcal • 15g protein • 43g carbohydrates of which 15g sugars • 14g fat of which 7g saturates • 6g fibre

150g macaroni
1 small courgette
4 Romano red peppers
175g low-fat soft cheese
2 tbsp snipped fresh chives
50g grated Parmesan cheese
1 tbsp olive oil
1 tsp paprika

ALTERNATIVE INGREDIENTS
• Use yellow or orange peppers instead of red ones.
• Try other pasta shapes instead of macaroni, such as spirals or shells.
• Use 100g mature Cheddar, Gruyère or Monterey Jack cheese instead of Parmesan, though this will raise the fat content.
• To increase your vegetable intake, add 1 grated carrot with the courgettes in step 2.
• Reduce the quantity of macaroni to 75g and add 50g frozen petit pois to the pan for the last 5 minutes of cooking. Bring the water back to the boil after adding the peas.

1 Preheat the grill to the hottest setting. Bring a large saucepan of water to the boil. Add the macaroni, bring back to the boil and stir. Reduce the heat, part cover the pan and boil for 12 minutes, or according to the packet instructions, until the macaroni is cooked.

2 Meanwhile, finely grate the courgette and cut the peppers in half lengthways, scraping out all of the seeds but leaving on the stalks. Mix together the soft cheese, grated courgette and snipped chives. Reserve 1 tablespoon of Parmesan cheese, stir the remainder into the mixture and set aside. Place the peppers on a baking sheet and grill, cut sides down, for 3 minutes or until the skins begin to blister. Turn over and grill for another 3 minutes before brushing with oil and grilling for a final 3 minutes or until tender.

3 Drain the macaroni, return it to the pan and stir in the cheese and courgette mixture. Spoon the macaroni into the peppers and sprinkle with paprika and the reserved Parmesan cheese. Place the peppers back under the grill for 5 minutes to warm through and crisp up on top.

COOK'S TIPS
★ During the final grilling, after brushing with a little oil, the peppers may well bubble up inside but they will shrink back when removed from the grill. Watch them closely to avoid burning the skins and rims.
★ Long, pointed Romano peppers make an attractive alternative to bell peppers. Grilling intensifies their flavour.

SUPERFOOD

LOW-FAT SOFT CHEESE
Much lower in fat than standard soft cheese, this dairy product provides valuable protein, phosphorus, some B vitamins, zinc, vitamin A and calcium, which is good for bone health. Three servings of low-fat dairy products per day – along with a diet rich in fibre and fruit and vegetables – helps to reduce high blood pressure and lowers the risk of strokes.

SUPERFOOD

Peppers

Whether eaten cooked or raw, sweet peppers, also known as capsicums, are packed full of goodness. They are one of the best sources of vitamin C and are crammed with beneficial carotenes that may protect against lung cancer.

Juicy veggie kebabs

Serves 4
Preparation 10 minutes Cooking 20 minutes

Each serving provides • 98kcal • 1g protein • 6g carbohydrates of which 5g sugars • 8g fat of which 1g saturates • 2g fibre

Preheat the grill to high. Cut **2 red peppers** in half and place them on the grill pan, skin side up. Brush with **1 tablespoon olive oil** and grill for 15 minutes, turning occasionally, until softened and with the skin starting to blister. Turn the grill down to medium. Remove the peppers, cool slightly and cut into bite-size squares. Crush **2 medium garlic cloves** with a little seasoning then stir in **1 tablespoon olive oil, ½ finely chopped red chilli** and **1 teaspoon balsamic vinegar**. Remove the stalks from **12 small chestnut mushrooms**. Use a brush to coat the mushrooms with the flavoured olive oil. Thread the mushrooms and peppers onto four metal or wooden skewers. Grill for 5 minutes, turning once and basting with any remaining oil.

COOK'S TIPS
★ Soak wooden skewers for 30 minutes in cold water before threading the vegetables to prevent the wood from charring under the hot grill.
★ Serve the kebabs as a starter on a bed of frisée lettuce with crusty wholemeal bread.

Smooth red pepper and tomato sauce

Serves 4
Preparation 10 minutes Cooking 6 minutes

Each serving provides • 158kcal • 4g protein • 11g carbohydrates of which 9g sugars • 11g fat of which 1g saturates • 3g fibre

Heat **1 tablespoon olive oil** in a saucepan over a medium heat. Add **1 finely chopped onion** and **2 diced red peppers** and cook for 5 minutes until softened. Stir in **2 crushed garlic cloves**. Fry for 1 minute, then pour in **200ml tomato juice**. Transfer to a blender, or to a mixing bowl and use a stick blender, and purée until smooth. Stir in **50g ground almonds** and blend for a further 5 seconds. Return the sauce to the pan and gently reheat but do not boil. Season to taste before serving.

COOK'S TIPS
★ This sauce makes a colourful accompaniment to grilled tuna steaks or any robust white fish.

★ The sweet flavour of the peppers and almonds also marries well with roast or grilled chicken.
★ Reduce the tomato juice to 25ml to transform the sauce into a rich dip with a light and refreshing taste. Serve with vegetable crudités and breadsticks or baked cheese straws.

Golden chicken and avocado salad

Serves 4
Preparation 10 minutes Cooking 15 minutes

Each serving provides • 333kcal • 18g protein • 7g carbohydrates of which 6g sugars • 26g fat of which 5g saturates • 4g fibre

Preheat the grill to medium-high. Cut **2 yellow peppers** lengthways into 5mm thick slices then halve the slices and transfer them to a large bowl. Pour **3 tablespoons olive oil, juice of ½ lime** and **1 teaspoon runny honey** into a small jug to make a dressing. Stir and season to taste then pour over the pepper slices. Grill **2 skinless chicken breasts** for 15 minutes or until cooked through and lightly golden. Cool for 1-2 minutes then cut into four or five slices. Peel and slice **2 ripe avocados**. Arrange a layer of **mixed salad leaves** on four plates. Layer the peppers, chicken and avocado slices on top. Drizzle over any remaining dressing and serve.

COOK'S TIPS
★ Serve the salad as a starter or double the quantity of chicken for a light lunch accompanied with minted new potatoes. Layer the peppers and avocado slices on top of the salad, then slice 4 grilled chicken breasts and place one breast on each plate.

Sesame-infused peppers with broccoli

Serves 4
Preparation 10 minutes Cooking 10 minutes

Each serving provides • 150kcal • 4g protein • 5g carbohydrates of which 4g sugars • 13g fat of which 2g saturates • 3g fibre

Heat **2 tablespoons sesame oil** in a frying pan. Thinly slice **2 large peppers, one green and one orange**. Add the peppers to the pan together with **150g broccoli florets**. Stir-fry over a medium-high heat for 8 minutes or until the peppers soften and turn brown at the edges, but the broccoli is still firm in the centre. Add **1 crushed**

garlic clove, **1 teaspoon finely chopped fresh root ginger, 2 teaspoons light soy sauce** and **2 teaspoons sesame seeds**. Stir for 1 minute. Season to taste and then transfer to four plates. Pour any pan juices over the vegetables and drizzle with **2 teaspoons sesame oil** and an additional **2 teaspoons sesame seeds**.

COOK'S TIPS
★ Serve as a healthy side dish with grilled turkey kebabs or a fish fillet. A jacket potato or spoonful of mash makes a filling accompaniment.
★ As an alternative to the broccoli, use 150g sugarsnap peas but omit the ginger and soy sauce.

Feta and chilli pepper sandwich spread

Serves 4
Preparation 10 minutes Cooking 10 minutes

Each serving provides • 142kcal • 6g protein • 3g carbohydrates of which 3g sugars • 12g fat of which 6g saturates • 1g fibre

Heat **1 tablespoon olive oil** in a small frying pan. Add **1 chopped red or orange pepper**. Stir over a medium-high heat for 8 minutes or until softened. Stir in **1 finely chopped fresh jalapeño pepper** and cook for 2 minutes more before adding **a dash of chilli sauce**. Crumble **150g feta cheese** into a bowl. Add the pepper mixture and mash with a fork to form a textured spread.

COOK'S TIPS
★ Use a jar of ready-grilled pepper pieces if fresh ones are not available.
★ Spread on chunks of crusty bread, use as a sandwich filling or as a canapé on small squares of toast.

Malaysian laksa with
prawns and vegetables

This simple version of a classic Far Eastern recipe is laden with vegetables in a broth just bursting with aromatic spices. Reduced-fat coconut milk provides the authentic background flavour.

Serves 4
Preparation 15 minutes
Cooking 10 minutes

Each serving provides • 663kcal • 24g protein • 94g carbohydrates of which 9g sugars • 21g fat of which 10g saturates • 3g fibre

1 onion
1 red chilli
60g fresh root ginger
300g Chinese cabbage
¼ cucumber, about 100g
1 spring onion
200g beansprouts
2 tbsp vegetable oil
2 garlic cloves, crushed
1 tsp ground turmeric
1 litre hot fish stock
400ml can light coconut milk
375g fine rice noodles
300g large peeled cooked prawns
8 chopped fresh mint leaves

ALTERNATIVE INGREDIENTS
• Use pak choi or choi sum instead of Chinese cabbage. Alternatively, add any frozen mixed stir-fry vegetables instead of fresh ones.
• For a touch of lemon sharpness, crush 1 piece of lemongrass and add it to the onion mixture in step 1. Remove before serving.

1 Thinly slice the onion, finely chop the chilli and grate the ginger. Shred the cabbage, cut the cucumber into thin strips and finely slice the spring onion. Thoroughly wash the beansprouts. Heat the oil in a large saucepan over a high heat. Add the garlic, onion and chilli, reduce the heat to medium and cook for 2 minutes.

2 Stir in the ginger, turmeric, fish stock and coconut milk and bring to the boil. Reduce the heat, cover and simmer for 5 minutes. Stir in the rice noodles, Chinese cabbage and beansprouts and simmer for a further 1 minute before adding the prawns.

3 Continue to cook for 30 seconds to warm the prawns, but do not allow the liquid to boil or the prawns will toughen. Ladle into bowls and sprinkle with cucumber, spring onion and mint before serving.

COOK'S TIPS
★ Frozen grated ginger is a great storecupboard ingredient. Buy good-quality fresh root ginger – look out for large, plump, smooth thin-skinned roots. Peel, chop in a food processor or grate using a metal grater, then spread the ginger on a plastic tray covered in cling film and freeze. When frozen, place the block of ginger in a freezer bag, seal and tap against a work surface to break it into pieces. Use the ginger from frozen.

SUPERFOOD

GARLIC
A member of the onion family, garlic is rich in allyl sulphur compounds, a group of antioxidants believed to play a role in reducing the risk of cancer by stimulating enzymes that help the body to get rid of harmful chemicals.

Thai **noodles** with **cashews** and stir-fried **vegetables**

Take a deliciously simple recipe for Thai stir-fry and experiment with readymade curry paste, sweet cashew nuts and creamy soya beans for a quick, super-healthy meal any day of the week.

Serves 4
Preparation 10 minutes
Cooking 10 minutes

1 onion
100g mushrooms
1 red pepper
200g pak choi
150g beansprouts
2 tbsp vegetable oil
2 garlic cloves, crushed
75g unsalted cashew nuts
100g frozen soya beans
1 tbsp Thai green curry paste
400g fresh egg noodles

Each serving provides • 649kcal
• 22g protein • 82g carbohydrates
of which 7g sugars • 28g fat of which
5g saturates • 8g fibre

ALTERNATIVE INGREDIENTS
• If time is short, cook the garlic and onion then add a 500g pack of mixed stir-fry vegetables in step 3 instead of the mushrooms, pepper, pak choi and beansprouts.
• Try unsalted peanuts as a change to cashew nuts.
• Stir-fry strips of raw chicken or pork with the onion in step 1 and omit the soya beans. The meat strips should be cooked through and lightly browned before adding the curry paste.

1 Finely slice the onion and mushrooms and dice the pepper. Wash and shred the pak choi and thoroughly wash the beansprouts. Heat the oil in a large frying pan or wok over a high heat. Add the garlic, onion, mushrooms and pepper.

2 Stir-fry the vegetables for 2 minutes, then stir in the cashew nuts and continue to cook for a further 3 minutes. Mix in the frozen soya beans and Thai green curry paste. Stir in the noodles, breaking them up with a spoon then add the pak choi.

3 Stir-fry the mixture for 2 minutes, adding 1-2 tablespoons of cold water if it becomes too dry and the pak choi does not wilt. Stir in the beansprouts and cook for a final 1 minute before serving.

COOK'S TIPS

★ A broad selection of red and green Thai curry pastes is available in the shops. They vary in precise spice mix and chilli heat, so try a few to find your favourite.
★ Frozen soya beans are bright green, creamy in flavour and firm. They make a good freezer standby for adding nutrition, delicious texture and flavour to meat-free meals.

SOYA BEANS
Vitamin and protein-rich soya beans are packed with nutrients that offer antioxidant-boosting and cholesterol-lowering benefits. They are a good source of fibre, vitamin C, iron and the B vitamins thiamin and folate, which help to maintain a healthy heart.

Indonesian fried **rice** with **egg** and **vegetables**

Known as *nasi goreng* in southeast Asia, delicious egg-topped fried rice is a traditional way of using up leftovers. Crunchy water chestnuts and bamboo shoots complement the soft rice perfectly.

Serves 4
Preparation 15 minutes
Cooking 28 minutes

Each serving provides • 434kcal • 13g protein • 54g carbohydrates of which 10g sugars • 20g fat of which 3g saturates • 5g fibre

200g brown rice
600ml hot vegetable stock
2 onions
2 small carrots
225g can water chestnuts
225g can sliced bamboo shoots
100g beansprouts
3 tbsp vegetable oil
1 tsp sesame oil
3 garlic cloves, crushed
100g frozen green beans, thawed
½ tbsp medium curry powder
1 spring onion
3 eggs
3 tbsp chopped fresh coriander

ALTERNATIVE INGREDIENTS
• Use fragrant Thai rice instead of brown rice and reduce the cooking time to 25 minutes, or according to the packet instructions.
• Use a 500g pack fresh mixed stir-fry vegetables instead of the carrots, green beans and beansprouts.

1 Place the rice in a large saucepan with the stock. Cover, bring to the boil and stir once. Reduce the heat and simmer for 25 minutes, or according to the packet instructions, until the rice is tender and the stock has been absorbed. Slice the onions. Thinly slice the carrots, slicing them at an angle, then drain and slice the water chestnuts, drain the bamboo shoots and wash the beansprouts.

2 Halfway through cooking the rice, heat 1 tablespoon vegetable oil in a frying pan over a high heat. Add the onions, reduce the heat to medium and fry for 7 minutes or until browned. Set aside and keep warm. When the rice is almost cooked, heat 1 tablespoon vegetable oil in the frying pan. Add the sesame oil, garlic, carrots, water chestnuts, bamboo shoots, green beans and curry powder. Stir-fry for 2 minutes or until the vegetables are tender. Add the beansprouts and stir-fry for 1 minute or until piping hot. Mix the vegetables into the rice and season to taste.

3 Slice the spring onion. Beat the eggs with the spring onion and coriander. Add the remaining 1 tablespoon oil to the frying pan over a high heat. Pour in the egg and cook for 1 minute on each side or until set. Cut the omelette into thin strips. Divide the rice between four bowls and top with the fried onions and omelette strips.

COOK'S TIPS
★ Boil the rice uncovered for a few seconds if there is any excess liquid left at the end of cooking in step 1.

SUPERFOOD

BROWN RICE
Wholegrains, including brown rice, consist of three elements – a fibre-rich outer layer (bran), a nutrient-packed inner area (germ) and the central starchy part (endosperm). Brown rice contains the entire grain, keeping all the nutrients intact and so offering full nutritional benefits.

Fruity **butternut squash** casserole with **papaya**

Succulent butternut squash, delicate papaya and firm borlotti beans make for a satisfying one-pot meal that helps to keep blood sugar levels steady. Serve with a side salad of mixed leaves.

Serves 4
Preparation 15 minutes
Cooking 10 minutes

½ butternut squash, about 600g
1 papaya, about 300g
1 red onion
1 tbsp vegetable oil
4-6 large fresh sage leaves
1 tsp ground cinnamon
juice of 1 large orange, about 100ml
400g can borlotti beans, drained

Each serving provides • 179kcal
• 7g protein • 29g carbohydrates of which 16g sugars • 4g fat of which 1g saturates • 9g fibre

ALTERNATIVE INGREDIENTS
• Try pumpkin if butternut squash is not available.
• Mango goes well with squash. Select a ripe but firm mango, peel and slice it off the stone and then cut the flesh into chunks. Whereas papaya mellows the flavour of the orange juice, mango accentuates its tanginess.
• Substitute chickpeas or cannellini beans for the borlotti beans.
• For a meaty version of this dish, grill and slice four Cumberland sausages, or French-style sausages seasoned with garlic, and gently stir them into the mixture before serving.

1 Peel and seed the butternut squash and dice the flesh into 2cm chunks. Seed and peel the papaya (see Cook's Tips below), then slice it and set aside. Thinly slice the onion.

2 Heat the oil in a large pan with a lid. Add the onion and butternut squash and cook over a high heat, stirring occasionally, for 1 minute. Reduce the heat to medium or medium-low, cover the pan and cook for 2 minutes.

3 Shred the sage leaves, then stir them into the pan with the cinnamon and orange juice. Bring to the boil, reduce the heat to low and cover again. Simmer for 5 minutes, stirring once, or until the butternut squash is tender but not soft.

4 Stir in the beans, re-cover the pan and heat gently for 2 minutes. Top with the papaya and serve immediately.

COOK'S TIPS
★ To prepare papaya, cut the fruit in half, then scoop out the round black seeds with a spoon. Peel the thin skin off the fruit with a knife.
★ Cutting onions in half before slicing them is far easier than slicing them whole as the cut side can be placed flat on a board to prevent it from slipping.

SUPERFOOD

BEANS
A good, low-fat source of protein, beans also have a low glycaemic index (GI) rating, so give a steady energy release without causing spikes in blood sugar levels. The borlotti beans in this recipe are rich in lysine, an essential protein-building amino acid that is often lacking in plant proteins.

Minted mixed grain salad

Add fresh summery salad stalwarts – plus lots of aromatic parsley, mint and lemon – to plump grains and you have a zesty lunchtime treat that is both refreshing and surprisingly filling.

Serves 4
Preparation 10 minutes,
  plus 15 minutes cooling
Cooking 15 minutes

Each serving provides • 267kcal • 7g protein • 32g carbohydrates of which 8g sugars • 13g fat of which 2g saturates • 3g fibre

75g bulgur wheat
75g quinoa
¼ cucumber
2 large tomatoes
1 large green pepper
2 spring onions
1 tsp sugar
grated zest and juice of 1 lemon
3 tsp olive oil
5 chopped large mint sprigs
60g chopped fresh parsley
1 romaine lettuce, to serve

ALTERNATIVE INGREDIENTS
• Use young raw courgettes instead of cucumber and add a crushed garlic clove in step 2.
• Try the vegetable and herb mixture with rice as a change to bulgur wheat and quinoa. Cook Thai rice for an aromatic salad or sushi rice for a delicious, slightly sticky dish.

1 Place the bulgur wheat and quinoa in a saucepan with 1 litre of boiling water. Bring back to the boil, reduce the heat, cover and simmer for 15 minutes until the bulgur wheat and quinoa are tender. Drain in a sieve if all of the water has not been absorbed. Finely dice the cucumber, tomatoes and pepper, and thinly slice the spring onions.

2 Mix the sugar, lemon zest and juice in a large bowl, stirring until the sugar dissolves. Whisk in the oil then add the cucumber, tomatoes, pepper and spring onions. Stir in the cooked bulgur wheat and quinoa, then cover and leave to cool for 15 minutes.

3 Stir the mint and parsley into the salad and season to taste just before serving. Divide the salad between four bowls and offer a selection of lettuce leaves for wrapping and scooping.

COOK'S TIPS

★ To finely dice cucumber, slice it lengthways, lay the slices flat together then cut them into strips and cut across the strips to make dice.
★ The easiest way to 'chop' herbs is to hold the large leaves in a bundle and shred them finely with scissors.

SUPERFOOD

QUINOA

Perfect in salads, quinoa provides wholegrain, high-fibre goodness to a meal. An excellent source of starchy carbohydrate for energy, quinoa is also rich in iron and zinc for a super-healthy immune system.

Seafood and vegetable rice

Delicious vegetables and seafood mix perfectly with savoury rice for a quick alternative to paella. With its colourful variety of ingredients, the dish also provides an all-round health boost.

Serves 4
Preparation 15 minutes
Cooking 35 minutes

2 onions
2 large peppers (1 yellow, 1 red)
1 tbsp vegetable oil
2 large garlic cloves, crushed
2 bay leaves
200g brown rice
600ml hot vegetable stock
200g frozen peas
200g frozen green beans
350g frozen cooked mixed seafood
lemon wedges and chopped fresh
   parsley, to garnish

Each serving provides • 397kcal
• 24g protein • 59g carbohydrates
of which 12g sugars • 9g fat of which
2g saturates • 11g fibre

ALTERNATIVE INGREDIENTS
• Frozen diced peppers make a good
storecupboard ingredient. Add them
with the rice at step 2 rather than
cooking them with the onions. Frozen
mixed vegetables can also be used
instead of the peas and beans.
• For a tomato-based version, reduce
the stock to 300ml in step 2, then add
a 400g can chopped tomatoes.
• If you do not like mixed seafood,
use 400g cooked large prawns.

1 Thinly slice the onions and peppers. Heat the oil in a large frying pan and add the onions, garlic and bay leaves. Add the peppers and cook, stirring, over a high heat for 2 minutes or until the vegetables soften slightly.

2 Stir in the rice and pour in the vegetable stock. Bring back to the boil and stir to mix the ingredients. Reduce the heat to low so that the liquid simmers. Cover the pan and cook for 20 minutes or until the liquid has almost evaporated.

3 Use a fork to lightly mix in the frozen peas and beans. Bring back to the boil, reduce the heat and cover the pan. Simmer gently for a further 5 minutes.

4 Sprinkle the frozen cooked seafood over the rice. Re-cover the pan and cook for a final 5 minutes until the rice is tender, but not soft, the seafood is hot and the majority of liquid has evaporated. Garnish with lemon wedges and chopped parsley. Season with ground black pepper before serving.

COOK'S TIPS
★ Garnish with mussels in their shells. Rinse and scrub the shells clean, then steam the mussels with 4 tablespoons white wine in a lidded pan for 5-7 minutes or until the shells open. Throw away any mussels that do not open.
★ Serve with a salad of lamb's lettuce and cherry tomatoes.

SUPERFOOD

SEAFOOD
Full of goodness, seafood contributes many nutrients to a balanced diet. It contains immune-boosting zinc and the antioxidant selenium, which helps to protect against heart disease. It is also a rich source of iodine that is needed for a healthy metabolism.

Sunshine kedgeree with
sweetcorn and **broccoli**

In an updated classic, the full-on flavour of smoky fish is balanced by refreshing vegetables. Exotic spices add warmth and colour – cumin is pungent and peppery, while turmeric turns the rice to gold.

Serves 4
Preparation 15 minutes, plus
  5 minutes standing
Cooking 25 minutes

Each serving provides • 537kcal • 31g protein • 68g carbohydrates of which 5g sugars • 17g fat of which 3g saturates • 4g fibre

1 large onion
300g skinless smoked
  haddock fillet
2 tbsp vegetable oil
250g basmati rice
1½ tsp cumin seeds
1½ tsp turmeric
1 litre hot fish stock
200g frozen sweetcorn
4 eggs
200g small broccoli florets
grated zest of 1 lemon
2 tbsp chopped fresh parsley

ALTERNATIVE INGREDIENTS
• Use smoked cod instead of haddock. Alternatively, chunks of fresh salmon are delicious in place of smoked fish.
• Omit the uncooked fish in step 2 and serve the rice topped with shredded smoked salmon, allowing 200g per person, or with smoked mackerel, allowing 300g per person.
• For a vegetarian kedgeree, leave out the smoked haddock and add 100g red lentils to the rice. Use vegetable stock in step 1 and increase the quantity to 1.3 litres.

1 Finely chop the onion and cut the smoked haddock into 2cm pieces. Heat the oil in a large saucepan over a high heat. Add the onion and cook for 2 minutes. Reduce the heat and stir in the rice, cumin seeds and turmeric. Pour in the stock, bring back to the boil and reduce the heat to low. Cover and simmer for 5 minutes.

2 Add the frozen sweetcorn and bring back to the boil. Mix in the fish, reduce the heat, cover and simmer for 15 minutes or until the stock has been absorbed by the rice. Meanwhile, cook the eggs for 8 minutes in a pan of boiling water. Remove the rice from the heat and leave it to stand, covered, for 5 minutes.

3 Drain the boiled eggs and rinse them under cold water, then shell and quarter them. Place the broccoli in a saucepan, add boiling water to cover and bring back to the boil. Reduce the heat and simmer for 3 minutes, then drain. Add the broccoli and lemon zest to the kedgeree. Top with the eggs and parsley and season with black pepper.

COOK'S TIPS
★ Smoked haddock is available either dyed, making it yellow, or undyed and paler, tinged yellow at the edges. Where you can, opt for the natural undyed version.
★ Running hard-boiled eggs under cold water stops the cooking process and prevents a grey ring from forming around the egg yolk.

SUPERFOOD

SWEETCORN
As well as containing the naturally occurring phytochemical lutein, good for eye health, sweetcorn is also a useful source of fibre, folate and antioxidants. All three of these are associated with a lower risk of cancer.

Savoury **bacon** pilaf with **berries** and **nuts**

Any dish based on wholesome brown rice is sure to taste deliciously nutty and to put goodness into your meal. The flavours of walnuts, cranberries and bacon combine to make a heart-warming plateful.

Serves 4
Preparation 15 minutes
Cooking 45 minutes

Each serving provides • 565kcal • 16g protein • 71g carbohydrates of which 10g sugars • 26g fat of which 3g saturates • 8g fibre

100g lean rindless bacon
100g walnuts
1 onion
2 celery sticks
350g cabbage
1 tbsp olive oil
300g brown rice
1 litre hot chicken stock
50g dried cranberries
4 tbsp snipped fresh chives

ALTERNATIVE INGREDIENTS
• Use thin slices of pepperoni or chorizo instead of bacon.
• For a vegetarian pilaf, omit the bacon and dry-fry 100g pine nuts, or roughly chopped macadamia nuts, in a frying pan until lightly browned. Remove and set aside, then add with the walnuts in step 4. Use hot vegetable stock in place of the chicken stock.
• Use chopped dried apricots or peaches instead of cranberries.

1 Cut the bacon into thin strips and coarsely chop the walnuts. Finely chop the onion and celery, then shred the cabbage. Place the bacon in a large frying pan over a medium-high heat. Dry-fry for 5 minutes until browned. Add the walnuts, stir-frying them with the bacon for 1 minute. Remove the bacon and walnuts and set aside.

2 Add the oil, onion and celery to the pan and fry over a high heat for 2 minutes or until the onion softens. Add the rice and continue to cook for 2 minutes, stirring frequently, until the rice grains are opaque.

3 Pour in 500ml chicken stock, bring to the boil, reduce the heat to medium, cover and simmer for 5 minutes. Add the remaining 500ml stock, bring back to the boil and cook for a further 10 minutes.

4 Pile the cabbage on top of the rice, cover and cook over a low heat for 20 minutes or until the rice is tender and the cabbage is cooked. Add the fried bacon and walnuts plus the cranberries for the last minute of cooking to warm through. Season to taste and divide the pilaf between four plates. Sprinkle with chives and serve.

COOK'S TIPS
★ Savoy or any green cabbage works well in this recipe. Spring greens or curly kale are also good choices.
★ Take care when adding the first batch of stock to the pan because it will sizzle and steam as the liquid hits the base of the hot pan.

SUPERFOOD

BROWN RICE
Research shows that the risk of both heart disease and Type 2 diabetes may be up to 30 per cent lower in people who regularly eat wholegrains such as brown rice as part of a low-fat diet and healthy lifestyle. It is the combination of health-promoting nutrients working together in brown rice that offers protection against these life-threatening disorders.

Greek salad with **chickpeas**

Food does not get much healthier than a salad low in fat, high in fibre and full of antioxidants. This dish conjures up lazy days and a long life in the sun, and delivers on taste with every mouthful.

Serves 4
Preparation 10 minutes

Each serving provides • 258kcal • 15g protein • 19g carbohydrates of which 6g sugars • 14g fat of which 7g saturates • 3g fibre

425g can chickpeas
1 small onion
1 green pepper
¼ cucumber
200g cherry tomatoes
200g feta cheese
2 tbsp olive oil
1 garlic clove, crushed
20 pitted black olives
4 tbsp chopped fresh parsley
250g mixed salad leaves
lemon wedges, to garnish

ALTERNATIVE INGREDIENTS
• Try adding miniature new potatoes, either instead of or as well as the chickpeas. Allow 250g potatoes, cook them in boiling water for 10 minutes until tender and toss with the oil and garlic dressing while still hot.
• Feta cheese is traditional in Greek salad, but try diced mozzarella for a lighter flavour. Alternatively, Spanish manchego, Cheshire cheese, Caerphilly or Wensleydale have full flavours that all taste great in this dish.

1 Drain the chickpeas and thinly slice the onion. Coarsely dice the pepper and cucumber. Cut the cherry tomatoes in half and crumble the feta cheese.

2 Mix the oil, garlic, olives, chickpeas, onion, pepper and cucumber together in a large bowl. Stir in the tomatoes and parsley. Gently stir in the feta cheese.

3 Divide the mixed salad leaves between four plates or bowls. Spoon the Greek salad over the leaves and garnish with lemon wedges.

COOK'S TIPS
★ Most of this salad can be prepared ahead, apart from adding the tomatoes, parsley and cheese. It can then be covered and set aside for several hours. Once complete, the salad is best served within 2-3 hours.
★ If you do not like raw garlic, follow the old-fashioned French method of giving a mild garlic flavour by rubbing a cut clove around the serving bowl before adding the salad. Another alternative is to cook the garlic in a little oil in a small pan over a low heat for 1-2 minutes to mellow its flavour. Cool, then add to the salad in step 1.

SUPERFOOD

OLIVE OIL
For decades, olive oil has been linked to good health. Recent research evidence shows people who follow a Mediterranean diet (olive oil, fruit, vegetables, wholegrains, nuts and fish) do indeed enjoy better health and live longer than people who follow a more traditional meat-based diet.

Three **bean** salad with **lemon** and **walnut** dressing

A fabulously tart dressing transforms a plate of mixed beans into a richly satisfying dish, served either as a main meal or as a side. Crispy croutons and lively lemon zest also add texture.

Serves 4
Preparation 10 minutes
Cooking 7 minutes

Each serving provides • 483kcal • 16g protein • 62g carbohydrates of which 16g sugars • 21g fat of which 2g saturates • 12g fibre

8 thick baguette slices
2 tbsp olive oil
grated zest of 2 lemons and juice of 1 lemon
3 tbsp honey
1 garlic clove, crushed
3 tbsp walnut oil
200g green beans
400g can red kidney beans
400g can butter beans

ALTERNATIVE INGREDIENTS
• Try soya beans or chickpeas instead of kidney beans and butter beans.
• Use hazelnut oil as a change to walnut oil.
• Close-textured light rye bread or Italian ciabatta are also good for making croutons.

1 Preheat the grill to the hottest setting. Place the slices of baguette on a grill pan and brush lightly with 1 tablespoon olive oil. Toast for around 2 minutes or until crisp and golden. Turn the slices, brush with the remaining 1 tablespoon olive oil and toast for a further 2 minutes. Cut into chunky croutons and set aside to cool.

2 To make the lemon and walnut dressing, whisk together the lemon zest and juice, honey, garlic and walnut oil in a large bowl. Then trim the green beans and drain the red kidney beans and butter beans.

3 Place the green beans in a saucepan. Pour in boiling water to cover and bring back to the boil. Reduce the heat slightly and simmer for 3 minutes, or until lightly cooked but still crunchy. Drain the beans, shaking off the cooking water, and toss them in the dressing.

4 Add the red kidney beans and butter beans to the dressing. Mix well and divide the salad between four bowls, spooning any remaining dressing in the bowl over the beans. Scatter with croutons and serve.

COOK'S TIPS

★ Canned butter beans are widely available in all major supermarkets. Alternatively, soak and cook dried butter beans, following the packet instructions. Drain the cooked beans and pack into freezer bags or containers while still hot, then chill and freeze. Thaw at room temperature before use.

SUPERFOOD

BUTTER BEANS

These large beans are a good source of protein and iron, which play an important role in physical well-being. Just 3 tablespoons count as one of your 5-a-day. Butter beans are also virtually fat free and packed with fibre to promote digestive health.

Chicken and ginger fried rice

Take a little cooked chicken breast, add some delightfully crunchy vegetables and warming fresh ginger, then combine with rice – and you have a simple supper dish that is really hard to beat.

Serves 4
Preparation 10 minutes
Cooking 25 minutes

50g fresh root ginger
350g cooked chicken breast
225g can water chestnuts
200g Chinese cabbage
200g beansprouts
4 spring onions
2 tbsp vegetable oil
2 garlic cloves, crushed
300g long-grain rice
1 tsp sesame oil
1 litre hot chicken stock
200g mangetout

Each serving provides • 555kcal • 37g protein • 76g carbohydrates of which 6g sugars • 14g fat of which 2g saturates • 4g fibre

ALTERNATIVE INGREDIENTS
• Brown rice works well in this recipe, but allow an additional 200ml stock and cook it for an extra 10 minutes in step 2.
• Instead of adding the cooked chicken in step 3, add 350g peeled cooked prawns in step 4, heating them briefly before serving.
• Add a diced red or green pepper with the mangetout in step 4.
• Try raw sugarsnap peas instead of mangetout, or add frozen peas or green beans in step 3.
• For vegetarian fried rice, replace the chicken stock with hot vegetable stock and add 350g Quorn pieces instead of the chicken.

1 Peel and grate the ginger and slice the chicken into small strips. Drain and slice the water chestnuts and finely shred the Chinese cabbage. Wash the beansprouts and slice the spring onions.

2 Heat the vegetable oil in a large saucepan over a high heat. Add the ginger, garlic and rice and cook, stirring, for 3 minutes or until the rice becomes opaque.

3 Pour in the sesame oil and chicken stock. Bring back to the boil, reduce the heat to low, cover and simmer for 10 minutes. Add the chicken, water chestnuts and Chinese cabbage, but do not stir them in. Making sure that the stock is simmering, cover the pan and cook gently for a further 7 minutes.

4 Add the mangetout, beansprouts and spring onions to the pan. Cover and cook for 2 minutes or until the beansprouts are piping hot. Fork the ingredients through the rice and serve.

COOK'S TIPS
★ This is a good recipe for using up leftover roast chicken. Remove all the meat from the bones and cut it into bite-size pieces, checking that there are no bones. Store cooked chicken in a sealed container in the fridge for up to three days.

SUPERFOOD

CHICKEN
Skinless, boneless chicken breast contains 30 per cent high-quality protein and is low in fat – great for weight control. Chicken also contains some B vitamins, especially niacin, and when eaten with carbohydrate foods, such as rice and pasta, it can help to fight fatigue and improve mood.

Asparagus and mushroom sushi

Sticky sushi rice is a perfect base for tender Japanese-style vegetables, topped with mineral-rich seaweed. This dish gives a real lift to chicken.

Serves 4
Preparation 10 minutes, plus
** 5 minutes standing**
Cooking 20 minutes

Each serving provides • 338kcal
• 7g protein • 46g carbohydrates of
which 5g sugars • 12g fat of which
1g saturates • 2g fibre

200g sushi rice
4 sheets roasted sushi nori
2 tbsp Japanese rice vinegar
¼ tsp salt
1 tbsp sugar
3 tbsp vegetable oil
200g asparagus tips
100g shiitake mushrooms
2 tbsp sake or dry sherry
1 tbsp soy sauce

ALTERNATIVE INGREDIENTS
• Sprinkle 200g shredded smoked
chicken or ham, or 150g diced smoked
salmon offcuts, over the rice instead
of, or as well as, asparagus tips.
• Stir-fry 450g raw large peeled prawns
instead of the asparagus tips. Cook for
2-4 minutes or until they turn pink.
Sprinkle them over the rice and omit
the asparagus tips.
• You can substitute 2 tablespoons
vegetable stock for the sake or sherry
if you prefer.

1 Place the rice in a large saucepan and pour in 300ml of boiling water. Bring back to the boil, stirring once, reduce the heat to low, cover and simmer for 15 minutes or until the water has been absorbed and the rice is moist.

2 Cut each sheet of nori into four strips, then across into fine shreds and set aside. Mix together the vinegar, salt and sugar and stir into the cooked rice. Cover the pan and set aside to infuse for 5 minutes.

3 Meanwhile, heat 1 tablespoon oil in a large frying pan over a high heat. Add the asparagus tips and cook for 3 minutes or until tender. Thinly slice the mushrooms. Heat the remaining 2 tablespoons oil in another pan, add the mushrooms and fry over a high heat for 2 minutes. Add the sake or sherry and soy sauce to the mushrooms and boil for a few seconds, turning the mushrooms in the liquid.

4 Divide the sushi rice between four plates, patting each portion into a neat oblong shape, and top with the asparagus tips. Transfer the mushrooms to the plates and sprinkle with the nori before serving.

COOK'S TIPS
★ Nori is an edible seaweed and sheets of roasted, or toasted, nori are available in the international section of most large supermarkets or in Chinese stores. Once opened, store the packet of nori in an airtight bag for 1-2 days, though it is best eaten on the day of opening.

SUPERFOOD

NORI
Rich in fibre, nori is good for aiding
digestive health. In addition, it is a
good source of protein, iron, vitamin
B12, potassium and iodine, which
together help to prevent anaemia
and regulate blood pressure. Rich
in carotenoids, nori has powerful
antioxidant properties, too.

Piquant **pepper** tabbouleh with **cranberries**

Marjoram, nutmeg and chilli bring a hint of warmth, with dried cranberries adding eye-catching colour, to a light version of a classic Middle Eastern salad. Serve with crisp lettuce leaves and soft tortilla wraps.

Serves 4
Preparation 10 minutes,
   plus 30 minutes soaking

Each serving provides • 309kcal
• 6g protein • 53g carbohydrates of which 14g sugars • 9g fat of which 1g saturates • 2g fibre

200g bulgur wheat
1 large red pepper
1 medium-hot red chilli
½ red onion
50g dried cranberries
1 tbsp red wine vinegar
2 tbsp olive oil
4 chopped fresh marjoram sprigs
pinch of grated nutmeg

ALTERNATIVE INGREDIENTS
• Make a colour change by using an orange pepper instead of a red one.
• Use walnut oil as an alternative to olive oil for a nuttier tabbouleh.
• Dried blueberries are just as tasty as cranberries in this dish. Currants, sultanas and raisins also work well.
• Try sprigs of thyme instead of marjoram. Alternatively, use a mixture of herbs such as parsley and fennel for an aromatic twist.
• For a tangy tabbouleh, add the grated zest and juice of 1 orange in step 2.

1 Place the bulgur wheat in a heatproof bowl and pour in plenty of boiling water to cover – a ratio of one part bulgur wheat to two parts water works well. Cover the bowl with clingfilm and leave it to soak for 30 minutes or until the bulgur wheat is plumped up to double in volume.

2 Meanwhile, finely dice the pepper and chilli and finely chop the onion. In a large bowl, mix together the pepper, chilli, onion, cranberries, vinegar, oil, marjoram and nutmeg. Cover and set aside until the bulgur wheat is ready.

3 Drain the bulgur wheat through a sieve to remove any excess water and stir it into the pepper mixture. Season to taste and serve.

COOK'S TIPS

★ The flavour of the tabbouleh is enhanced by leaving it to infuse for 2 hours or more before eating. If you have time to plan ahead, prepare and cover the tabbouleh, then store it in the fridge until needed – it will stay fresh for up to 2 days when chilled.
★ Tabbouleh goes well with barbecued food, either as a first course or a side dish. It is also great in packed lunches or picnics.

SUPERFOOD

CRANBERRIES
Similar to other red berries such as raspberries and strawberries, cranberries are rich in a phytochemical called ellagic acid. Some studies have shown that ellagic acid can help to prevent the growth of cancerous cells. With fibre, too, cranberries can lend support to a healthy digestive system.

Fluffy **quinoa** with vibrant summer **vegetables**

The creamy, slightly crunchy texture and nutty taste of quinoa make it a great partner for sweet beans and juicy tomatoes. Sprinkle mild Gouda cheese on top and serve with salad leaves.

Serves 4
Preparation 5 minutes
Cooking 18 minutes

Each serving provides • 333kcal
• 15g protein • 35g carbohydrates
of which 7g sugars • 16g fat of
which 5g saturates • 5g fibre

200g quinoa
400ml hot chicken stock
200g baby broad beans, thawed
  if frozen
4 spring onions
400g cherry tomatoes
2 tbsp olive oil
6 fresh basil sprigs
60g Gouda cheese, grated or pared

ALTERNATIVE INGREDIENTS
• Try pearl barley if you cannot buy
quinoa. Cook pearl barley in boiling
water for 30 minutes, allowing
600ml water to 200g pearl barley.
• Use frozen soya beans instead
of broad beans, adding them to the
quinoa from frozen and increasing
the cooking time by 2 minutes.
• Look out for firm-textured mature
Gouda cheese. Alternatively, try
Spanish Manchego, Gruyère or mature
Cheddar cheese. For a completely
different flavour, use Bavarian smoked
cheese or add crumbled feta.

1 Put the quinoa in a large saucepan and pour in the hot stock. Cover the pan, bring to the boil, reduce the heat to medium and simmer for 10 minutes. Add the baby broad beans to the pan. Re-cover, bring back to the boil and simmer for another 5 minutes.

2 Turn up the heat and boil the mixture, uncovered, for 1 minute to evaporate excess stock. If any remains in the pan after this time, drain the quinoa through a fine-meshed sieve.

3 Thinly slice the spring onions and cut the tomatoes in half. Pour the oil into a serving bowl and add the spring onions and tomatoes. Shred the basil leaves on top then transfer the cooked quinoa and beans to the mixture and stir to combine. Season to taste, divide between four bowls and top with Gouda cheese shavings.

COOK'S TIPS
★ Quinoa is cooked when the grains burst open and the germ (inside the grain) has formed into an opaque curl. It should be soft but not stodgy. Quinoa is gluten-free, so this recipe is suitable for coeliacs and people sensitive to gluten.
★ Baby broad beans can be eaten in their skins, but you may like to pop them out to reveal the delicate pulses. Larger broad beans benefit from this method as the skins can be quite tough.

SUPERFOOD

QUINOA
Pronounced 'keen-wah', quinoa is a wholegrain with a low glycaemic index (GI) value that produces a slow rise in blood sugar levels and may help to protect against Type 2 diabetes. It is also a source of magnesium, needed for healthy bones, muscle and nerve functions, and high in protein – good news for vegetarians.

Pearl barley pilaf with emerald vegetables

Wholegrain pearl barley is mixed with blueberries and pine nuts for an unusual ensemble that really works. With fresh-flavoured green vegetables, it is as easy on the eye as it is on the palate.

Serves 4
Preparation 10 minutes
Cooking 30 minutes

Each serving provides • 59kcal
• 16g protein • 79g carbohydrates
of which 17g sugars • 22g fat of
which 3g saturates • 6g fibre

200g pearl barley
1 bay leaf
300g leeks
3 celery sticks
3 tbsp olive oil
250g spinach
1 garlic clove, crushed
50g pine nuts
70g dried blueberries

ALTERNATIVE INGREDIENTS
• As a change, use a mix of brown rice and pearl barley, which have similar water absorption and cooking times. Other types of rice that taste good in a pilaf include Camargue red rice or wild rice.
• Try raisins or sultanas instead of dried blueberries, and sunflower seeds instead of pine nuts.
• Baby turnips make a tasty alternative to spinach. Thinly slice 400g baby turnips and cook them in the olive oil in step 3 with the pine nuts and garlic.

1 Place the pearl barley in a large saucepan with the bay leaf and pour in 600ml of boiling water. Bring back to the boil, stir once, reduce the heat, part cover the pan and cook for 25 minutes or until the water has been absorbed and the pearl barley is tender.

2 Meanwhile, thinly slice the leeks and celery. Heat 2 tablespoons oil in a frying pan over a high heat. Add the leeks and celery and fry, stirring frequently, for 5 minutes or until the vegetables are tender. Stir into the cooked barley and season to taste.

3 Pour the remaining 1 tablespoon oil into the pan. Add the spinach and cook over a medium heat for 3 minutes or until wilted. Add the garlic, pine nuts and dried blueberries and cook for 1 minute. Remove the bay leaf and divide the barley between four plates. Top with spinach, blueberries and pine nuts and serve.

COOK'S TIPS

★ If you do not have a garlic crusher, peel the garlic, flatten the clove on a board with the side of a large knife blade and then chop it. Whether garlic is crushed, chopped or sliced influences its flavour in the finished dish. Crushed garlic gives the most intense result.

SUPERFOOD

PEARL BARLEY
A member of the grain family, pearl barley contains many nutrients, including B vitamins and folate, which help to produce healthy red blood cells and prevent a type of anaemia known as macrocytic anaemia. Pearl barley also contains some soluble dietary fibre that is effective in lowering cholesterol.

Spinach

SUPERFOOD

Dark leafy greens, especially spinach, have a rich supply of carotenoids – a group of plant compounds with strong antioxidant properties. Eaten often, vegetables that contain carotenoids help to build the body's resistance to diseases. Spinach is also a good source of heart-healthy folate.

Squash, spinach and hazelnut gratin

Serves 4
Preparation 15 minutes Cooking 35 minutes

Each serving provides • 250kcal • 14g protein • 24g carbohydrates of which 8g sugars • 11g fat of which 5g saturates • 6g fibre

Preheat the oven to 190°C (170°C fan oven), gas 5. Peel **1 small butternut squash**, halve lengthways and remove the seeds, then cut into 1.5cm slices. Cut **300g potatoes** into small cubes. Steam the squash and potato together for 8 minutes or until just tender. Season with ground black pepper. Meanwhile, wilt **500g fresh spinach** with 1 tablespoon of water in a large saucepan over a medium-high heat, stirring, for 5 minutes. Take off the heat when the spinach leaves have turned dark green, but have not yet disintegrated. Drain off any liquid, stir in **1 teaspoon grated nutmeg** and set aside. Spoon half of the squash and potato mix into a shallow, oiled baking dish and top with half the spinach. Sprinkle with **2 tablespoons chopped hazelnuts**. Continue layering the dish and top with a creamy sauce made by combining **150g Greek yogurt, 1 beaten egg, 25g grated Parmesan cheese** and **50g crumbled feta cheese**. Sprinkle **2 tablespoons wholemeal breadcrumbs** over the top and bake for 25 minutes or until golden.

COOK'S TIPS

★ Try sweet potato instead of white potatoes.
★ If you do not have a steamer, place the butternut squash and potatoes in a colander set over a large pan of boiling water. Cover with a lid and steam as above. Alternatively, boil them for 5 minutes then drain, but be sure not to overcook them or the gratin will be mushy.

Eggs florentine

Serves 4
Preparation 15 minutes Cooking 15 minutes

Each serving provides • 311kcal • 19g protein • 11g carbohydrates of which 6g sugars • 22g fat of which 11g saturates • 4g fibre

Preheat the grill to the hottest setting. Make a cheese sauce by melting **20g butter** in a nonstick pan with **25g plain flour**. Stir over a medium heat for 2 minutes then gradually beat in **300ml semi-skimmed milk** until it forms a smooth sauce. Stir in **50g grated Cheddar cheese** and **1 teaspoon French mustard**. Wilt **600g** baby spinach leaves with 1 tablespoon of water in a large pan over a medium-high heat for 5 minutes. Drain thoroughly and beat in **15g butter**. Divide between four individual ovenproof dishes, or gratin dishes, and make a hollow in the centre of each portion. Poach **4 eggs** in a pan of simmering water until the whites are cooked, then remove the eggs using a slotted spoon, drain on kitchen paper and place one in each spinach hollow. Pour the sauce over the spinach and egg, sprinkle each with **1 tablespoon grated Cheddar cheese** and grill for 2 minutes or until golden.

COOK'S TIPS

★ This dish makes a hearty starter, or serve it as a light supper with crusty bread.

Savoury spinach with peas

Serves 4
Preparation 5 minutes Cooking 8 minutes

Each serving provides • 122kcal • 6g protein • 5g carbohydrates of which 4g sugars • 9g fat of which 1g saturates • 8g fibre

Cook **150g petit pois** for 3 minutes in a small pan of boiling water. Drain and set aside. Meanwhile, heat **1 tablespoon olive oil** in a large pan. Add **8 chopped spring onions** and fry over a medium heat for 5 minutes or until softened. Add **500g fresh spinach** and an extra **1 tablespoon olive oil**, stirring until wilted. Stir in the peas and the **juice of ½ lemon** and serve.

COOK'S TIPS

★ As an alternative to petit pois, use fresh shelled peas. They must be sweet and small – large peas contain more starch and can taste floury.

Filled filo tartlets

Serves 4
Preparation 15 minutes Cooking 20 minutes

Each serving provides • 213kcal • 13g protein • 14g carbohydrates of which 3g sugars • 11g fat of which 5g saturates • 3g fibre

Preheat the oven to 190°C (170°C fan oven), gas 5. Wash **500g baby spinach leaves** in a colander, then shake dry and cook in a large saucepan for 5 minutes over a medium heat, with just the water clinging to the leaves. Drain the spinach, if necessary, then transfer it to a large bowl with **200g ricotta cheese, 2 egg yolks**

and **1 crushed garlic clove**. Stir to combine, season with ground black pepper and set aside. Chop **2 slices prosciutto** into 1cm strips. Cut **4 filo pastry sheets** into four squares each and lightly brush with a little **olive oil**. Layer four squares of pastry into four individual metal flan dishes and fill with the spinach mixture. Top each tart with a few slices of prosciutto and sprinkle **1 tablespoon grated Parmesan cheese** over each. Bake for 15 minutes or until the pastry is golden and the filling has set.

COOK'S TIPS

★ Serve the tarts warm or cold, with a mixed green salad or a tomato and onion salad.

Rustic spinach and mushroom pasta

Serves 4
Preparation 5 minutes Cooking 12 minutes

Each serving provides • 558kcal • 17g protein • 61g carbohydrates of which 5g sugars • 29g fat of which 4g saturates • 6g fibre

Cook **300g penne** in a saucepan of boiling water for 10 minutes or until the pasta is tender but still with some bite in the centre, then drain. Meanwhile, heat **2 tablespoons olive oil** in a large frying pan and then add **2 finely chopped shallots, 200g sliced mushrooms** and **2 crushed garlic cloves**. Stir over a medium heat until softened. Add **400g baby spinach leaves** and **1 teaspoon grated nutmeg**. Stir until the spinach has wilted, then mix in an additional **1 tablespoon olive oil**. Stir the vegetables into the hot pasta and season to taste. Divide between four plates and sprinkle each portion with **½ tablespoon grated Parmesan cheese** and **½ tablespoon pine nuts**.

COOK'S TIPS

★ For a creamy dish, add 100ml half-fat crème fraîche instead of the last tablespoon of olive oil.

Summer **chicken** risotto with green **peas**

The creaminess of Italian arborio rice develops with the slow cooking of this mouth-watering and simple dish. The clean sweetness of fresh young peas adds an uplifting final flourish.

Serves 4
Preparation 20 minutes, plus
 5 minutes standing
Cooking 28 minutes

1 onion
400g skinless chicken breast fillets
400g fresh peas or 200g frozen
 petit pois
2 tbsp olive oil
250g arborio risotto rice
900ml hot chicken stock

Each serving provides • 460kcal
• 32g protein • 60g carbohydrates
of which 4g sugars • 11g fat of
which 2g saturates • 3g fibre

ALTERNATIVE INGREDIENTS
• For a richer risotto, try a combination
of wine and stock. Add 300ml dry
white wine in step 2 and reduce the
chicken stock to 600ml. Top each
portion of risotto with Parmesan
cheese shavings before serving.
• Asparagus works well instead of
peas. Trim off any woody ends from
8 asparagus spears then slice them
and add to the pan in step 2 before
pouring in the stock.

1 Finely chop the onion and cut the chicken into 2cm chunks. Shell the peas, if using fresh ones. Heat the oil in a large saucepan over a high heat. Add the onion, reduce the heat to medium and cook for 1 minute. Mix in the chicken and cook, stirring, for 5 minutes or until the pieces of chicken are firm and white in colour.

2 Add the rice and cook for 1 minute, stirring to coat the rice in the oil. Pour 500ml of the stock into the pan and bring to the boil, stirring once or twice. Reduce the heat to medium or low so that the stock simmers steadily and cook for 10 minutes.

3 Add the peas if using fresh and stir in the remaining 400ml stock. Bring back to the boil, reduce the heat again to medium or low and simmer steadily for 10 minutes. If using frozen petit pois, add them for the final 5 minutes of cooking time. Stir once or twice to ensure that the rice cooks evenly. By the end of the cooking time, the majority of stock should be absorbed but still with a little excess.

4 Season to taste, cover the pan and remove it from the heat. Leave the risotto to stand for 5 minutes – the rice will finish cooking and absorb the excess liquid, leaving it moist and creamy.

COOK'S TIPS
★ Simmer the stock gently for an authentic, creamy risotto. Do not allow it to bubble furiously or the stock will evaporate rather than be absorbed by the rice.

SUPERFOOD

PEAS
These little green wonders are bursting with antioxidants, including lutein, which can protect your eyesight by lowering the risk of age-related cataract development. Peas are also starchy and high in fibre – good for promoting a healthy heart and digestive system.

Herby **bulgur wheat** with **chorizo**

Moist grains flavoured with herbs, peppers and cucumber make a welcome change to everyday salads. A little chorizo adds a lot of punch, with cooling yogurt served on the side.

Serves 4
Preparation 10 minutes,
  plus 30 minutes soaking

200g bulgur wheat
400ml hot chicken stock
½ cucumber
2 red peppers
125g chorizo
4 tbsp snipped fresh chives
2 tbsp chopped fresh dill
8 chopped large fresh mint sprigs
120g plain yogurt

Each serving provides • 343kcal • 14g protein • 47g carbohydrates of which 8g sugars • 12g fat of which 5g saturates • 2g fibre

ALTERNATIVE INGREDIENTS
• Use a variety of cooked meats – spicy or full-flavoured varieties work best – such as beef pastrami, garlic sausage or salami.
• Mixed grains, such as spelt with barley and buckwheat, make an ideal change to bulgur wheat. Follow the packet instructions for individual soaking and cooking times.
• For a meat-free alternative, top the yogurt with chopped hard-boiled egg, allowing one egg per portion and omitting the chorizo and mint. Replace the chicken stock with vegetable.

1 Place the bulgur wheat in a heatproof bowl and pour in the stock. Cover with clingfilm and leave to soak for 30 minutes or until the bulgur wheat is tender and doubled in volume.

2 Meanwhile, dice the cucumber and peppers and shred the chorizo. Remove any excess liquid from the bulgur wheat by draining it through a sieve. Return it to the pan and stir in the cucumber, peppers, chives, dill and mint and season to taste.

3 Divide the bulgur wheat between four bowls. Top each serving with yogurt and sprinkle with the chorizo.

COOK'S TIPS
★ Use kitchen scissors to shred the chorizo into thin strips.
★ If you need to measure yogurt, it is helpful to know that the volume in millilitres is equivalent to the weight, so 120g of yogurt can be measured as 120ml in a jug.

SUPERFOOD

RED PEPPERS
As fibre providers, red peppers are good for promoting a healthy digestive system, and contain potassium to help regulate blood pressure. They are also packed with powerfully antioxidant carotenes, which help to protect the body against some cancers.

Desserts

Exotic fruits, juicy berries and other high-fibre,
high-energy foods combine in these scrumptious
sweet dishes that are easy to make and simply
perfect for family meals at any time.

Raspberry creams with mango and honey sauce

The whole family will love such a lusciously smooth yet quick and healthy dessert. Not only that, its bright jewel-like colours would look great on any dinner party table.

Serves 4
Preparation 10 minutes

250g low-fat soft cheese
2 tbsp icing sugar
1 large ripe mango
1 tbsp honey
260g raspberries

Each serving provides • 172kcal
• 6g protein • 21g carbohydrates
of which 20g sugars • 7g fat of
which 5g saturates • 3g fibre

ALTERNATIVE INGREDIENTS
• Use a variety of fruit instead of raspberries – try sliced strawberries, whole blueberries, pitted cherries, halved black or green grapes, kiwi fruit, pineapple chunks or sliced bananas.
• Swap the low-fat soft cheese for ricotta cheese, beating it thoroughly with the icing sugar in step 1 to remove its 'grainy' texture.
• As a change to mango, peaches, nectarines and plums all make tasty purées to complement the raspberries. Use 350g fruit in total for the purée.

1 Mix together the soft cheese with the icing sugar. Cut the mango off the stone, chop into small chunks and purée in a blender or food processor. Stir the honey into the mango purée.

2 Set aside 8 raspberries and reserve 4 teaspoons of the sweetened soft cheese. Divide the remainder of the raspberries between four glass dishes and top with the soft cheese mixture. Use a knife or the back of a spoon to create an even surface.

3 Spoon the mango purée over the soft cheese to cover. Top each portion with 1 teaspoon of the reserved sweetened soft cheese and decorate with 2 raspberries.

COOK'S TIPS
★ To measure runny honey accurately, dip a metal spoon into boiling water, shake off the water and scoop up the honey – it will easily slide off the hot spoon. For set honey, use a round-bladed knife to fill the bowl of a measuring spoon and then to scrape the honey into the mango purée.

SUPERFOOD

RASPBERRIES
Like other berry fruits, raspberries are rich in anthocyanins and ellagic acid, powerful antioxidants that protect against cancers and heart disease. Raspberries also have a low glycaemic index (GI) value, which means their natural sugars are released slowly into the bloodstream, helping to keep blood sugar levels steady.

Warm spiced **plums** with **hazelnut** yogurt

Speedy cooking brings out the best in firm plums, especially when they are sprinkled with a little cinnamon. Toasted hazelnuts, mixed with yogurt, add a burst of fibre and vitamin E goodness.

Serves 4
Preparation 10 minutes
Cooking 5 minutes

Each serving provides • 382kcal • 10g protein • 28g carbohydrates of which 27g sugars • 26g fat of which 8g saturates • 4g fibre

100g chopped toasted hazelnuts
400g Greek-style yogurt
2 tbsp runny honey
1 tbsp granulated sugar
½ tsp cinnamon
500g firm ripe plums

ALTERNATIVE INGREDIENTS
• Use chopped pecan nuts and maple syrup rather than hazelnuts and honey.
• Grill 8 ripe pear halves in place of plums. Use a little grated nutmeg instead of the cinnamon, which has too strong a flavour for the pears. Halve 1 pear per portion, remove the cores and place cut-sides up in the dish. Sprinkle with the juice of ½ lemon and the spiced sugar before grilling in step 2.
• For a weekend breakfast, serve the plums on heated waffles or pancakes and top with the hazelnut yogurt.

1 Preheat the grill to the hottest setting. Reserve 4 tablespoons of hazelnuts and mix the remaining hazelnuts into the yogurt. Trickle in the honey, mix gently, cover and set aside in the fridge while preparing the plums.

2 Mix the sugar and cinnamon. Halve and stone the plums (see Cook's Tips), cutting the halves in quarters if they are large. Place the plums in an ovenproof dish and sprinkle with the cinnamon sugar. Grill for 5 minutes or until the sugar has dissolved and the plums begin to brown. The cooking time will depend on the ripeness of the fruit.

3 Divide the plums between four serving plates and pour over any cooking juices. Add a spoonful of hazelnut yogurt and sprinkle with the reserved hazelnuts.

COOK'S TIPS

★ To stone plums, cut the fruit in half from the top, following the natural dimple. Twist the halves and they will separate easily, leaving the stone on one half. Use a small pointed knife to cut out the stone.
★ To toast your own hazelnuts, place the nuts on a baking sheet and roast in the oven for 5 minutes at 220°C (200°C fan oven), gas 6, or until browned, checking regularly to make sure they don't burn.
★ Prepare the hazelnut yogurt in advance – handy for making an easy weekend breakfast treat.

SUPERFOOD

HAZELNUTS
Highly nutritious, hazelnuts are rich in heart-healthy fats. They are also a good source of some B vitamins, especially thiamine (B1) and B6. Full of fibre, the nuts help to maintain digestive health and just a handful will provide your daily dose of vitamin E.

Juicy **apples** with **oat** and **seed** crunch

A delicious and fibre-rich take on the classic crumble, these lightly stewed apples and prunes with a golden oaty topping are a special treat with a spoonful of yogurt or piping-hot custard.

Serves 4
Preparation 5 minutes
Cooking 8 minutes

450g cooking apples
100ml apple juice
100g ready-to-eat prunes
25g butter
50g whole rolled oats
25g sunflower seeds
25g demerara or raw cane sugar
4 tbsp plain yogurt

Each serving provides • 273kcal
• 6g protein • 41g carbohydrates of which 31g sugars • 11g fat of which 4g saturates • 5g fibre

ALTERNATIVE INGREDIENTS
• Almost any dried fruit can be used to sweeten the apples instead of prunes: peaches, pears, apricots, sultanas, raisins, cranberries or even mixed dried fruit.
• Add 50g chopped walnuts with the sugar in step 3.
• Ordinary rolled oats work well instead of the slightly larger 'whole' type in this recipe.
• Try mixed seeds, such as sesame, sunflower and pumpkin, or use a combination of chopped mixed nuts and seeds.

1 Peel, core and cut the apples into 1cm slices. Place in a saucepan and pour in the juice. Bring to the boil, reduce the heat and cover the pan with a lid. Simmer for around 5 minutes, stirring occasionally, until soft but not pulpy. Slice the prunes into quarters and gently stir in the pieces. Cover and set aside off the heat.

2 Melt the butter in a frying pan over a medium heat. Add the oats and sunflower seeds, increase the heat to medium-high and cook, stirring, for about 2 minutes or until the oats and seeds are browned.

3 Add the sugar and stir until it melts and coats the mixture. Remove the pan from the heat. Divide the apple between four dishes and top with the oat mixture. Add 1 tablespoon of yogurt to each dish and serve hot or warm.

COOK'S TIPS
★ Make double the quantity and freeze in individual portions. You can also do this if you have a surplus of stewed apple. The crunchy topping can be frozen separately and sprinkled over ice cream or yogurt.

SUPERFOOD

APPLES
Fruit is good for heart health as it contains soluble fibre known to help to lower blood cholesterol. Apples have a low glycaemic index (GI) score, meaning they release glucose steadily rather than rapidly into the bloodstream, which helps to regulate blood sugar levels.

Chocolatey **orange** and **blueberry** soufflés

A gooey soufflé, with its tempting deep cocoa colour, is baked over a vitamin-filled blueberry base, proving that even such an irresistible pudding can be good for you.

Serves 4
Preparation 10 minutes
Cooking 12 minutes

250g blueberries
2 eggs
4 tbsp caster sugar
3 tbsp plain flour
2 tbsp unsweetened cocoa powder
grated zest and juice of 1 orange
½ tsp icing sugar, to dust

Each serving provides • 208kcal
• 7g protein • 35g carbohydrates of
which 23g sugars • 5g fat of which
2g saturates • 3g fibre

ALTERNATIVE INGREDIENTS
• When fresh blueberries are not
available, use frozen ones or try a
frozen forest fruit mix.

1 Preheat the oven to 220°C (200°C fan oven), gas 7. Place four 250ml (9cm diameter) ramekins on a baking sheet and divide the blueberries between them.

2 Separate the eggs, pouring the whites into a thoroughly clean bowl and placing the yolks in a separate bowl. Add the sugar, flour, cocoa powder, orange zest and juice to the egg yolk and beat to form a smooth batter. Whisk the egg whites until they stand in stiff peaks. Use a large metal spoon to fold the egg whites into the batter.

3 Spoon the batter over the blueberries, level each surface and bake for 12 minutes or until the soufflés are risen and set. Dust with icing sugar and serve immediately.

COOK'S TIPS
★ When whisking egg whites, the bowl and beaters must be totally clean and grease-free or the whites will not stiffen.
★ If you are preparing this dessert ahead of time, mix the chocolate batter a couple of hours in advance, then cover and set aside until needed. Place the egg whites in a separate bowl and whisk them just before folding into the batter.

SUPERFOOD

BLUEBERRIES
Acclaimed as one of the ultimate
superfoods, blueberries are packed
full of phytochemicals, especially
anthocyanins, which are thought to
have anti-inflammatory effects in the
body. Researchers believe that the
berries may help to protect against
some cancers and heart disease.

Zesty **orange** and **banana** medley

Cinnamon and orange are a perfect match for banana in a quick, refreshing and filling dessert full of flavour, essential vitamins and minerals. Serve with a dollop of vanilla ice cream.

Serves 4
Preparation 10 minutes
Marinating 10-15 minutes
Cooking 2 minutes

4 large seedless oranges
50g raisins or sultanas
1 cinnamon stick
2 large or 4 small bananas

Each serving provides • 180kcal
• 4g protein • 43g carbohydrates
of which 41g sugars • 1g fat
(no saturates) • 6g fibre

ALTERNATIVE INGREDIENTS
• Use dried cranberries or cherries instead of raisins or sultanas.
• Try strawberries as a change to bananas, leaving the strawberries whole or halving large ones.
• Spiced pineapple is a refreshing alternative to banana and orange. Use 1 ripe pineapple, with the ends and peel removed, 1 star anise and ¼ teaspoon ground cinnamon.

1 Use a zester to remove the zest of 1 orange, then halve the orange and squeeze out the juice. Add water, if necessary, to make the juice up to 150ml. Pour the juice into a saucepan. Add the zest, raisins or sultanas, and the cinnamon stick (use just half a stick if long). Bring to the boil, then remove from the heat, cover and set aside.

2 Slice the ends off the remaining 3 oranges, then cut away the peel in wide strips, working down the fruit to remove all the pith. Slice the oranges, discarding any pips.

3 Place the sliced oranges in a serving dish, adding any juices that run out during preparation. Pour the orange juice mixture over the fruit. Cover and set aside for 10-15 minutes.

4 Peel and slice the bananas and add them to the oranges just before serving, mixing to coat the slices in the orange juice mixture so that they do not discolour.

COOK'S TIPS
★ The banana and orange medley can also be served warm, especially when using a good-quality fresh cinnamon stick, which will provide plenty of flavour. Prepare the recipe as above but do not set aside the syrup or the fruit in either step 1 or step 3.
★ The oranges can be prepared, cooled and chilled overnight in an airtight container.

SUPERFOOD

ORANGES
The orange is renowned for its high content of vitamin C, which, as well as being a powerful antioxidant, is good for eye health and the immune system. One glass of pure orange juice counts as one of your 5-a-day.

SUPERFOOD

Bananas

The fibre in bananas, both soluble and insoluble, helps to protect the body against bowel cancer, stabilise blood sugar levels and lower harmful blood cholesterol. Bananas also contain vitamin B6, important for making red blood cells and breaking down protein and fats.

Fruity tea bread

Makes 8 slices
Preparation 10 minutes Cooking 40 minutes

Each serving provides • 275kcal • 8g protein • 31g carbohydrates of which 14g sugars • 14g fat of which 2g saturates • 3g fibre

Preheat the oven to 180°C (160°C fan oven), gas 4. Oil and line a 900g loaf tin with baking parchment. In a bowl, combine **100g self-raising flour, 75g wholemeal self-raising flour, 75g ground almonds, ½ teaspoon baking powder** and **½ teaspoon ground ginger**. In another bowl, combine **3 very ripe mashed bananas, 2 eggs, 50ml runny honey** and **100ml semi-skimmed milk**. Stir the dry ingredients into the wet ingredients, then fold in **75g chopped pecan nuts**. Pour the tea bread mixture into the prepared loaf tin and bake for 40 minutes or until golden and a skewer comes out clean when pushed into the centre of the tea bread. Cool before slicing.

COOK'S TIPS

★ This is a healthy alternative for tea time, picnics and lunchboxes. If desired, spread with butter or low-fat spread before serving.

Apricot and banana crumble

Serves 4
Preparation 10 minutes Cooking 35 minutes

Each serving provides • 342kcal • 7g protein • 54g carbohydrates of which 37g sugars • 12g fat of which 4g saturates • 6g fibre

Preheat the oven to 190°C (170°C fan oven), gas 5. Simmer **150g dried apricots** in sufficient water to cover for 15 minutes or until tender. Meanwhile, peel and slice **3 bananas** and place them in an ovenproof dish. Spoon in the juice of **1 lemon**. Drain the cooked apricots, reserving the cooking liquid, chop into quarters and spoon them over the sliced bananas. Pour in 4 tablespoons of the reserved cooking liquid. In a bowl, combine **75g rolled oats** with **25g chopped mixed nuts** and **1 tablespoon sunflower seeds**. In a small saucepan, add **1 tablespoon honey, 25g butter** and **1 tablespoon soft brown sugar**. Warm over a medium heat until the sugar has melted. Mix together and pour over the dry ingredients, stirring everything together. Spoon the oaty topping over the fruit and bake for 20 minutes or until the crumble topping is cooked and golden.

★ When melting the sugar with the honey and butter, do not place the pan over a high heat or the sugar may burn on the base of the pan and make the crumble topping taste bitter. Stir the mixture regularly.

Banana split with iced yogurt

Serves 4
Preparation 10 minutes, plus 30 minutes cooling
Cooking 5 minutes Freezing 5 hours

Each serving provides • 410kcal • 13g protein
• 81g carbohydrates of which 79g sugars • 6g fat
of which 3g saturates • 4g fibre

Make the iced yogurt by first melting **100g caster sugar** in **3 tablespoons hot water** in a pan for 5 minutes over a low heat. Take off the heat and cool for 30 minutes. Combine this sugar syrup with **700g full-fat plain yogurt** and **½ teaspoon vanilla extract**. Freeze in an ice-cream maker following the manufacturer's instructions, or transfer to a plastic lidded container and freeze for at least 5 hours, removing every hour and beating to prevent ice crystals from forming. Whizz **300g fresh raspberries** in a blender with **50g caster sugar** and the **juice of 1 lemon**. Pass the purée through a fine-meshed sieve to remove the pips, stirring in 1 tablespoon of water to thin slightly, if necessary. Peel **4 ripe bananas**, halve them lengthways and arrange in four dishes. Top each banana with a scoop of iced yogurt, **75g fresh raspberries**, **1 tablespoon chopped almonds** and 2 tablespoons of the purée.

COOK'S TIPS
★ If short on time, use readymade raspberry coulis and shop-bought iced yogurt or ice cream.
★ Use vanilla essence if extract is not available, but for a powerful vanilla boost, try vanilla bean paste.

Sunshine smoothie

Serves 4
Preparation 5 minutes Chilling 30 minutes

Each serving provides • 136kcal • 4g protein
• 30g carbohydrates of which 29g sugars • 1g fat
(no saturates) • 1g fibre

Put **2 ripe bananas** into a blender with **2 tablespoons honey**, **½ teaspoon ground cinnamon** and **1 heaped tablespoon wheatgerm**. Blend for 10 seconds, then add **200ml low-fat plain yogurt**, **300ml orange juice**

and the **juice of ½ lemon**. Blend again until smooth. Chill for 30 minutes in the fridge before pouring into four tall glasses.

COOK'S TIPS
★ Wheatgerm is a tiny part of the wheat kernel that is high in protein, vitamin E and potassium. Find it in the cereal aisle in the supermarket, or in health food shops.
★ This smoothie is best drunk within an hour of making because it will thicken as the wheatgerm expands and the vitamin C content will begin to deteriorate.

Pan-fried bananas in a sweet citrus sauce

Serves 4
Preparation 5 minutes Cooking 5 minutes

Each serving provides • 163kcal • 1g protein
• 28g carbohydrates of which 26g sugars • 6g fat
of which 2g saturates • 1g fibre

Cut **4 just-ripe bananas** into bite-size diagonal chunks. Heat **15g butter** in a large frying pan with **2 teaspoons sunflower oil**. Add the banana chunks to the pan and fry for 3 minutes over a medium heat until golden, then add the **juice of 1 orange, 1 level tablespoon soft dark brown sugar** and a **dash of orange liqueur (optional)**. Stir for 2 minutes until bubbling then transfer to four plates and serve with the pan juices spooned over.

COOK'S TIPS
★ For an oven-cooked suzette, place 4 whole bananas in an ovenproof dish with the flavourings and bake at 180°C (160°C fan oven), gas 4, for 20 minutes, basting once or twice. Remove from the oven and sprinkle with 1 teaspoon desiccated coconut per portion.
★ A spoonful of crème fraîche makes a tasty partner to the bananas.

Kiwi fruit cheesecake with lime honey

Sinfully yummy – but not sinfully calorific – a healthy take on traditional cheesecake balances low-fat cheese with toasty muesli and a lime and kiwi fruit combo bursting with vitamin C.

Serves 4
Preparation 10 minutes
Cooking 2 minutes

100g muesli
250g low-fat soft cheese
1 tsp icing sugar
grated zest of 2 limes
   and juice of 1 lime
2 tbsp honey
4 ripe kiwi fruit

Each serving provides • 248kcal
• 8g protein • 34g carbohydrates of
which 21g sugars • 9g fat of which
5g saturates • 3g fibre

ALTERNATIVE INGREDIENTS
• Try 3 crushed chocolate-chip cookies
per portion instead of muesli.
• To make a red berry cheesecake,
use a handful of raspberries or ripe
strawberries per portion and leave out
the kiwi fruit.
• For a more substantial dessert,
coarsely mash 2 bananas and mix
them with the soft cheese in step 1.

1 Preheat the grill to the hottest setting. Cover the grill pan with foil and sprinkle the muesli evenly over it. Toast the museli under the grill for 2 minutes, turning it once or twice to prevent it from burning. Mix the soft cheese with the icing sugar and zest of 1 lime. Mix the lime juice with the honey. Peel and slice the kiwi fruit.

2 Divide half of the toasted muesli between four dessert plates or bowls, spooning the cereal into small mounds. Top with the soft cheese and sprinkle with the remaining half of the muesli. Flatten each portion into a 'cake' using a round-bladed knife or the back of a spoon.

3 Arrange the kiwi slices on top of each cheesecake and sprinkle with the remaining zest of 1 lime. Drizzle with the lime and honey mixture just before serving.

COOK'S TIPS
★ The exact weight of the muesli may vary slightly depending on the brand and its precise content. As a guide, each cheesecake uses roughly 2 tablespoons of muesli.
★ Instead of shaping the cheesecakes on plates, layer the muesli, cheese and fruit into 7cm cooking rings to form a tidy construction. Remove the rings just before serving.

SUPERFOOD

LIMES
Like all citrus fruit, limes are packed
with vitamin C, which is essential for
healthy skin, muscles and bones,
and a booster for the body's immune
system. Vitamin C also offers
protection from some cancers and
heart disease, and helps the body
to absorb essential iron.

Warm **berries** on toasted **brioche**

A vibrant fruit mix, poured over buttery brioche and served with creamy mascarpone, makes a flavour-drenched dessert. Even better, it is bursting with vitamins and fibre for good health.

Serves 4
Preparation 5 minutes
Cooking 4 minutes

Each serving provides • 257kcal • 4g protein • 37g carbohydrates of which 23g sugars • 12g fat of which 8g saturates • 4g fibre

50g demerara sugar
40g butter
4 brioche rolls, about 35g each
250g black forest fruits mix, thawed
  if frozen
2 large chopped fresh mint leaves
120g mascarpone
4 mint sprigs, to garnish

ALTERNATIVE INGREDIENTS
• When berry fruits are in season, this recipe can be made using fresh fruit. Choose from blackcurrants, black cherries, raspberries, redcurrants, blackcurrants and strawberries.
• Greek-style yogurt makes a good alternative to mascarpone.

1 Preheat the grill to the hottest setting. Beat half of the sugar into the butter. Trim the rounded ends off the brioche rolls, then cut each one at a slant into four slices. Toast the slices under the grill on one side.

2 Place the fruit in a small saucepan. Add 2 tablespoons of water and the remaining 25g of sugar, then bring to the boil over a medium heat, stirring frequently. Cook for 1-2 minutes until the sugar dissolves and the fruit releases its juices. Remove the pan from the heat and add the chopped mint.

3 Spread the untoasted sides of the brioche with the sweetened butter. Toast under the grill for 1 minute until the sugar melts and the edges of the slices are crisp and browned.

4 Transfer the brioche to four plates and spoon over the hot mixed fruit. Top with a large spoonful of mascarpone and garnish with a sprig of mint before serving.

COOK'S TIPS
★ Cook the mixed fruit over a medium rather than high heat to avoid boiling the juices rapidly, which will toughen the skins. Remove the pan from the heat as soon as the juice boils.
★ Currants and berries freeze well and can be cooked from frozen if time is short. Allow an extra 3-5 minutes cooking time in step 2 if using frozen fruit. If you are a keen gardener, grow raspberries, strawberries and blackcurrants. Rinse and freeze them as soon as possible after picking.

SUPERFOOD

MIXED BERRIES
Vividly coloured berries contain natural compounds called anthocyanins, which can help to counter the effects of potentially damaging free radicals. These are unstable molecules that can alter or damage cells in the body, which may lead to the development of cancer.

Strawberry, grape and pistachio flowers

What a tempting dessert. Simply arrange fresh strawberry 'petals' around a rosewater and cinnamon-infused grape centre for an enticing bouquet of summertime treats.

Serves 4
Preparation 10 minutes

Each serving provides • 268kcal • 9g protein • 30g carbohydrates of which 30g sugars • 13g fat of which 7g saturates • 2g fibre

¼ tsp ground cinnamon
1 tsp rosewater
2 tbsp honey
175g seedless black grapes
1 tbsp icing sugar
½ tsp vanilla extract
500g fromage frais
300g strawberries
20g chopped pistachio nuts

ALTERNATIVE INGREDIENTS
• Use Greek-style yogurt instead of fromage frais for a sharper flavour.
• Try sliced and quartered oranges instead of grapes, removing the bitter pith before mixing them with the cinnamon, rosewater and honey.
• Sliced ready-to-eat dried peaches or pears make great alternatives to the grapes. Allow two pieces of dried fruit per portion.

1 Mix together the ground cinnamon, rosewater and honey in a large bowl. Cut the grapes in half and stir them into the honey mixture.

2 In another bowl, lightly beat the icing sugar and vanilla extract with the fromage frais and divide between four ice-cream glasses or tall glass dessert dishes. Level the surface of the fromage frais with the back of a spoon or a round-bladed knife.

3 Hull the strawberries and then chop them in half, slicing any large fruit into smaller pieces. Position the strawberries around the edge of each glass to look like the petals of a flower. Spoon the grape mixture into the centre of each portion and sprinkle with pistachio nuts.

COOK'S TIPS
★ Rosewater contributes a flowery flavour that tastes perfect with honey. It is usually stocked in the cake baking aisle in the supermarket.
★ If you cannot buy ready-chopped pistachio nuts, buy whole nuts and whizz them in a food processor for 10 seconds or until finely chopped.

SUPERFOOD

STRAWBERRIES
A summer favourite, strawberries are rich in vitamin C, helping to boost the body's immune system and protect against ageing. Strawberries also contain ellagic acid, an antioxidant found in berry fruits and thought to have anti-cancer properties.

Cool **pineapple** and **kiwi** medley with **gingernut** cream

Mint and preserved ginger are the surprise ingredients in a refreshing exotic fruit dessert. The kiwi and pineapple pieces are sweetly sharp, while crunchy, biscuity fromage frais adds just a hint of indulgence.

Serves 4
Preparation 20 minutes

Each serving provides • 145kcal • 4g protein • 21g carbohydrates of which 16g sugars • 6g fat of which 3g saturates • 1g fibre

½ pineapple
4 kiwi fruit
4 pieces preserved stem ginger
6 large fresh mint leaves
4 gingernut biscuits
200g fromage frais
4 fresh mint sprigs, to garnish

ALTERNATIVE INGREDIENTS
• Instead of kiwi fruit use 200g seedless green grapes, cutting them in half first.
• Try ginger or chocolate shortbread biscuits as a change to gingernuts, or use almond macaroons if you want a softer texture.
• Candied ginger is more economical than preserved stem ginger. Use 1 heaped teaspoon chopped candied ginger per portion.

1 Peel, core and slice the pineapple into wedges (see Cook's Tips), then peel and thickly slice the kiwi fruit and cut each slice in half. Thinly slice the preserved stem ginger. Shred the mint leaves and mix them with the pineapple and kiwi fruit.

2 In a bowl or plastic bag, crush the gingernut biscuits with the end of a rolling pin to make fine crumbs. Stir the gingernut crumbs into the fromage frais.

3 Arrange the pineapple and kiwi on four plates with a large spoonful of biscuity fromage frais at the side. Top the fromage frais with sliced ginger and garnish each portion with a mint sprig.

COOK'S TIPS

★ To prepare a whole pineapple, cut off the leafy top and stalk end. Slice off the skin with a sharp knife, working down the fruit to remove any eyes and spines. Divide the pineapple in half lengthways and remove the tough core from both halves. Slice into semi-circles then cut into wedges.

SUPERFOOD

PINEAPPLE
Like all fruit, the tropical pineapple is a low-calorie, health-promoting food. It contains fibre and potassium to help to regulate the body's blood pressure and fluid balance. With a glycaemic index (GI) value that is relatively high for a fruit, pineapple is best eaten in combination with low GI food such as low-fat fromage frais.

Delectable **red berry** pancakes

From brunch through tea time to weekday family suppers, warm fruity pancakes make a feast for any meal. Be generous with the rich red berries, and finish with a little Greek yogurt.

Serves 4
Preparation 15 minutes
Cooking 8 minutes

100g self-raising flour
1 tsp granulated sugar
1 egg
75ml semi-skimmed milk
125g redcurrants
12 strawberries
25g unsalted butter
2-3 tsp caster sugar
8 tbsp low-fat Greek yogurt

Each serving provides • 276kcal
• 10g protein • 32g carbohydrates
of which 14g sugars • 13g fat of
which 8g saturates • 2g fibre

ALTERNATIVE INGREDIENTS
• Try fresh or frozen blackcurrants instead of redcurrants.
• Seasonal raspberries, blackberries or pitted cherries make very tasty alternatives to strawberries.
• For a lactose-free dessert, make up the batter with 75ml unsweetened fruit juice, such as cranberry, apple or orange juice, instead of milk.

1 Sift the flour into a bowl and stir in the sugar. Beat in the egg and a little of the milk to form a thick paste. Gradually add the rest of the milk, beating to remove any lumps until it forms a smooth, thick batter. Pull the stalks off the redcurrants, if necessary, and stir the berries into the batter. Hull and halve the strawberries.

2 Heat a large frying pan over a medium heat and add half the butter to melt. Use shaped moulds (see Cook's Tips) to make the pancakes or cook four heaped dessertspoons of batter, spacing them well apart, for 2 minutes or until they are firm, set and golden underneath.

3 Flip and cook for another 1 minute, turning the heat down if the pancakes begin to burn. Transfer the pancakes to a dish and keep warm. Carefully wipe any juice from the berries off the pan with kitchen paper, add the remaining butter and fry four more pancakes using up the rest of the batter. Transfer the pancakes to the dish and keep warm.

4 Add the strawberries to the hot pan for 30 seconds to warm through. Transfer the pancakes to four plates, add the strawberries, sprinkle with a little caster sugar and serve with Greek yogurt.

COOK'S TIPS
★ To create shaped pancakes, place four heatproof moulds in the frying pan, carefully spoon the batter into each mould, then leave to cook and firm up. Then, carefully remove the moulds and flip the pancakes to cook the other side.
★ If using home-grown redcurrants, remove the stalks by gently scraping the fruit against the prongs of a fork, placing a bowl underneath. Shop-bought redcurrants should already have their stalks removed.

SUPERFOOD

REDCURRANTS
This versatile fruit, often used to make jelly, is rich in nutrients and high in health-promoting fibre. Redcurrants also contain potassium, which helps to regulate blood pressure, and vitamin C for healthy bones, teeth and gums.

Quick mixed **berry** and **almond** delights

A nutty but light topping of fibre-rich almonds and oats transforms a packet of frozen mixed fruit into a supercharged dessert that blissfully marries comfort eating with healthy treating.

Serves 4
Preparation 10 minutes
Cooking 20 minutes

400g frozen summer fruits
100g ground almonds
50g porridge oats
2 eggs
2 tbsp runny honey
5 tbsp semi-skimmed milk
½ tsp almond extract

Each serving provides • 325kcal • 12g protein • 29g carbohydrates of which 19g sugars • 19g fat of which 2g saturates • 6g fibre

ALTERNATIVE INGREDIENTS
• Try black forest fruits instead of summer fruits, though larger fruit such as grapes and cherries will need an extra 5 minutes to cook.
• For a lactose-free dish, use apple juice instead of milk.

1 Preheat the oven to 200°C (180°C fan oven), gas 6. Divide the frozen summer fruits between four 250ml (9cm diameter) ramekins.

2 Mix the ground almonds and oats in a bowl and make a well in the centre. Separate the eggs, placing the yolks in the almond mixture and the whites in a separate, clean bowl. Pour the honey, milk and almond extract into the well and beat the ingredients together to form a soft, dropping consistency (see Cook's Tips).

3 Whisk the egg whites until stiff and beat one-third of them into the almond mixture. Use a metal spoon to fold in the remaining egg whites. Spoon the pudding mixture over the frozen summer fruits, levelling the top.

4 Place the ramekins on a baking sheet and bake for 20 minutes or until the mixture browns, rises and is slightly cracked and firm to the touch. Serve hot.

COOK'S TIPS
★ A dropping consistency is achieved when the mixture drops easily off your spoon when tapped against the side of the bowl. The mixture should be firm and not sloppy.

SUPERFOOD

ALMONDS
There is good evidence that a handful (30g) of nuts, especially almonds, when eaten daily can lower harmful cholesterol. Almonds contain 7g fibre per 100g, which is good news because high-fibre foods may protect against bowel cancer.

Spiced **rhubarb** and **blueberry** compote

Ginger delivers a delicious spike to this versatile compote that can be served warm or chilled, for breakfast or dessert – perfect with a scoop of ice cream or yogurt. The fruit offers up a mouthwatering cocktail of vitamins.

Serves 4
Preparation 5 minutes
Cooking 10 minutes
Chilling 30 minutes (optional)

600g rhubarb
3 tbsp granulated sugar
40g crystallised stem ginger
125g blueberries

Each serving provides • 83kcal
• 1g protein • 20g carbohydrates of which 19g sugars • no fat • 3g fibre

ALTERNATIVE INGREDIENTS
• Frozen blueberries can be used in place of fresh ones, but the rhubarb must be fresh, not canned.
• Strawberries also taste terrific with the rhubarb.
• Serve the rhubarb and blueberry compote with muesli and yogurt for a nutritious breakfast.
• Stone 250-350g red cherries and add them to the rhubarb, omitting the blueberries and ginger and adding an extra tablespoonful of sugar.
• Serve as a healthy topping for pancakes or waffles.

1 Cut the rhubarb into 2-3cm lengths and place in a large saucepan. Sprinkle the sugar over the fruit and add 1 tablespoon of water. Cook over a high heat for 30 seconds or until the sugar begins to dissolve.

2 Reduce the heat to medium or medium-low, so that the fruit simmers. Cover the pan and simmer for 5-8 minutes, stirring once, until the rhubarb is tender but not mushy.

3 Cut the crystallised stem ginger into 1-2mm slices. Remove the pan from the heat and add the ginger and blueberries. Stir gently and divide between four bowls. Serve immediately or chill for 30 minutes.

COOK'S TIPS
★ Small, fresh sticks of rhubarb are usually tender and only need the ends of the stalks trimmed and the leaves removed. Larger or older sticks should be thinly peeled to remove the skin, which can be stringy.
★ Make the stewed rhubarb and keep it in a covered dish in the fridge for up to 3 days. Add the blueberries and ginger just before serving.

SUPERFOOD

RHUBARB
A low sugar content, and therefore a low glycaemic index (GI) rating, means that rhubarb can help to steady blood sugar levels, which is great for weight control and keeping hunger at bay. With fibre and potassium as extra nutritional benefits, rhubarb helps to maintain a healthy digestive system.

Blueberries

SUPERFOOD

A nutritional supernova, blueberries are bursting with antioxidants that can offer protection against long-term health problems such as some cancers and heart disease. As fibre providers, blueberries do their bit to support a healthy digestive system.

Individual summer puddings

Serves 4
Preparation 5 minutes Cooking 5 minutes
Chilling 1½ hours

Each serving provides • 175kcal • 5g protein • 35g carbohydrates of which 20g sugars • 3g fat of which 1g saturates • 5g fibre

Poach **225g blueberries** and **225g raspberries** in a pan with 3 tablespoons of water, **3 tablespoons caster sugar** and the **juice of 1 lemon** for 5 minutes or until the juices run free. Line four dariole moulds with cling film. Remove the crusts from **5 thin brown bread slices**, then cut each slice into four squares and use them to line the darioles, placing one square on each base and four around the sides. Spoon the fruit and juice into the lined moulds, wrap with cling film and chill in the fridge for 1½ hours. Lift the summer puddings out of each mould using the cling film and transfer to four plates. Spoon **1 tablespoon half-fat crème fraîche** over the top of each pudding and serve.

COOK'S TIPS
★ When pouring the fruit juice into the moulds, make sure that it covers as much of the bread as possible.

Berry iced yogurt

Serves 4
Preparation 5 minutes Cooking 15 minutes
Freezing 5 hours

Each serving provides • 309kcal • 11g protein • 56g carbohydrates of which 55g sugars • 6g fat of which 2g saturates • 3g fibre

Place **400g blueberries** in a small pan with **25g caster sugar** and 2 tablespoons of cold water. Bring to the boil over a high heat, lower the heat and simmer the fruit for 5 minutes. Leave to cool. Whisk **2 egg yolks** in a bowl with **75g caster sugar** and **200g low-fat Greek yogurt**. Transfer to a small pan and warm gently over a low heat, stirring continuously, for 10 minutes or until the mixture thickens slightly. Remove the pan from the heat. Mash **1 ripe banana** with **¼ teaspoon ground cinnamon, juice of ½ lemon** and **200g low-fat plain yogurt**. Stir this mixture into the pan. Add the blueberries and any juice then stir again. Freeze in an ice-cream maker following the manufacturer's instructions, or transfer to a plastic lidded container and freeze for at least 5 hours, removing from the freezer every hour and beating to remove any ice crystals. When ready to serve, leave the iced yogurt at room temperature for 15 minutes to thaw slightly then cut into slices or scoop into bowls.

COOK'S TIPS

★ Serve two scoops of iced yogurt in a glass bowl with a crunchy biscuit or wafer per person.

Colour-burst crème brûlée

Serves 4
Preparation 5 minutes Cooking 12 minutes
Chilling 1 hour

Each serving provides • 185kcal • 2g protein • 16g carbohydrates of which 12g sugars • 13g fat of which 8g saturates • 1g fibre

Preheat the grill to the hottest setting. Place **125g blueberries**, 1 tablespoon of water and **2 teaspoons caster sugar** in a saucepan over a medium-high heat and simmer for 2 minutes. Spoon the blueberries, and any juice that has run out, into the base of four 250ml (9cm diameter) ramekins. Crush **2 digestive biscuits** by putting them into a plastic bag and crushing them with a rolling pin. Gently beat **300ml half-fat crème fraîche** with **1 teaspoon vanilla extract** in a bowl and stir in the biscuit crumbs. Spoon the mixture over the blueberries and level the surface with a flat-edged knife or spatula. Sprinkle **1 level tablespoon brown sugar** evenly over each ramekin and grill for 10 minutes or until the sugar caramelises. Cool slightly before transferring to the fridge to chill for 1 hour or until the tops harden.

COOK'S TIPS

★ For a nutty crème brûlée, replace the biscuits with 2 tablespoons chopped blanched almonds.

Blueberry and buttermilk muffins

Makes 6
Preparation 20 minutes, plus 15 minutes cooling
Cooking 25 minutes

Each serving provides • 287kcal • 9g protein • 52g carbohydrates of which 18g sugars • 6g fat of which 1g saturates • 4g fibre

Preheat the oven to 180°C (160°C fan oven), gas 4. In a large bowl, combine **100g self-raising flour** with **100g wholemeal self-raising flour, 1 teaspoon baking powder, zest of ½ lemon** and **50g light soft brown sugar**. In another bowl, beat **1 egg** and stir in **150ml buttermilk** and **1 tablespoon sunflower oil**. Using a large metal spoon, gently stir the wet ingredients into the dry ingredients. Add **125g blueberries**. Spoon the mixture into six muffin cases placed in a muffin tin and bake for 25 minutes or until risen and golden. Cool in the tin for 15 minutes then transfer to a wire rack.

COOK'S TIPS

★ Use skimmed milk or low-fat pouring yogurt if you cannot get buttermilk.
★ The muffins will keep fresh for 48 hours in an airtight container but are best eaten soon after baking.

Fruit explosion muesli

Serves 4
Preparation 10 minutes, plus 15 minutes standing

Each serving provides • 295kcal • 8g protein • 41g carbohydrates of which 22g sugars • 12g fat of which 1g saturates • 6g fibre

Place **100g rolled oats** in a large bowl and then stir in **1 tablespoon sunflower seeds, 1 tablespoon pumpkin seeds, 25g chopped hazelnuts, 25g chopped almonds** and **1 tablespoon finely chopped ready-to-eat dried apricots**. Add **2 grated dessert apples** with the skins still on and **125g blueberries**. Pour in **200ml orange juice**, stir again and leave to soak for 15 minutes. When ready to serve, divide the muesli between four bowls and add **½ teaspoon brown sugar** and **1 heaped tablespoon plain yogurt** to each bowl.

COOK'S TIPS

★ For variety, include a mix of wholegrains, such as wheat or rye flakes, in addition to the rolled oats.
★ For a muesli with added crunch, roughly chop the apricots and leave the almonds whole.

Poached **peaches** and **pears** in a **blueberry** jus

Few things are more mouth-watering than a juicy peach and a ripe pear, and poaching is a great way to make them extra delectable. Using nothing but the goodness of fresh fruit and juice guarantees a sweet but healthy dessert.

Serves 4
Preparation 5 minutes
Cooking 30 minutes

Each serving provides • 194kcal
• 1g protein • 48g carbohydrates of which 47g sugars • no fat • 5g fibre

1 litre blueberry juice drink
2 large firm peaches
2 large pears
120g blueberries

ALTERNATIVE INGREDIENTS
• A smart way to combine the first pears of the season with late-fruiting raspberries is to use raspberry juice drink instead of blueberry juice drink and top the peaches and pears with 120g raspberries in place of blueberries.
• Try dried peaches or mango slices instead of fresh peaches. Use 2 ready-to-eat dried peach halves per portion or 3 mango slices. Poach the dried fruit with the pears for 5 minutes.

1 Pour the blueberry juice drink into a large saucepan. Halve and stone the peaches, leaving on the skins, then add them to the pan as they are prepared. Peel, halve and core the pears and add them to the pan.

2 Bring the blueberry juice drink to the boil over a high heat, reduce the heat to medium so that the juice is simmering and poach the fruit for 10 minutes or until tender – test the fruit with the point of a knife. Use a draining spoon to transfer the fruit to a bowl, then set aside.

3 Increase the heat to high again and boil the blueberry juice drink for 20 minutes or until it is reduced to a thick glaze. Watch it carefully after 10 minutes to ensure it does not boil over. Divide the fruit between four bowls and spoon a little glaze over each portion. Top with fresh blueberries and serve.

COOK'S TIPS

★ Firm peaches do not shed their skins when cooked but become tender and juicy. They also retain their heat better than peeled fruit and should remain warm while the juice drink is boiled down.
★ For a healthy breakfast treat, prepare the glazed fruit the day before, then cool, cover and store in the fridge overnight.

SUPERFOOD

PEACHES
Low in calories, peaches make a perfect healthy snack or dessert, with vitamin C to fortify the body's immune system. Peaches also contain beta-carotene, which the body converts to vitamin A for healthy skin and eyes.

Wicked **chocolate** and **pecan** dip

Rich dark chocolate, crunchy nuts and sticky honey combine for a tempting dip that is actually chock full of healthy fruit. A little goes a long way – so, take it easy and you will be more saint than sinner.

Serves 4
Preparation 10 minutes
Cooking 5 minutes

Each serving provides • 386kcal • 6g protein • 49g carbohydrates of which 48g sugars • 20g fat of which 7g saturates • 3g fibre

120g dark plain chocolate
4 tsp runny honey
50g pecan nuts
120g fromage frais
fresh fruit to serve, such as physalis, cherries, pineapple, mandarin segments, strawberries, banana, about 180g per person

ALTERNATIVE INGREDIENTS
• Use maple syrup instead of honey.
• Walnuts make a great alternative to pecan nuts.
• For added warmth, add a pinch of ground cinnamon, ground mixed spice or grated nutmeg to the chocolate with the nuts.

1 Break the chocolate into 2cm pieces and place them in a small heatproof bowl. Drizzle in the honey and place the bowl over a saucepan of simmering water set over a low heat for 5 minutes, stirring occasionally, until the chocolate has melted. Finely chop the pecans.

2 Remove the bowl from the pan and cool slighty. Stir in 2 tablespoons of the fromage frais and the pecans. Gradually stir in the remaining fromage frais and transfer the dipping sauce to one large serving bowl or four individual bowls. Serve the sauce warm with the fresh fruit to dip.

3 Prepare a selection of fresh fruit for serving with the chocolate and nut dipping sauce. Cut the fruit into bite-size pieces and arrange them on a serving dish.

COOK'S TIPS
★ To prevent chocolate splitting when it is being melted, use a small pan that fits neatly under the bowl. It is essential to avoid getting water or steam in the chocolate because this will make the fat separate from the chocolate solids. Do not overheat chocolate.

SUPERFOOD

PECAN NUTS
Rich in beneficial cholesterol-lowering unsaturated fats, pecans are good for the heart. In addition, they are high in fibre, omega-3 oils, some B vitamins and vitamin E for healthy skin. Pecans also contain flavonoids, potent plant-based antioxidants that may help to protect against cancer.

Hot **fruit puds** topped with **hazelnut praline**

Succulent dried pears, tart cooking apples and luscious raspberries nestle under a layer of creamy yogurt, sprinkled with a crunchy nut praline. Each mouthful promises plenty of vitamins and calcium.

Serves 4
Preparation 5 minutes, plus
  2 minutes standing
Cooking 10 minutes
Chilling 30 minutes

350g cooking apples
100g dried pears
200g raspberries
500g Greek-style yogurt
100g roasted chopped hazelnuts
50g granulated sugar

Each serving provides • 409kcal
• 11g protein • 41g carbohydrates of
which 40g sugars • 24g fat of which
6g saturates • 6g fibre

ALTERNATIVE INGREDIENTS
• Pitted cherries make a succulent
replacement for raspberries.
• Flaked almonds are a good
alternative to hazelnuts. Buy them
ready toasted or grill for 1 minute
under a medium-hot heat before
adding the sugar.

1 Peel, core and slice the apples into 1cm wedges and place in a large saucepan. Add 4 tablespoons of boiling water and bring back to the boil over a high heat. Cover the pan, reduce the heat and simmer for 4 minutes, stirring once.

2 Slice the dried pears into 1cm wedges. Stir the pears into the apples and remove the pan from the heat. Mix in the raspberries and divide the fruit between four bowls. Spoon the yogurt over the fruit. Cover and leave to cool, then chill in the fridge for 30 minutes, ready for finishing with the nut topping.

3 To make the praline, mix the hazelnuts and sugar in a heavy-based frying pan. Place over a high heat for 1-2 minutes until the sugar begins to melt. Shake the pan and continue to cook, stirring frequently, for a further 1-2 minutes or until the sugar turns golden brown.

4 Working quickly so that the sugar does not burn on the hot pan, spoon the praline on top of the desserts. Then leave to stand for 1-2 minutes so the praline is not too hot when served.

COOK'S TIPS

★ Praline is a crunchy sweet made by boiling nuts in sugar. If serving the desserts in glass dishes, turn the praline out onto a lightly oiled baking tray to cool slightly as the heat may crack the glass.
★ The praline topping can be made, cooled and stored in an airtight jar. It will keep for several months, ready for sprinkling over fruit compotes or yogurt.

SUPERFOOD

YOGURT
One small pot of yogurt a day provides
nearly one-third of your daily calcium
needs. Bio-yogurt (probiotic) contains
lactobacillus and bifido bacteria, which,
if eaten regularly, can boost 'friendly'
bacteria in the bowel and colon,
helping to maintain and promote
healthy digestion.

Warm **cherry** and **chocolate** trifle

Biscotti make a crunchy base for a medley of cherries and blueberries, coated in a smooth chocolate sauce. The fruit bursts with potassium, helping to keep blood pressure under control.

Serves 4
Preparation 10 minutes
Cooking 5 minutes

6 biscotti, about 180g
425g can pitted cherries
   in juice or syrup
150g blueberries
2 tbsp cornflour
2 tbsp cocoa powder
300ml semi-skimmed milk
1 tsp vanilla extract
2 tbsp granulated sugar
40g white chocolate chips

Each serving provides • 479kcal • 9g protein • 89g carbohydrates of which 52g sugars • 11g fat of which 6g saturates • 2g fibre

ALTERNATIVE INGREDIENTS
• Use amaretti biscuits or almond macaroons instead of biscotti.

1 Break the biscotti biscuits in half and divide them between four dishes (3 halves per dish). Drain the cherries using a bowl to catch the juice. Spoon the juice over the biscotti and then leave to soak for 5 minutes before topping with the cherries and blueberries.

2 Whisk the cornflour and cocoa powder with a little of the milk in a small saucepan. Gradually whisk in the remaining milk. Use a spatula to scrape up any cornflour from the bottom of the pan.

3 Put the pan on a medium to medium-high heat and bring the sauce to the boil, whisking continuously. Reduce the heat and simmer, stirring gently, for 2 minutes. Whisk in the vanilla extract and sugar.

4 Pour the sauce over the fruit. Sprinkle with the chocolate chips and use the tip of a knife to swirl the chocolate around as it melts.

COOK'S TIPS
★ Try flavoured biscotti, such as almond and chocolate or ones that contain pistachios.
★ Check that the cherries are pitted before buying them. Some bottled and canned cherries contain stones.
★ Adding sugar to the milk and cocoa sauce at the end of cooking helps to prevent it from browning and sticking to the pan. The milk and cocoa sauce may seem too thick before the sugar is added, but as the sugar melts, your sauce will thin to the correct consistency.
★ Instead of chocolate chips, break a bar of chocolate into squares, place in a bowl, then use a rolling pin to crush into tiny pieces.

SUPERFOOD

CHERRIES
High in fibre, cherries are good for digestive health. They are rich in health-protecting anthocyanins, and also contain plenty of potassium that can help to regulate blood pressure.

Index

Superfoods are shown in **bold**. Page numbers in *italic* indicate where superfood nutritional information can be found.

A

almonds *73, 268*
banana split with iced yogurt 257
creamy avocado and aubergine stacks 82
fruit explosion muesli 273
fruity tea bread 256
golden squash with peppers and almonds 66
Indian lamb with apricots 169
quick mixed berry and almond delights 268
smooth red pepper and tomato sauce 206-7
spring greens stir-fry with ham and toasted almonds 73
trout with almonds and vibrant peppers 104
winter barley soup 147
apples *90, 251*
apple and ginger smoothie 91
baked oaty apples 90
carrot, apple and beetroot salad 91
fig, apple and cinnamon compote 91
fruit explosion muesli 273
fruity chicory and apple salad 88
gorgeous pasta salad 147
hot fruit puds topped with hazelnut praline 279
juicy apples with oat and seed crunch 251
tender pork steaks with blueberry and apple sauce 190
walnut and apple stuffing 90-91
apricots *140, 169*
apricot and banana crumble 256-7
fruit explosion muesli 273
ginger and apricot rarebit 51
Indian lamb with apricots 169
tarragon chicken with tangy apricot sauce 140
asparagus *47*
asparagus and ham grill 47
asparagus and mushroom sushi 231
herby asparagus omelettes 69
aubergines *79*
creamy avocado and aubergine stacks 82
lightly spiced vegetable medley 92
ratatouille with feta gratin 79
avocados *82*
creamy avocado and aubergine stacks 82
creamy lentil soup with croutons 27

golden chicken and avocado salad 207
oat-crunch fish with avocado salsa 114
summer seafood salad 57
Tex-Mex chicken wraps 147

B

bacon (and pancetta)
delicate sole wraps with grapes and savoury white sauce 121
savoury bacon pilaf with berries and nuts 223
wilted greens, crispy bacon and pine nuts on polenta 95
bananas *60, 256*
banana split with iced yogurt 257
berry iced yogurt 272-3
fruity banana and date breakfast bagel 60
fruity tea bread 256
pan-fried bananas in a sweet citrus sauce 257
scrumptious raspberry, banana and oat smoothie 62
sunshine smoothie 257
wicked chocolate and pecan dip 276
zesty orange and banana medley 254
beans *38, 214*
crispy coriander mackerel with zesty beans 107
fresh tuna and zesty bean salad 37
fruity butternut squash casserole with papaya 214
light and spicy turkey chilli 152
rich chicken and bean hotpot 39
spicy Caribbean rice 39
summer bean risotto 38-39
three bean salad with lemon and walnut dressing 226
see also **broad beans; flageolet beans; green beans**
beansprouts
chicken and ginger fried rice 229
Indonesian fried rice with egg and vegetables 213
Malaysian laksa with prawns and vegetables 208
Oriental chicken stir-fry with cashew nuts 138
spinach, beef and beansprout stir-fry 175
Thai noodles with cashews and stir-fried vegetables 210
beef *174, 176 (red meat)*
beef and vegetable bolognese sauce 174-5
devilled steak with pepper batons 172
Italian summer casserole 174
paprika beef fajitas 175
sizzling beef and sweet pepper burgers 176

spinach, beef and beansprout stir-fry 175
steak and beetroot stroganoff 178
sweet potato and mushroom cottage pie 175
beetroot *43, 178*
beetroot and cranberry borscht 22
beetroot and mozzarella with raspberry dressing 43
carrot, apple and beetroot salad 91
steak and beetroot stroganoff 178
berries *261*
quick mixed berry and almond delights 268
warm berries on toasted brioche 261
see also **blueberries; cranberries; raspberries; strawberries**
blueberries *261 (mixed berries), 272*
berry iced yogurt 272-3
blueberry and buttermilk muffins 273
chocolatey orange and blueberry soufflés 252
colour-burst crème brûlée 273
fruit explosion muesli 273
individual summer puddings 272
pearl barley pilaf with emerald vegetables 236
poached peaches and pears in a blueberry jus 274
spiced rhubarb and blueberry compote 270
tender pork steaks with blueberry and apple sauce 190
warm cherry and chocolate trifle 281
broad beans *38 (beans), 87*
chunky fish and vegetable soup 34
fluffy quinoa with vibrant summer vegetables 234
warm citrus bean salad 38
warm potato and broad bean salad 87
broccoli *74, 76*
broccoli, carrot and mushroom stir-fry 77
broccoli mash with poached egg 74
broccoli pâté 76
brown rice, lentil and carrot salad 19
gorgeous pasta salad 147
Italian pasta with pine nuts 77
lamb medallions with redcurrant jus 166
salmon and broccoli risotto 110-11
sesame-infused peppers with broccoli 207
summer broccoli and lemon soup 76

sunshine kedgeree with sweetcorn and broccoli 220
sweet potato, broccoli and lentil salad 77
brown rice *213, 223*
brown rice, lentil and carrot salad 19
cheesy-crust baked tomatoes 56
chicken and rice broth with shredded omelette 21
Indonesian fried rice with egg and vegetables 213
savoury bacon pilaf with berries and nuts 223
seafood and vegetable rice 218
spicy Caribbean rice 39
turkey souvlaki with grilled vegetables 154
bulgur wheat
herby bulgur wheat with chorizo 242
minted mixed grain salad 216
piquant pepper tabbouleh with cranberries 232
butternut squash *66*
fruity butternut squash casserole with papaya 214
golden squash with peppers and almonds 66
squash, spinach and hazelnut gratin 238

C

cabbages *22, 190*
beetroot and cranberry borscht 22
chilli prawn and pea stir-fry 124
fruity pork steaks with glazed plums and red cabbage 194
ham and sweet potato bubble and squeak 183
herbed chicken with cranberry coleslaw 143
savoury bacon pilaf with berries and nuts 223
tender pork steaks with blueberry and apple sauce 190
wilted greens, crispy bacon and pine nuts on polenta 95
carrots *16, 18*
aromatic pork kebabs 186
beef and vegetable bolognese sauce 174-5
broccoli, carrot and mushroom stir-fry 77
brown rice, lentil and carrot salad 19
carrot, apple and beetroot salad 91
carrot pancakes with prosciutto and silky mango 40
chicken and rice broth with shredded omelette 21
chilled carrot and orange soup 16
chunky vegetable soup with pasta 14

creamy lentil soup with croutons 27

gamy venison sausages with sweetcorn relish 162

herbed chicken with cranberry coleslaw 143

herby carrot and coriander soup 18

honey-braised carrots with petit pois 19

Indonesian fried rice with egg and vegetables 213

layered veggie casserole 18-19

light and spicy turkey chilli 152

lightly spiced vegetable medley 92

one-pot fish casserole with spicy yogurt 101

Oriental chicken stir-fry with cashew nuts 138

sausages and supermash with onion relish 193

sizzling beef and sweet pepper burgers 176

springtime vegetable soup 25

sweet and sour noodles 19

sweet potato and mushroom cottage pie 175

warming cock-a-leekie soup with kale 30

winter barley soup 147

cashew nuts *138*

broccoli, carrot and mushroom stir-fry 77

carrot, apple and beetroot salad 91

Oriental chicken stir-fry with cashew nuts 138

Thai noodles with cashews and stir-fried vegetables 210

cauliflower *130*

lightly spiced vegetable medley 92

prawn goulash with cauliflower and beans 130

celery *202*

beef and vegetable bolognese sauce 174-5

beetroot and cranberry borscht 22

chicken and rice broth with shredded omelette 21

chunky vegetable soup with pasta 14

citrus fish with sautéed leeks and courgettes 117

creamy lentil soup with croutons 27

delicate sole wraps with grapes and savoury white sauce 121

fiery Italian vegetable pasta 202

lightly spiced vegetable medley 92

minted celery houmous 52

one-pot fish casserole with spicy yogurt 101

Oriental chicken stir-fry with cashew nuts 138

pearl barley pilaf with emerald vegetables 236

pepper and tomato soup with a spicy egg 33

rich chicken and bean hotpot 39

savoury bacon pilaf with berries and nuts 223

sesame squid with Oriental vegetables 132

winter barley soup 147

cheese *51*

beetroot and mozzarella with raspberry dressing 43

cheesy vegetable frittata 54

colourful tofu-stuffed peppers 70

creamy avocado and aubergine stacks 82

eggs florentine 238-9

filled filo tartlets 239

fluffy quinoa with vibrant summer vegetables 234

ginger and apricot rarebit 51

sweet pepper and turkey grill with glazed mango 151

warm berries on toasted brioche 261

see also feta cheese; mozzarella cheese; Parmesan cheese; **soft cheese**

cherries *180, 281*

veal escalopes in brandy sauce with sour cherries 180

warm cherry and chocolate trifle 281

wicked chocolate and pecan dip 276

chicken *144, 146, 229*

aromatic chicken with zesty grilled vegetables 137

chicken and ginger fried rice 229

chicken and rice broth with shredded omelette 21

golden chicken and avocado salad 207

gorgeous pasta salad 147

herbed chicken with cranberry coleslaw 143

lazy days bake 146-7

Oriental chicken stir-fry with cashew nuts 138

rich chicken and bean hotpot 39

sophisticated chicken salad 146

Spanish chicken with peppers and olives 144

summer chicken risotto with green peas 240

tarragon chicken with tangy apricot sauce 140

Tex-Mex chicken wraps 147

warming cock-a-leekie soup with kale 30

winter barley soup 147

chicken livers *148*

sherry-infused chicken livers with mushrooms and beans 148

chickpeas *52*

Greek salad with chickpeas 224

minted celery houmous 52

chicory *88*

fruity chicory and apple salad 88

potato and courgette medley with pickled herring 128

chillies

chilli prawn and pea stir-fry 124

feta and chilli pepper sandwich spread 207

fiery Italian vegetable pasta 202

ginger salmon kebabs 111

Italian pasta with pine nuts 77

juicy veggie kebabs 206

light and spicy turkey chilli 152

Malaysian laksa with prawns and vegetables 208

paprika beef fajitas 175

pepper and tomato soup with a spicy egg 33

piquant pepper tabbouleh with cranberries 232

sesame squid with Oriental vegetables 132

spicy Caribbean rice 39

spicy Punjabi peas with lamb 126

spinach, beef and beansprout stir-fry 175

sweet and sour noodles 19

tropical mango and salmon salad 111

turkey souvlaki with grilled vegetables 154

chocolate

chocolatey orange and blueberry soufflés 252

warm cherry and chocolate trifle 281

wicked chocolate and pecan dip 276

citrus fruit *188*

see also **grapefruit**; **lemons**; **limes**; **oranges**

clementine and red onion chutney 189

coconut milk

Malaysian laksa with prawns and vegetables 208

spicy Caribbean rice 39

tropical mango and salmon salad 111

courgettes *137*

aromatic chicken with zesty grilled vegetables 137

cheesy vegetable frittata 54

citrus fish with sautéed leeks and courgettes 117

pepper shells with cheesy pasta 205

potato and courgette medley with pickled herring 128

ratatouille with feta gratin 79

sausages and supermash with onion relish 193

sesame squid with Oriental vegetables 132

cranberries *261 (mixed berries), 143, 232*

beetroot and cranberry borscht 22

herbed chicken with cranberry coleslaw 143

piquant pepper tabbouleh with cranberries 232

savoury bacon pilaf with berries and nuts 223

walnut and apple stuffing 90-91

cucumbers

aromatic chicken with zesty grilled vegetables 137

Chinese duck with pancakes 158

chunky fish and vegetable soup 34

Greek salad with chickpeas 224

herby bulgur wheat with chorizo 242

Malaysian laksa with prawns and vegetables 208

minted mixed grain salad 216

sophisticated chicken salad 146

spring greens stir-fry with ham and toasted almonds 73

tropical mango and salmon salad 111

turkey souvlaki with grilled vegetables 154

curries

Indian lamb with apricots 169

spicy Punjabi peas with lamb 126-7

Thai noodles with cashews and stir-fried vegetables 210

D

duck

Chinese duck with pancakes 158

succulent duck with chestnuts and prunes 156

E

eggs *21, 69*

berry iced yogurt 272-3

broccoli mash with poached egg 74

broccoli pâté 76

carrot pancakes with prosciutto and silky mango 40

cheesy vegetable frittata 54

chicken and rice broth with shredded omelette 21

chocolatey orange and blueberry soufflés 252

citrus pancakes 188-9

eggs florentine 238-9

filled filo tartlets 239

fruity tea bread 256

healthy mixed grill with tomatoes 80

herby asparagus omelettes 69

Indonesian fried rice with egg and vegetables 213

pepper and tomato soup with a spicy egg 33

quick mixed berry and almond delights 268
salmon niçoise 110
sizzling beef and sweet pepper burgers 176
squash, spinach and hazelnut gratin 238
sunshine kedgeree with sweetcorn and broccoli 220
walnut and apple stuffing 90-1

F

feta cheese
feta and chilli pepper sandwich spread 207
glazed pears with feta cheese 84
Greek salad with chickpeas 224
ratatouille with feta gratin 79
squash, spinach and hazelnut gratin 238
fish *34*
chunky fish and vegetable soup 34
citrus fish with sautéed leeks and courgettes 117
delicate sole wraps with grapes and savoury white sauce 121
herb and walnut crusted fish fillets 118
oat-crunch fish with avocado salsa 114
one-pot fish casserole with spicy yogurt 101
potato and courgette medley with pickled herring 128
sunshine kedgeree with sweetcorn and broccoli 220
see also **herring; mackerel; salmon; sardines; seafood; trout; tuna**
flageolet beans *166*
lamb medallions with redcurrant jus 166

G

garlic *208*
ginger *158*
apple and ginger smoothie 91
brown rice, lentil and carrot salad 19
chicken and ginger fried rice 229
chilli prawn and pea stir-fry 124
Chinese duck with pancakes 158
cool pineapple and kiwi medley with gingernut cream 264
ginger and apricot rarebit 51
ginger salmon kebabs 111
Malaysian laksa with prawns and vegetables 208
sesame-infused peppers with broccoli 207
spiced rhubarb and blueberry compote 270
spicy Punjabi peas with lamb 126
spinach, beef and beansprout stir-fry 175

sweet potato, broccoli and lentil salad 77
grapefruit *188 (citrus fruit)*
pink grapefruit and pomegranate salad 189
sunrise fruit salad 188
grapes *121*
delicate sole wraps with grapes and savoury white sauce 121
strawberry, grape and pistachio flowers 263
sunrise fruit salad 188
green beans *38 (beans)*, *171*
healthy mixed grill with tomatoes 80
Indonesian fried rice with egg and vegetables 213
Mediterranean green beans 39
prawn goulash with cauliflower and beans 130
salmon niçoise 110
sautéed lamb and green beans with creamy caper sauce 171
seafood and vegetable rice 218
sherry-infused chicken livers with mushrooms and beans 148
three bean salad with lemon and walnut dressing 226

H

ham
asparagus and ham grill 47
ham and sweet potato bubble and squeak 183
spring greens stir-fry with ham and toasted almonds 73
sweet pepper and turkey grill with glazed mango 151
see also prosciutto
hazelnuts *248*
fruit explosion muesli 273
hot fruit puds topped with hazelnut praline 279
squash, spinach and hazelnut gratin 238
warm spiced plums with hazelnut yogurt 248
herring *128*
potato and courgette medley with pickled herring 128
honey
baked oaty apples 90
beetroot and mozzarella with raspberry dressing 43
broccoli, carrot and mushroom stir-fry 77
citrus pancakes 188-9
fruity banana and date breakfast bagel 60
fruity tea bread 256
gamy venison sausages with sweetcorn relish 162
golden chicken and avocado salad 207
honey-braised carrots with petit pois 19

kiwi fruit cheesecake with lime honey 258
quick mixed berry and almond delights 268
raspberry creams with mango and honey sauce 246
scrumptious raspberry, banana and oat smoothie 62
strawberry, grape and pistachio flowers 263
sweet and sour noodles 19
three bean salad with lemon and walnut dressing 226
warm spiced plums with hazelnut yogurt 248
wicked chocolate and pecan dip 276

K

kidney beans
light and spicy turkey chilli 152
kiwi fruit
cool pineapple and kiwi medley with gingernut cream 264
kiwi fruit cheesecake with lime honey 258

L

lamb
Indian lamb with apricots 169
lamb medallions with redcurrant jus 166
sautéed lamb and green beans with creamy caper sauce 171
spicy Punjabi peas with lamb 126
leeks *30*
chunky fish and vegetable soup 34
citrus fish with sautéed leeks and courgettes 117
crispy coriander mackerel with zesty beans 107
delicate sole wraps with grapes and savoury white sauce 121
ham and sweet potato bubble and squeak 183
Italian spirals with watercress and olive dressing 198
lamb medallions with redcurrant jus 166
Mediterranean seafood pie 123
minted pesto with leeks and peas 127
one-pot fish casserole with spicy yogurt 101
pearl barley pilaf with emerald vegetables 236
sesame squid with Oriental vegetables 132
spring greens stir-fry with ham and toasted almonds 73
sweet and sour noodles 19
tender pork steaks with blueberry and apple sauce 190
warming cock-a-leekie soup with kale 30

lemons *188 (citrus fruit)*
apricot and banana crumble 256-7
aromatic chicken with zesty grilled vegetables 137
banana split with iced yogurt 257
berry iced yogurt 272-3
blueberry and buttermilk muffins 273
broccoli mash with poached egg 74
chunky fish and vegetable soup 34
citrus pancakes 188-9
creamy avocado and aubergine stacks 82
creamy lentil soup with croutons 27
crispy coriander mackerel with zesty beans 107
fiery Italian vegetable pasta 202
fresh tuna and zesty bean salad 37
ginger salmon kebabs 111
golden squash with peppers and almonds 66
herby carrot and coriander soup 18
individual summer puddings 272
Italian spirals with watercress and olive dressing 198
lazy days bake 146-7
lemon and pea sauce 127
lightly spiced vegetable medley 92
minted celery houmous 52
minted mixed grain salad 216
pan-fried salmon on a bed of baby spinach 108
savoury spinach with peas 239
sesame squid with Oriental vegetables 132
sherry-infused chicken livers with mushrooms and beans 148
summer bean risotto 38-9
summer broccoli and lemon soup 76
sunshine kedgeree with sweetcorn and broccoli 220
sunshine smoothie 257
tangy sardine pâté 44
three bean salad with lemon and walnut dressing 226
warm citrus bean salad 38
lentils *27*
brown rice, lentil and carrot salad 19
creamy lentil soup with croutons 27
sweet potato, broccoli and lentil salad 77
limes *188 (citrus fruit) 258*
glazed pears with feta cheese 84
golden chicken and avocado salad 207
kiwi fruit cheesecake with lime honey 258

pork fillets with lime
gremolata 189
spring greens stir-fry with ham
and toasted almonds 73
tropical mango and salmon
salad 111

M

mackerel *107*
crispy coriander mackerel with
zesty beans 107
mangetout
chicken and ginger fried rice 229
creamy Italian mangetout with
pasta 127
Oriental chicken stir-fry with
cashew nuts 138
spring greens stir-fry with ham
and toasted almonds 73
mangos *40*
carrot pancakes with prosciutto
and silky mango 40
raspberry creams with mango
and honey sauce 246
sweet pepper and turkey grill with
glazed mango 151
tropical mango and salmon
salad 111
mozzarella cheese
beetroot and mozzarella with
raspberry dressing 43
tricolore tomato towers 57
mushrooms *48, 152*
asparagus and mushroom
sushi 231
broccoli, carrot and mushroom
stir-fry 77
cheesy-crust baked tomatoes 56
chunky vegetable soup with
pasta 14
creamy mushroom feast with
tagliatelle 200
healthy mixed grill with
tomatoes 80
juicy garlic mushrooms with sun-
dried tomatoes 48
juicy veggie kebabs 206
light and spicy turkey chilli 152
one-pot fish casserole with spicy
yogurt 101
Oriental chicken stir-fry with
cashew nuts 138
rustic spinach and mushroom
pasta 239
seared tuna steaks in a warm
herb dressing 103
sherry-infused chicken livers with
mushrooms and beans 148
steak and beetroot
stroganoff 178
sweet potato and mushroom
cottage pie 175
Thai noodles with cashews and
stir-fried vegetables 210
veal escalopes in brandy sauce
with sour cherries 180
winter barley soup 147

N

nectarines *161*
pan-fried venison with nectarine
chutney 161
noodles
Malaysian laksa with prawns and
vegetables 208
sweet and sour noodles 19
Thai noodles with cashews and
stir-fried vegetables 210
nori *231*
asparagus and mushroom
sushi 231
nuts
apricot and banana
crumble 256-7
Indonesian satay pork with
peppers 185
see also individual nut entries

O

oats *114, 172*
apricot and banana
crumble 256-7
baked oaty apples 90
devilled steak with pepper
batons 172
fruit explosion muesli 273
juicy apples with oat and seed
crunch 251
oat-crunch fish with avocado
salsa 114
quick mixed berry and almond
delights 268
scrumptious raspberry, banana
and oat smoothie 62
sizzling beef and sweet pepper
burgers 176
olive oil *59, 224*
olives
broccoli mash with poached
egg 74
fiery Italian vegetable pasta 202
Greek salad with chickpeas 224
Italian spirals with watercress
and olive dressing 198
pan-fried salmon on a bed of
baby spinach 108
Spanish chicken with peppers
and olives 144
onions *185, 193*
oranges *117, 188 (citrus fruit), 254*
aromatic pork kebabs 186
chilled carrot and orange
soup 16
chocolatey orange and blueberry
soufflés 252
citrus fish with sautéed leeks
and courgettes 117
citrus pancakes 188-9
clementine and red onion
chutney 189
fig, apple and cinnamon
compote 91
fruit explosion muesli 273
fruity butternut squash casserole
with papaya 214

pan-fried bananas in a sweet
citrus sauce 257
succulent duck with chestnuts
and prunes 156
sunrise fruit salad 188
sunshine smoothie 257
tarragon chicken with tangy
apricot sauce 140
wicked chocolate and pecan
dip 276
zesty orange and banana
medley 254

P

pak choi
chicken and rice broth with
shredded omelette 21
sesame squid with Oriental
vegetables 132
Thai noodles with cashews and
stir-fried vegetables 210
Parmesan cheese
asparagus and ham grill 47
broccoli pâté 76
cheesy-crust baked tomatoes 56
chunky vegetable soup with
pasta 14
creamy Italian mangetout with
pasta 127
fiery Italian vegetable
pasta 202
filled filo tartlets 239
Italian pasta with pine nuts 77
Italian spirals with watercress
and olive dressing 198
Mediterranean seafood pie 123
pepper shells with cheesy
pasta 205
rustic spinach and mushroom
pasta 239
salmon and broccoli risotto
110-11
squash, spinach and hazelnut
gratin 238
summer bean risotto 38-39
walnut and basil pesto pasta 59
parsley *25*
beetroot and mozzarella with
raspberry dressing 43
broccoli mash with poached
egg 74
brown rice, lentil and carrot
salad 19
carrot pancakes with prosciutto
and silky mango 40
cheesy vegetable frittata 54
cheesy-crust baked tomatoes 56
creamy mushroom feast with
tagliatelle 200
fiery Italian vegetable pasta 202
fresh tuna and zesty bean
salad 37
Greek salad with chickpeas 224
healthy mixed grill with
tomatoes 80
herb and walnut crusted fish
fillets 118

Italian spirals with watercress
and olive dressing 198
Italian summer casserole 174
juicy garlic mushrooms with
sun-dried tomatoes 48
layered veggie casserole 18-19
lemon and pea sauce 127
minted mixed grain salad 216
no-cook tomato sauce with
pasta 56-57
one-pot fish casserole with spicy
yogurt 101
pork fillets with lime
gremolata 189
ratatouille with feta gratin 79
rich chicken and bean hotpot 39
salmon and broccoli
risotto 110-11
sautéed lamb and green beans
with creamy caper sauce 171
sherry-infused chicken livers with
mushrooms and beans 148
Spanish chicken with peppers
and olives 144
springtime vegetable soup 25
sunshine kedgeree with
sweetcorn and broccoli 220
walnut and apple stuffing 90-91
warm citrus bean salad 38
winter barley soup 147
pasta
creamy Italian mangetout with
pasta 127
creamy mushroom feast with
tagliatelle 200
fiery Italian vegetable pasta 202
Italian spirals with watercress
and olive dressing 198
no-cook tomato sauce with
pasta 56-57
pepper shells with cheesy
pasta 205
rustic spinach and mushroom
pasta 239
peaches *274*
poached peaches and pears in a
blueberry jus 274
pearl barley *236*
pearl barley pilaf with emerald
vegetables 236
winter barley soup 147
pears *84*
glazed pears with feta cheese 84
hot fruit puds topped with
hazelnut praline 279
poached peaches and pears in a
blueberry jus 274
peas *124, 126, 240*
chilli prawn and pea stir-fry 124
honey-braised carrots with petit
pois 19
lemon and pea sauce 127
light and spicy turkey chilli 152
minted pesto with leeks and
peas 127
peas à la française 126
savoury spinach with peas 239

seafood and vegetable rice 218
seared tuna steaks in a warm
	herb dressing 103
spicy Punjabi peas with
	lamb 126-7
spinach and pea soup with minty
	yogurt 28
summer chicken risotto with
	green peas 240
sweet potato medallions with
	minted pea purée 97
see also mangetout
pecan nuts 276
	fruity tea bread 256
	wicked chocolate and pecan
		dip 276
peppers 186, 206, 242
	aromatic pork kebabs 186
	Chinese duck with pancakes 158
	chunky vegetable soup with
		pasta 14
	colourful tofu-stuffed peppers 70
	devilled steak with pepper
		batons 172
	feta and chilli pepper sandwich
		spread 207
	gamy venison sausages with
		sweetcorn relish 162
	ginger salmon kebabs 111
	golden chicken and avocado
		salad 207
	golden squash with peppers and
		almonds 66
	gorgeous pasta salad 147
	Greek salad with chickpeas 224
	herby bulgur wheat with
		chorizo 242
	Indonesian satay pork with
		peppers 185
	Italian summer casserole 174
	juicy veggie kebabs 206
	light and spicy turkey chilli 152
	minted mixed grain salad 216
	oat-crunch fish with avocado
		salsa 114
	paprika beef fajitas 175
	pepper and tomato soup with a
		spicy egg 33
	pepper shells with cheesy
		pasta 205
	piquant pepper tabbouleh with
		cranberries 232
	seafood and vegetable rice 218
	sesame squid with Oriental
		vegetables 132
	sesame-infused peppers with
		broccoli 207
	sizzling beef and sweet pepper
		burgers 176
	smooth red pepper and tomato
		sauce 206-7
	Spanish chicken with peppers
		and olives 144
	spicy Caribbean rice 39
	summer seafood salad 57
	sweet pepper and turkey grill with
		glazed mango 151

Thai noodles with cashews and
	stir-fried vegetables 210
trout with almonds and vibrant
	peppers 104
turkey souvlaki with grilled
	vegetables 154
pine nuts 95
	crunchy baked salmon 111
	fig, apple and cinnamon
		compote 91
	Italian pasta with pine nuts 77
	pearl barley pilaf with emerald
		vegetables 236
	rustic spinach and mushroom
		pasta 239
	tarragon chicken with tangy
		apricot sauce 140
	tricolore tomato towers 57
	wilted greens, crispy bacon and
		pine nuts on polenta 95
pineapple 264
	cool pineapple and kiwi medley
		with gingernut cream 264
	wicked chocolate and pecan
		dip 276
pistachio nuts
	fruity chicory and apple salad 88
	Italian spirals with watercress
		and olive dressing 198
	strawberry, grape and pistachio
		flowers 263
plums 194
	fruity pork steaks with glazed
		plums and red cabbage 194
	warm spiced plums with hazelnut
		yogurt 248
pomegranates 112
	pink grapefruit and pomegranate
		salad 189
	succulent salmon with tangy
		pomegranate glaze 112
pork
	aromatic pork kebabs 186
	fruity pork steaks with glazed
		plums and red cabbage 194
	Indonesian satay pork with
		peppers 185
	pork fillets with lime
		gremolata 189
	sausages and supermash with
		onion relish 193
	tender pork steaks with blueberry
		and apple sauce 190
potatoes
	lamb medallions with redcurrant
		jus 166
	layered veggie casserole 18-19
	lightly spiced vegetable
		medley 92
	Mediterranean seafood pie 123
	one-pot fish casserole with spicy
		yogurt 101
	potato and courgette medley with
		pickled herring 128
	springtime vegetable soup 25
	squash, spinach and hazelnut
		gratin 238

summer broccoli and lemon
	soup 76
warm potato and broad bean
	salad 87
prawns
	chilli prawn and pea stir-fry 124
	Malaysian laksa with prawns and
		vegetables 208
	prawn goulash with cauliflower
		and beans 130
prosciutto
	carrot pancakes with prosciutto
		and silky mango 40
	filled filo tartlets 239
prunes 156
	juicy apples with oat and seed
		crunch 251
	succulent duck with chestnuts
		and prunes 156
	warming cock-a-leekie soup with
		kale 30

Q
quinoa 216, 234
	fluffy quinoa with vibrant summer
		vegetables 234
	minted mixed grain salad 216

R
raspberries 261 (mixed berries),
		62, 246
	banana split with iced yogurt 257
	beetroot and mozzarella with
		raspberry dressing 43
	hot fruit puds topped with
		hazelnut praline 279
	individual summer puddings 272
	raspberry creams with mango
		and honey sauce 246
	scrumptious raspberry, banana
		and oat smoothie 62
red meat 176
	see also **beef**; duck; lamb;
		venison
redcurrants 261 (mixed berries) 266
	delectable red berry
		pancakes 266
	lamb medallions with redcurrant
		jus 166
rhubarb 270
	spiced rhubarb and blueberry
		compote 270

S
salads
	beetroot and mozzarella with
		raspberry dressing 43
	brown rice, lentil and carrot
		salad 19
	carrot, apple and beetroot
		salad 91
	fresh tuna and zesty bean
		salad 37
	fruity chicory and apple salad 88
	glazed pears with feta cheese 84
	golden chicken and avocado
		salad 207

gorgeous pasta salad 147
Greek salad with chickpeas 224
minted mixed grain salad 216
pink grapefruit and pomegranate
	salad 189
salmon niçoise 110
sophisticated chicken salad 146
summer seafood salad 57
sunrise fruit salad 188
sweet potato, broccoli and lentil
	salad 77
three bean salad with lemon and
	walnut dressing 226
tropical mango and salmon
	salad 111
warm citrus bean salad 38
warm potato and broad bean
	salad 87
salmon 108, 110
	crunchy baked salmon 111
	ginger salmon kebabs 111
	one-pot fish casserole with spicy
		yogurt 101
	pan-fried salmon on a bed of
		baby spinach 108
	salmon and broccoli
		risotto 110-11
	salmon niçoise 110
	succulent salmon with tangy
		pomegranate glaze 112
	tropical mango and salmon
		salad 111
sardines 44
	tangy sardine pâté 44
sausages
	gamy venison sausages with
		sweetcorn relish 162
	sausages and supermash with
		onion relish 193
seafood 123, 218
	Mediterranean seafood pie 123
	seafood and vegetable rice 218
	sesame squid with Oriental
		vegetables 132
	summer seafood salad 57
sesame seeds 132
	brown rice, lentil and carrot
		salad 19
	sesame squid with Oriental
		vegetables 132
	sesame-infused peppers with
		broccoli 207
smoothies
	apple and ginger smoothie 91
	scrumptious raspberry, banana
		and oat smoothie 62
	sunshine smoothie 257
soft cheese 205
	asparagus and ham grill 47
	creamy Italian mangetout with
		pasta 127
	creamy mushroom feast with
		tagliatelle 200
	delicate sole wraps with grapes
		and savoury white sauce 121
	fruity banana and date breakfast
		bagel 60

kiwi fruit cheesecake with lime honey 258
pepper shells with cheesy pasta 205
raspberry creams with mango and honey sauce 246
sautéed lamb and green beans with creamy caper sauce 171
sweet potato medallions with minted pea purée 97
tangy sardine pâté 44
soups
beetroot and cranberry borscht 22
chicken and rice broth with shredded omelette 21
chilled carrot and orange soup 16
chunky fish and vegetable soup 34
chunky vegetable soup with pasta 14
classic tomato soup 57
creamy lentil soup with croutons 27
herby carrot and coriander soup 18
pepper and tomato soup with a spicy egg 33
spinach and pea soup with minty yogurt 28
springtime vegetable soup 25
summer broccoli and lemon soup 76
warming cock-a-leekie soup with kale 30
winter barley soup 147
soya beans *210*
Thai noodles with cashews and stir-fried vegetables 210
spinach *28, 92, 238*
eggs florentine 238-9
filled filo tartlets 239
lightly spiced vegetable medley 92
pan-fried salmon on a bed of baby spinach 108
pearl barley pilaf with emerald vegetables 236
rustic spinach and mushroom pasta 239
savoury spinach with peas 239
spinach and pea soup with minty yogurt 28
spinach, beef and beansprout stir-fry 175
squash, spinach and hazelnut gratin 238
wilted greens, crispy bacon and pine nuts on polenta 95
strawberries *261 (mixed berries), 263*
delectable red berry pancakes 266
strawberry, grape and pistachio flowers 263
wicked chocolate and pecan dip 276

sweet potatoes *97, 183*
ham and sweet potato bubble and squeak 183
lazy days bake 146-7
sweet potato, broccoli and lentil salad 77
sweet potato medallions with minted pea purée 97
sweet potato and mushroom cottage pie 175
sweetcorn *162, 220*
gamy venison sausages with sweetcorn relish 162
seared tuna steaks in a warm herb dressing 103
sunshine kedgeree with sweetcorn and broccoli 220
Tex-Mex chicken wraps 147

T
tofu *70*
colourful tofu-stuffed peppers 70
tomatoes *33, 56, 80*
beef and vegetable bolognese sauce 174-5
brown rice, lentil and carrot salad 19
cheesy vegetable frittata 54
cheesy-crust baked tomatoes 56
chunky fish and vegetable soup 34
chunky vegetable soup with pasta 14
classic tomato soup 57
colourful tofu-stuffed peppers 70
fiery Italian vegetable pasta 202
fluffy quinoa with vibrant summer vegetables 234
Greek salad with chickpeas 224
healthy mixed grill with tomatoes 80
Italian summer casserole 174
juicy garlic mushrooms with sun-dried tomatoes 48
light and spicy turkey chilli 152
Mediterranean green beans 39
Mediterranean seafood pie 123
minted mixed grain salad 216
no-cook tomato sauce with pasta 56-57
oat-crunch fish with avocado salsa 114
pan-fried salmon on a bed of baby spinach 108
pepper and tomato soup with a spicy egg 33
prawn goulash with cauliflower and beans 130
ratatouille with feta gratin 79
rich chicken and bean hotpot 39
salmon niçoise 110
sophisticated chicken salad 146
Spanish chicken with peppers and olives 144
spicy Caribbean rice 39

spicy Punjabi peas with lamb 126-7
summer seafood salad 57
sweet potato and mushroom cottage pie 175
sweet potato, broccoli and lentil salad 77
Tex-Mex chicken wraps 147
tricolore tomato towers 57
tortillas
paprika beef fajitas 175
Tex-Mex chicken wraps 147
trout *104*
trout with almonds and vibrant peppers 104
tuna *37, 103*
fresh tuna and zesty bean salad 37
seared tuna steaks in a warm herb dressing 103
turkey *151, 154*
light and spicy turkey chilli 152
sweet pepper and turkey grill with glazed mango 151
turkey souvlaki with grilled vegetables 154
turnips *54*
cheesy vegetable frittata 54

V
veal escalopes in brandy sauce with sour cherries 180
venison
gamy venison sausages with sweetcorn relish 162
pan-fried venison with nectarine chutney 161

W
walnuts *118*
creamy mushroom feast with tagliatelle 200
gorgeous pasta salad 147
herb and walnut crusted fish fillets 118
savoury bacon pilaf with berries and nuts 223
three bean salad with lemon and walnut dressing 226
walnut and apple stuffing 90-91
walnut and basil pesto pasta 59
water chestnuts
chicken and ginger fried rice 229
Indonesian fried rice with egg and vegetables 213
watercress *198*
ginger and apricot rarebit 51
Italian spirals with watercress and olive dressing 198
sophisticated chicken salad 146
white rice
chicken and ginger fried rice 229
salmon and broccoli risotto 110-11
Spanish chicken with peppers and olives 144
summer bean risotto 38-39

summer chicken risotto with green peas 240
sunshine kedgeree with sweetcorn and broccoli 220
wholewheat pasta *14*
chunky vegetable soup with pasta 14
gorgeous pasta salad 147
Italian pasta with pine nuts 77
walnut and basil pesto pasta 59

Y
yogurt *101, 279*
apple and ginger smoothie 91
banana split with iced yogurt 257
beetroot and cranberry borscht 22
berry iced yogurt 272-3
chilled carrot and orange soup 16
delectable red berry pancakes 266
fruit explosion muesli 273
gorgeous pasta salad 147
herbed chicken with cranberry coleslaw 143
herby bulgur wheat with chorizo 242
herby carrot and coriander soup 18
hot fruit puds topped with hazelnut praline 279
Indian lamb with apricots 169
juicy apples with oat and seed crunch 251
lightly spiced vegetable medley 92
one-pot fish casserole with spicy yogurt 101
potato and courgette medley with pickled herring 128
prawn goulash with cauliflower and beans 130
seared tuna steaks in a warm herb dressing 103
spicy Punjabi peas with lamb 126-7
spinach and pea soup with minty yogurt 28
squash, spinach and hazelnut gratin 238
steak and beetroot stroganoff 178
summer broccoli and lemon soup 76
sunshine smoothie 257
turkey souvlaki with grilled vegetables 154
warm spiced plums with hazelnut yogurt 248

Vivat Direct Project Team
Editor John Andrews
Art Editor Anne-Marie Bulat

For Vivat Direct
Editorial Director Julian Browne
Art Director Anne-Marie Bulat
Managing Editor Nina Hathway
Picture Resource Manager Sarah Stewart-Richardson
Pre-press Technical Manager Dean Russell
Product Production Manager Claudette Bramble
Senior Production Controller Jan Bucil
Colour origination Fresh Media Group
Printing and binding Neografia

Originated by **Creative Plus Publishing Limited**
Creative Director Gary Webb
Editorial Director Annette Love
Project Manager Katharine Goddard
Recipe development Bridget Jones
Registered Dietician and Nutritionist Jill Scott

Photographer David Munns
Art Directors Tracy Killick, Luis Peral
Food Stylists Lizzie Harris, Lorna Brash, Bridget Sargeson
Props Stylists Wei Tang, Rob Merrett

Designers Suzie Bacon, Kirsty Poole
Additional recipes and writing Judith Wills
Nutritional values Pat Bacon
Picture Researcher Claire Coakley
Proofreader Miren Lopategui
Indexer Marie Lorimer
Recipe Testers
Neil Baker, Tim Baker, Claudia Houghton, William Houghton, Helen Hutchinson, David Love, Margaret Maino, Patsy North, Ian Warmsley, Nicky Webb, Trudi Webb

Picture credits
All photography David Munns, copyright The Reader's Digest Association, except for the following.
t=top, l=left, c=centre, b=bottom
8 tl Elizabeth Watt; **13 ct** Elizabeth Watt; **18 tl** Cultura Creative/Alamy; **cl** iStockphoto.com/Denis Pogostin; **bl** iStockphoto.com/tirc83; **38 tl** iStockphoto.com/RawFile; **cl** iStockphoto.com/RawFile; **bl** iStockphoto.com/Patrick Heagney; **56 tl** GAP Photos/FhF Greenmedia; **cl** iStockphoto.com/Liza McCorkle; **bl** iStockphoto.com/Steve Debenport; **64 ct** Martin Poole/Digital Vision/Getty Images; **76 tl** GAP Photos/Juliette Wade; **cl** iStockphoto.com/Bruce Block; **bl** iStockphoto.com/Michael Sleigh; **90 tl** iStockphoto.com/yalax; **cl** GAP Photos/Pernilla Bergdahl; **bl** GAP Photos/Maxine Adcock; **98 tl** Elizabeth Watt; **99 tc** Elizabeth Watt; **110 tl** iStockphoto.com/Vladimir Kolobov; **cl** Jodi Pudge/Gettyimages; **bl** iStockphoto.com/Lehner; **126 tl** GAP Photos/Paul Debois; **cl** GAP Photos/Lee Avison; **bl** Martin Poole/Gettyimages; **144 br** iStockphoto.com/Eggimann; **146 tl** iStockphoto.com/Karl Barrett; **cl** Howard Shooter/Gettyimages; **bl** iStockphoto.com/Magdalena Kucova; **174 tl** iStockphoto.com/Linda Bair; **cl** Tom Grill/Gettyimages; **bl** Photography by Paula Thomas/Gettyimages; **188 tl** iStockphoto.com/amit erez; **cl** iStockphoto.com/Kristen Johansen; **bl** iStockphoto.com/Elena Workman; **196 tl** Elizabeth Watt; **197 tc** Elizabeth Watt; **206 tl** GAP Photos/Graham Strong; **cl** GAP Photos/Howard Rice; **bl** A ROOM WITH VIEWS/Alamy; **229 bl** iStockphoto.com/John Shepherd; **238 tl** GAP Photos/Andrea Jones; **cl** iStockphoto.com/Bruce Block; **bl** Uwe Bender/Gettyimages; **245 tl** Elizabeth Watt; **256 tl** GAP Photos/David Dixon; **cl** Foodcollection/Gettyimages; **bl** Johner Images/Alamy; **272 tl** KAZUHIRO TOMARU/a.collectionRF/Gettyimages; **cl** Jim Franco Photography/Gettyimages; **bl** Alexandra Grablewski Gettyimages

SUPERFOODS SUPEREASY edited and produced in 2012 in the United Kingdom by Vivat Direct Limited (t/a Reader's Digest), 157 Edgware Road, London W2 2HR, using the services of Creative Plus Publishing Limited, for The Reader's Digest Association, Inc.

SUPERFOODS SUPEREASY is owned and under licence from The Reader's Digest Association, Inc. All rights reserved.

We are committed both to the quality of our products and the service we provide to our customers. We value your comments, so please contact us on **0871 351 1000** or via our website at **www.readersdigest.co.uk**

If you have any comments or suggestions about the content of our books, email us at **gbeditorial@readersdigest.co.uk**

ISBN 978 1 78020 054 5
Book code 400-459 UP0000-1
Concept code AU0667/IC